LEARNING RESOURCES CTR/NEW ENGLAND TECH.
GEN   P90.R87 1994
Rushkoff, Do   Media virus! :

3 0147 0002 0752
W9-DBD-635

NEW ENGLAND INSTITUTE
OF TECHNOLOGY
LEARNING RESOURCES CENTER

MEDIA VIRUS !

NEW ENGLAND INSTITUTE
OF TECHNOLOGY
LEARNING RESOURCES CENTER

ALSO BY THE AUTHOR

*The GenX Reader**
Cyberia: Life in the Trenches of Hyperspace
Free Rides

*Published by Ballantine Books

MEDIA VIRUS!

HIDDEN AGENDAS IN POPULAR CULTURE

DOUGLAS RUSHKOFF

BALLANTINE BOOKS • NEW YORK

NEW ENGLAND INSTITUTE
OF TECHNOLOGY
LEARNING RESOURCES CENTER

12/95

#30354877

Copyright © 1994 by Douglas Rushkoff

All rights reserved under International and Pan-American
Copyright Conventions. Published in the United States by
Ballantine Books, a division of Random House, Inc., New
York, and simultaneously in Canada by Random House of
Canada Limited, Toronto.

Rushkoff, Douglas.
  Media virus / Douglas Rushkoff.
  p. I cm.
  Includes index.
  ISBN 0-345-38276-5
  1. Mass media. 2. Popular culture. I. Title.
P90.R87 1994
302.23—dc20   94-12133
                                                    CIP

Text design by Alex Jay/Studio J

Manufactured in the United States of America

First Edition: October 1994

10 9 8 7 6 5 4 3 2 1

To my mom and dad,
for letting me watch as much TV as I wanted.

CONTENTS

ACKNOWLEDGMENTS

Thanks so much to all of you who shared yourselves and your work with me for this book. I learned a lot and have great respect for your efforts.

I also want to thank everyone I met on the physical and virtual tours for my last book. Call me an optimist, but I have faith we are all absolutely on the right path.

Special thanks are due to the staff of the David Vigliano Agency for marketing my writing into a career; Mary South for seeing the value in viruses and authors who write about them; Sherri Rifkin for adopting me and making me her own; Leslie Rossman for putting me on the map and Alison Pratt for keeping me there; Noam Chomsky, Arthur Kroker, Timothy Leary, Geert Lovink, Terence McKenna, Michael Murphy, Genesis P-Orridge, and Howard Rheingold for developing this turf and teaching me how to navigate it; the WELL, particularly members of the Writers and GenX conferences; George Sheanshang and Heather for keeping the ship afloat; Bill Hayward, for photos that make me look cool; Michael Krantz for exhibiting God-like powers; Andrew Mayer for eliminating the notion of evil; David Feuer for slowing things down; and, as always, Walter Kirn— friend, ally, and fellow media transient.

MEDIA VIRUS!

INTRODUCTION

THE NATURE OF INFECTION

The average American home has more media-gathering technology than a state-of-the-art newsroom did ten years ago. Satellite dishes spot the plains of Nebraska, personal computers equipped with modems are standard equipment in a teenager's bedroom, cable boxes linking families to seventy or more choices of programming are a suburban necessity, and camcorders, Xerox machines, and faxes have become as accessible and easy to operate as public pay phones. Household television-top interactive multimedia centers are already available, promising easy access to the coming "data superhighway." Like it or not, we have become an information-based society.

We live in an age when the value of data, images, and ideologies has surpassed that of material acquisitions and physical territory. Gone are the days when a person's social stature could be measured by the distance he had to walk to see smoke from his neighbor's campfire. We've finally reached the limits of our continental landmasses; we've viewed the earth from space over national broadcast television. The illusion of boundless territorial frontiers has been destroyed forever. There's simply no more room, nothing left to colonize. While this may keep real-estate prices high, it also demands that real growth—and the associated accumulation of wealth and power—occur on some other level.

The only place left for our civilization to expand—our only real frontier—is the ether itself: the media. As a result, power today has little to do with how much property a person owns or commands; it is instead determined by how many minutes of prime-time television or pages of news-media attention she can access or occupy. The ever-expanding media has become a true region—a place as real and seemingly open as the globe was five hundred years ago. This new space is called the datasphere.

The datasphere, or "mediaspace," is the new territory for human interaction, economic expansion, and especially social and political machination. It has become our electronic social hall: Issues that were formerly reserved for hushed conversations on walks home from church choir practice are now debated openly on afternoon talk shows, in front of live audiences composed of people "just like us." Good old-fashioned local gossip has been replaced by nationwide coverage of particularly resonant sex scandals. The mediaspace has also developed into our electronic town meeting (to use Ross Perot's expression). Traditional political debate and decisions have been absorbed by the ever-expanding forums of call-in radio and late-night variety shows. Today's most media-savvy politicians announce their candidacies on Larry King and explain their positions on Rush Limbaugh or, better yet, prime-time "infomercials."

It has become fashionable to bemoan the fact that "Saturday Night Live's" Dana Carvey's latest impersonation of a political celebrity means as much to the American voter as the candidate's official platform or that kids today can get passionate about the styles and attitudes depicted in the latest MTV video but may never have watched an evening news broadcast. We worry that our media industry has developed a generation of couch potatoes who are incapable of making an intelligent decision and too passive to act on one if they did.

That's not what is going on. True, the construction of

the American media machine may have been fostered by those hoping to market products and develop a consumer mindset in our population. As media analysts from Marshall McLuhan to Noam Chomsky have shown, television and printed news cater to the corporate and political entities who created them and keep them in business. You don't need a conspiracy theory to figure out the basic operating principles of Madison or Pennsylvania Avenues. But even if the original intentions of the media were to manipulate the American psyche by deadening our senses and winning over our hearts and minds to prepackaged ideologies, this strategy has finally backfired.

Nielsen "peoplemeters" may indicate which channels we're watching, but they tell little about our relationship to the media as a whole. Just because a family is "tuned in" doesn't mean it hasn't turned on and dropped out, too. No, the media web has neither captured nor paralyzed the American individual. It has provided her with the ability to chart and control the course of her culture. She's been empowered.

The first step toward empowerment is to realize that no one takes the mainstream media any more seriously than you do. Having been raised on a diet of media manipulation, we are all becoming aware of the ingredients that go into these machinations. Children raised hearing and speaking a language always understand it better than adults who attempt to learn its rules. This is why, educators believe, our kids understand computers and their programming languages better than the people who designed them. Likewise, people weaned on media understand its set of symbols better than its creators and see through the carefully camouflaged attempts at mind control. And now Americans feel free to talk back to their TV sets with their mouths, their remote controls, their joysticks, their telephones, and even their dollars. Television has become an interactive experience.

The advent of do-it-yourself (DIY) technology makes direct feedback even more far-reaching. Today, homemade camcorder cassettes are as likely to find their way onto CNN as professionally produced segments. Tapes ranging from "America's Funniest Home Videos" to the world-famous Rodney King beating are more widely distributed through the datasphere than syndicated reruns of "I Love Lucy." Alternative media channels like the computer networks or even telephone and fax "trees" (distribution lists) permit the dissemination of information unacceptable to or censored by mainstream channels and have been heralded as the new tools of revolution in countries as "un-American" as Romania and Communist China. Pirate media, like illegal radio broadcasts and cable or satellite jamming, are even more blatant assertions of the power of individuals to hack the data network.

To appreciate the media as facilitator rather than hypnotizer, we must learn to decode the information coming into our homes through mainstream, commercial channels. We, the television audience, have already been trained as media theorists. We must acknowledge this education if we ever hope to gain command over the language being used to influence us. The first chapters of this book will examine some of our most popular cultural icons in the context of the mediaspace in which they live and the agendas they hope to promote.

In doing so, we'll come to know a new generation of media activists, whose techniques demonstrate a keen awareness of psychology, conditioning, sociology, and marketing. These children of the fifties, sixties, and seventies were willing participants in a great social experiment in which the world behind the television screen was presented as a depiction of reality—or at least a reality to which they should aspire. This was a dangerous perception to instill. Spending most of their energy trying to conform to media representations, these kids eventually determined that the easiest way to change the world is to change the television image. Now that these kids have grown up, we find our most imaginatively influential programming developed, written, and produced by people who were themselves products of the media age. They are in command of the most sophisticated techniques of thought control, pattern recognition, and neuro-linguistic programming and use them to create television that changes the way we view reality and thus reality itself.

This mainstream media subversion is accomplished through careful and clever packaging. Commercial television activism means hiding subversive agendas in palatable candy shells. Most of us do not suspect that children's programs like "Pee-Wee's Playhouse" or "The Ren & Stimpy Show" comment on gay lifestyles or that "The Simpsons" and "Liquid Television" express a psychedelic world-view. Children's television and MTV, in fact, are the easiest places to launch countercultural missiles. The more harmless or inane the forum, the more unsuspecting the audience.

The messages in our media come to us packaged as Trojan horses. They enter our homes in one form, but behave in a very different way than we expect once they are inside. This is not so much a conspiracy against the viewing public as it is a method for getting the mainstream media to unwittingly promote countercultural agendas that can actually empower the individuals who are exposed to them. The people who run network television or popular magazines, for example, are understandably unwilling to run stories or images that directly criticize the operating principles of the society that its sponsors are seeking to maintain. Clever young media strategists with new, usually threatening ideas need to invent new nonthreatening forms that are capable of safely housing these dangerous concepts until they have been successfully delivered to the American public as part of our daily diet of mainstream media.

This requires tremendous insight into the way media works. Today's activists understand the media as an extension of a living organism. Just as ecologists now understand the life on this planet to be part of a single biological organism, media activists see the datasphere as the circulatory system for today's information, ideas, and images. The datasphere was created over the past two or three decades as the households and businesses of America were hard-wired together through devices like cable television, telephone systems, and personal computer modems. As individuals we are each exposed to the datasphere whenever we come into contact with communications technology such as television, computer networks, magazines, video games, fax machines, radio shows, CDs, or videocassettes.

People who lack traditional political power but still seek to influence the direction of our culture do so by infusing new ideas into this ever-expanding datasphere. These information "bombs" spread throughout the entire information net in a matter of seconds. For instance, a black man is beaten by white cops in Los Angeles. The event is captured on a home camcorder and within hours the beating is replayed on the televisions of millions. Within days it's the topic of an afternoon talk show; within weeks it's a court case on the fictional "L.A. Law"; within months it's a TV movie; before the end of the year it's the basis of a new video game, a comic book, and set of trading cards. Finally, what began as a thirty-second video clip emerges as the battle cry for full-scale urban rioting. This riot, in turn, is amplified on more talk shows, radio call-ins, and new episodes of "L.A. Law"! A provocative image or idea—like Rodney King getting beaten or even Pee-Wee Herman masturbating in a porno theater—spreads like wildfire. The event attracts our attention and generates media for several seconds, minutes, or even months . . . but its influence on us doesn't stop there.

Within every media sensation are ideas, issues, and agendas—often purposefully placed—that influence us less directly. A home video of police beating a black man, for example, initiates a series of responses in the viewer. Questions of racism, police brutality, the First Amendment, Los Angeles politics, drug abuse, even the power of consumer-grade electronics—to name a few—are all released by the single media image in its media context. Similarly, a media icon like Pee-Wee Herman attracts attention because he is bizarre and funny, but hidden in the image and forcing us to respond are questions about homosexuality, consumerism run amok, the supposed innocence of childhood, and the farce of "adulthood."

If we are to understand the datasphere as an extension of a planetary ecosystem or even just the breeding ground for new ideas in our culture, then we must come to terms with the fact that the media events provoking real social change are more than simple Trojan horses. They are media viruses.

This term is not being used as a metaphor. These media events are not *like* viruses. They *are* viruses. Most of us are familiar with biological viruses like the ones that cause the flu, the common cold, and perhaps even AIDS. As they are currently understood by the medical community, viruses are unlike bacteria or germs because they are not living things; they are simply protein shells containing genetic material. The attacking virus uses its protective and sticky protein casing to latch onto a healthy cell and then inject its own genetic code, essentially genes, inside. The virus code mixes and competes for control with the cell's own genes, and, if victorious, it permanently alters the way the cell functions and reproduces. A particularly virulent strain will transform the host cell into a factory that replicates the virus.

It's really a battle for command of the cell, fought between the cell's own genetic programming (DNA) and the virus's invading code. Wherever the cell's existing codes are weak or confused, the virus will have a better chance of taking over. Further, if the host organism has a weak immune system, its susceptibility to invasion is dramatically increased. It can't recognize that it is being attacked and can't mobilize its defenses. The protein shell of a virus is the Trojan horse. The genetic codes are the soldiers hidden inside, battling our own genes in an attempt to change the way our cells operate. The only "intention" of the virus, if it can be said to have one, is to spread its own code as far and wide as possible—from cell to cell and from organism to organism.

Media viruses spread through the datasphere the same way biological ones spread through the body or a community. But instead of traveling along an organic circulatory system, a media virus travels through the networks of the mediaspace. The "protein shell" of a media virus might be an event, invention, technology, system of thought, musical riff, visual image, scientific theory, sex scandal, clothing style or even a pop hero—as long as it can catch our attention. Any one of these media virus shells will search out the receptive nooks and crannies in popular culture and stick on anywhere it is noticed. Once attached, the virus injects its more hidden agendas into the datastream in the form of *ideological code*—not genes, but a conceptual equivalent we now call "memes."* Like real genetic material, these memes infiltrate the way we do business, educate ourselves, interact with one another—even the way we perceive reality.

Media viruses spread rapidly if they provoke our interest, and their success is dependent on the particular strengths and weaknesses of the host organism, popular culture. The more provocative an image or icon—like the videotaped police beating or a new rap lyric, for that matter—the further and faster it will travel through the datasphere. We do not recognize the image, so we cannot respond automatically to it. Our interest and fascination is a sign that we are not culturally "immune" to the new virus. The success of the memes within the virus, on the other hand, depends on our legal, moral, and social resiliency. If our own attitudes about racism, the power of police, drug abuse, and free speech are ambiguous—meaning our societal "code" is faulty—then the invading memes within the media virus will have little trouble infiltrating our own confused command structure.

There appear to be three main kinds of media viruses. The most obvious variety, like publicity stunts or activist pranks, are constructed and launched intentionally, as a way of spreading a product or ideology. There are also what we can call co-opted or "bandwagon" viruses—the Woody Allen/ Mia Farrow debacle or the AIDS epidemic—that no one nec-

* See Dawkins, Richard, "Universal parasitism and the co-evolution of extended phenotypes," *Whole Earth Review* 62:90, Spring 1989.

essarily launches intentionally, but which are quickly seized upon and spread by groups who hope to promote their own agendas. (Republicans used the Woody affair to criticize New York's family values; ultraright conservatives used the AIDS epidemic to equate homosexuality with evil). Finally, there are completely self-generated viruses—like the Rodney King beating, the Tonya Harding/Nancy Kerrigan affair, or even new technologies like virtual reality and scientific discoveries—that elicit interest and spread of their own accord because they hit upon a societal weakness or ideological vacuum.

Today's media activists understand the properties of media viruses. The designers of intentional viruses take into account both the aspects of the status quo they wish to criticize, as well as the kinds of packaging that will permit the distribution of their critique. Most, but certainly not all, intentional media viruses are cultivated from scratch. The "smart drugs" virus is an excellent example of such designer memes. By the late 1980s a small group of AIDS activists, pharmaceutical industry critics, and psychedelics advocates felt the need to call our current drug paradigm into question. The AIDS activists were upset by laws limiting the domestic use of unapproved or experimental drugs from overseas. The pharmaceutical industry critics were frustrated by the way that the profit motives of drug companies could limit rather than expand the number of helpful medications and nutrients available to the public. The psychedelics advocates were disturbed by the "just say no" drug abuse publicity campaign, which denies the possibility of any value to experimentation with mind-altering substances.

The virus began with the carefully conceived phrase "smart drugs." Like many of the media viruses we'll be exploring—virtual reality, techno-shamanism, ecological terrorism—smart drugs is an oxymoron. By juxtaposing two words or ideas that do not normally go together, the phrase demands thought: "Drugs are smart?" Utilizing a hypnosis technique first developed by Milton Erickson, the contradictory phrase creates its own unique conceptual slot in the minds of people who hear it. The longer the phrase demands conscious attention, the more opportunity the virus has to inject its memes. If it makes us think, then we cannot be immune to it. Like a deer in a car's headlights, we freeze in our tracks.

The term "smart drugs" is meant to refer to a group of nutrients and prescription drugs that have long been shown to enhance memory functioning in senile people. A few doctors and nutritionists began to experiment with these substances on normally functioning people to see if they could induce superior mental functioning and found some positive results in their tests. These doctors ran up against many obstacles when they tried to publicize their findings and get research dollars for further study. AIDS, pharmaceutical industry, and psychedelics activists adopted this cause as their own and came up with "smart drugs" as part of an overall media strategy.

The next task was to develop what we can call the "syringe" for the virus. The way a virus is administered is as important as the construction of the virus itself. Often the way in which a virus spreads communicates as much as the memes within the virus. The smart drugs activists decided to create "The Smart Bar," a dispensary for over-the-counter cognitive-enhancing substances, right on the dance floor of a popular nightclub.

Within minutes after The Smart Bar opened, computer bulletin boards carried news of the smart drugs. Within weeks, *Rolling Stone*, *GQ*, "Larry King Live," "Nightline," and a host of other media outlets were covering the event. Other clubs began to sell smart drugs, health stores stocked up on cognitive-enhancing nutrients, and a lot of people and agencies became alarmed—not only because smart drugs were sweeping the nation, but because controversial memes within the smart drugs virus were spreading themselves throughout the datasphere.

While these drugs may or may not make a person smarter, their infusion into the datasphere as an idea has called our FDA laws, pharmaceutical industry, drug use policies, and medical mind-set into question. The smart drugs themselves are the Trojan horse—the sticky shell of the virus getting all the attention. As the smart drugs virus spread, one of its creators, John Morgenthaler, was asked to appear on "Larry King Live." Once safely nested on the studio set, he used the forum to explain how information about many smart substances has been ignored or even suppressed by the American pharmaceutical industry for years. The young, unassuming, and well-dressed man explained (to an audience whose appetite had already been whetted by the term "smart drugs" and video footage of the smart bars) how current FDA regulations require that millions of dollars of tests be done before these substances can be prescribed for cognitive purposes. Because the patents for many of these chemicals expired before the pharmaceutical companies realized their value, no firm today is willing to spend research dollars on a chemical it can't own.

This particular meme—we can call it the "patent law meme" within the smart drugs virus—burrows deeply into the existing medical business paradigm. As smart drugs promoters go on the air to discuss the problems caused by patent-motivated medical decisions, they convince viewers that the pharmaceutical industry is dangerous to the population it claims to serve. Along with smart drugs, says an AIDS activist friend of Morgenthaler's who appeared on "Nightline" a few weeks later, several potentially effective AIDS medications have been suppressed because they, too, cannot be patented. Whether or not smart drugs prove effective at all, the memes within the smart drugs media virus have infiltrated the existing conceptual framework for drug legalization.

The inconsistencies of our AIDS drug policies were exposed by the smart drugs virus—first on computer bulletin boards, then in magazines, then on cable television, and finally on national network news. The attraction to the idea and sound of smart drugs and smart bars opened the necessary media channels for the virus to spread. The immune response of our culture to the virus was weak because of our ambivalent attitudes toward drug use. The memes themselves were able to infiltrate because of our ambiguous laws and policies—our faulty societal code.

But not all media viruses are constructed purposefully. The Woody Allen/Mia Farrow scandal was—most probably, anyway—not created as a publicity stunt. The particularly New York story broke, however, during the Democratic Convention for Bill Clinton. The Republicans, who had already been denouncing New York as a hotbed of morally decadent and "cultural elitist" attitudes, were quick to capitalize on the Allen/Farrow media virus. Introductions for Bush's campaign speeches made reference to Woody Allen, hoping to reinterpret the memes that had already spread—child molestation, movie stars not being as they appear, New York confusion—as condemning evidence of Democratic family values.

Finally there exist what countercultural activists would consider "self-generated" viruses. These are concepts or events that arise in the media quite spontaneously, but spread widely because they strike a very resonant chord or elicit a dramatic response from those who are exposed to them. If all of civilization is to be seen as a single organism, then these self-generated viruses can be understood as self-corrective measures. They are ways for the organism to correct or modify its own code. This is what is known in evolutionary circles as "mutation."

One such self-generated virus, the theories of chaos math, come to us from deep in the computer departments of major universities, but their implications have reignited enthusiasm for ancient pagan and antiauthoritarian values. This new, highly heralded form of mathematics works without the straight lines and linear equations we have used to interpret reality for the past dozen or so centuries and instead paints a picture of our universe as a quite random, discontinuous field of natural phenomena. Chaos math is now used to analyze systems as complex as the stock market or the weather with astonishingly accurate results.

The famous phrase "a butterfly flapping its wings in China can create a hurricane in New York" means that a tiny event in one remote area can lead to huge repercussions in another. It is no wonder that those attempting to demonstrate the fall of hierarchical systems and to debunk the notion of top-down control cherish the memes of the chaos math virus, which contradict these orderly notions of natural behavior. Activists love evidence that supports their minuteman tactics.

It is the media activists, most of all, who depend on a world-view that accepts that a tiny virus, launched creatively and distributed widely, can topple systems of thought as established as organized religion and institutions as well rooted as, say, the Republican Party or even the two-party system altogether. This is why it is so important that we understand that, at least as far as media activists are concerned, viruses are not a "bad thing." True, biological viruses, when successful, can destroy the host organism. If they invade and take control of enough cells, they redirect vital functions that the host needs in order to survive. Media viruses do target a host organism, but that beast is not culture as whole; they target the systems and faulty code that have taken control of culture and inhibited the natural, chaotic flow of energy and information.

A media virus may be designed to fight a political party, a religion, an institution, an economy, a business, or even a system of thought. Just as scientists use viruses to combat certain diseases within the human body or to tag dangerous cells for destruction by the person's own antibodies, media activists use viruses to combat what they see as the enemies of our culture. Media viruses, whether intentional, co-opted, or spontaneous, lead to societal mutation and some sort of evolution. The purpose of this book is not to cast judgment on any of the issues these activists raise, but rather to examine the methods they use to promote what they see as positive, evolutionary change.

Interestingly enough, however, to come to grips with the efficacy of media viruses in our present datasphere, we

must also accept, or at least acknowledge, the basic principles of the datasphere as these activists view them. To understand media viruses, we must allow ourselves to become
infected.

PART 1

ON GETTING
CULTURED

CHAPTER 1

THE DATASPHERE

FROM PUBLIC RELATIONS TO PRIMORDIAL SOUP

Fall 1992. A quick surf through the TV channels on a weekday afternoon reveals that Geraldo, Donahue, and two other wireless-mike hosts are, simultaneously, doing shows about the Amy Fisher story. Geraldo's playing clips from the *three* television movies to be aired this week about the "Long Island Lolita" scandal—one from Amy's point of view, one from Joey Buttafuoco's, and one "neutral." One of the movie clips begins with a reenactment of a "Hard Copy" press conference, where actors playing the tabloid news show's producers screen a tape they will air on the program that night. The tape of the evening's episode rolls, announcing that "Hard Copy" has come into exclusive possession of a revealing videocassette: Amy Fisher speaking with her boyfriend, a gym employee, about ways they will be able to have sex even after she has been put in jail. This tape, we learn from the "Hard Copy" narrator, was secretly recorded by the boyfriend with his camcorder. The TV movie cuts from the actual videotape of Amy and her boyfriend to another television monitor, this one in the dramatized home of Amy Fisher, played by Drew Barrymore, who is watching the episode of "Hard Copy" in her living room, shocked.

So on our TV we watch Geraldo watch a monitor play a TV movie enacting a press conference where a tape is rolled of a TV show that in turn plays a tape—the actual, real-world tape purchased for the movie—made by a guy cashing in on a media scandal, only to pull out and reveal a third-generation American actress pretend to react as the real Amy Fisher might have. By this time Geraldo takes a commercial break, during which an evening news special is pitched that promises to air a brand-new Amy Fisher tape made by another of her boyfriends. Flip the channel and you get to watch an ad for an exclusive interview with Joey and his lawyer, who are upset about the way they were made to appear on the "Donahue" show earlier in the week. Of course, all these media events are being discussed concurrently on computer bulletin boards throughout the country and the story has turned up in the form of an Amy Fisher comic book.

This house of mirrors within mirrors is the American mediascape. It is more than a mirror of our culture; it *is* our culture. It is where we spend our time, our money, and our thought. But as we examine the nature of the datasphere more closely, we find it is a self-referential cut-and-paste of itself. Most of media is media commenting on media commenting on media. Even if one real event just happens to occur—a girl shoots the wife of a man she has slept with, a woman cuts off her husband's penis, two brothers shoot their millionaire parents, or an Olympic skater's bodyguard attacks her rival—it soon becomes part of the overall self-reflexive pastiche of media.

Something is going on in media all its own that reflects less on the particular events being reported than it does on the nature of our cultural preoccupations and the ways in which we process them. Media is saying something in the way it finds its stories, churns them out, swallows them again, redigests them, and spits them out once again. This is more than a simple cultural bulimia. This is a complex but, on some level, effective form of mass catharsis and self-observation that our society employs to monitor and then modify itself.

Most social theorists still consider the media a dung

heap of cultural waste. They believe that the media, having nothing better to do, keeps chewing on the same predigested matter. There's so much time to fill on so many stations and only a few real stories to tell. This is a simplistic view of media shared mostly by philosophers who grew up before television. They view media and even technology, for that matter, as somehow outside the realm of the natural. To them, media can only display or comment on something real. They cannot acknowledge that the media is something real itself— something that exists on its own and that might have its own needs and agendas. Even forward thinkers like media philosopher Marshall McLuhan insisted in *Understanding Media* (1964) that every media extension of man is akin to a biological "amputation." The advent of rock music made musicians deaf, and televisions or virtual reality goggles may eventually be found to damage our optic nerves and make us blind. This older generation of theorists even objects to the word "media" being used as a singular noun. The media, to these people, are merely the channels through which we communicate: TV, print, bumper stickers, telegraph, telephone. We are to see media as a set of artificial technologies that mediate and ultimately compromise human interaction.

But those who grew up after the development of the datasphere see the media very differently. More than a set of tools, the media is an entity unto itself that must be reckoned with on its own terms. The initiators of media viruses depend on a very optimistic vision of how the web of media nodes can serve to foster new cultural growth. Rather than stunting our natural development by amputating our limbs and numbing our senses, the media can accelerate evolution. The activists we are about to encounter believe the media can extend the human, or even the planetary, spirit.

THE END OF THE AGE OF PUBLIC RELATIONS

As our conceptual forefathers explain, the datasphere was put into place by authoritarian forces as a means of controlling the public. Noam Chomsky, a Massachusetts Institute of Technology media theorist and political scientist, has exposed over his long career the way the United States government developed the science of public relations in order to convince its population which wars were worth fighting and which labor unions threatened our national security. For example, in 1916, Woodrow Wilson was elected by a pacifistic public on a peace platform. But once his administration became committed to war, he needed to alter public opinion and created a propaganda group called the Creel Commission. Through creative use of the press, the commission successfully got America enthusiastic about fighting the Germans. Even more important it developed the primary propaganda techniques still used today for controlling mass sentiment. These techniques constitute a gigantic top-down media hierarchy, which, now that it is in place, has begun to work against its original purpose.

People like Chomsky have made us aware of these techniques and the underlying assumptions that keep them functional. Again, it is important to remember that the people involved in propaganda do not necessarily believe they are doing anything inherently evil. They simply perform according to their world-view. One of the first assumptions media controllers (as opposed to media activists) make is that our nation functions best as a "spectator democracy." The liberal intellectuals of the thirties and forties believed that the general populace is too stupid to understand the intricacies of running a country. Instead a select group of well-meaning intellectuals needs to determine the best course of action and then "manufacture consent" of the citizens for things they don't want, but that are in their best interest.[1] Rather than persuading the public through intellectual argument, public relations experts seek only to oversimplify issues and evoke an emotional response from the spectators.

Chomsky and others have shown that the commitment of the public relations industry was to "control the public mind."[2] Their techniques matured in the late thirties, when a surge of union organization threatened to bring true democracy back to the common populace. Then big business joined with government public relations experts to create a more persuasive campaign than simply beating up union organizers or bashing heads at labor strikes. These actions only unified the public against management. The Mohawk Valley formula (first used in the 1930s against a steelworker strike in Pennsylvania) was a landmark effort in a more subtle form of persuasion. Instead of attacking unions directly, businesses sought to influence public opinion through the media. This self-proclaimed "scientific method of strike breaking"[3] was a conceptual campaign, oversimplifying the labor issue into a single, easy-to-understand message: Strikers hurt us all. They disrupt American harmony. The simple propaganda formula was to equate union activity with something bad, namely, disunity and un-American (communist) activity. This had nothing to do with the real issues at hand—wages, conditions, the right to organize—but rather reframed the issue in a headline-length, easy-to-photograph image: Striking is un-American. And thus the "sound bite" was born.

Note how this simple technique—distraction and oversimplification—is exactly what the Bush administration used in the modern nineties to keep public sentiment in favor of the Persian Gulf War. Congressional Democrats were afraid to voice any protest against the war. To protest the war meant "endangering our troops." The oversimplification of the issue was coined in the simple phrase "Support our troops." But there is no real data in this slogan. There is no information with which one can make an informed decision. "Support our troops" distracts the populace from the real question: "Do you support this war?"

But according to the strategy, this is just the point: Citizens are unqualified to answer such questions. They should not be kept informed about policy decisions. They should be fed easy-to-understand but meaningless slogans to rally behind.

Even the Kuwaitis hired state-of-the-art public relations teams, who conducted a brilliant media campaign on the American people complete with rumors of heinous atrocities by the Iraquis, including disconnecting infants from medical apparatus. To oppose the war was equated with promoting torture of infants. This technique is called *marginalizing* and is still frequently used, especially in organized reactions to media viruses. In order to generate public support for an illogical policy, leaders need to name and demonize an enemy, then whip up an emotional fury against the demon. Anyone remaining against the proposed policy needs to be minimalized, sidelined, or marginalized. This way people who oppose the public relations objectives are made to feel absolutely alone. Anyone who believes, for example, that network news presents an accurate picture of the world does not know that, even during the Reagan "landslide," three fifths of the American public hoped that his policies—like military spending—would *not* be enacted.[4] But these people perceived themselves as part of a tiny, unvoiced minority. There was supposed to be a "landslide" going on. They assumed they were on the marginalized sidelines of a spectator democracy and watched world affairs continue behind the glass of the television screen.

As long as people feel they have no power over the images presented to them over the media, they will feel they have no power over events in the real world. By presenting news and media as a clean, uncomplicated, top-down, inaccessible, linear, sound-bite continuum, public relations artists prevent individuals who have independent feelings from getting any positive feedback from the world around them. Dissidents must be made to feel that they are alone.

The last and probably most debilitating effect of media propaganda is that it intentionally misrepresents reality. We may not believe everything we read—MARTIAN DOLPHIN STEALS TWO-HEADED BABY banner headlines on tabloid newspapers have made us more critical of the printed word—but what we see on TV in sound and pictures still seems real. Video is convincing. Even fictional images, like the POW camps in the movie *Rambo*, can appeal to the emotions and affect public opinion. When America fights a war, Hollywood—whether intentionally or not—aids the propaganda effort by "mirroring public sentiment" and depicting heroic battles against evil fascist forces. *Red Dawn* (1984), for example, the movie about kids who fight an invading Russian-Cuban army, came at the height of the Reagan/Bush effort to increase military spending.

These fictionalized, hate-mongering images reach their peak of absurdity in television programs like "World Wrestling Federation," where clean-cut American wrestlers exchange body slams with other wrestlers costumed as insane Iraquis or weapon-wielding Russians. The outrageousness of these images, however, ultimately exposes the strategy behind more subtle war-mongering propaganda. The producers or choreographers of television wrestling are not part of any conscious propaganda effort. But their appropriation of war-mongering emotional pandering into the fictional ring serves to reduce this strategy's efficacy on the public at large. By encouraging co-option of the propaganda effort by the fictional media, the forces attempting to control public opinion undermine the credibility of their own campaigns. The world of fictional imagery is anybody's game.

The current mishmash between tabloid television and made-for-television movies demonstrates the hazy line between reality and fiction in today's media and how mixing the two can lead to public relations backfires. By borrowing real news footage and inserting it into fact-based but fictionalized movies (Jim and Tammy Baker, Amy Fisher, Tonya Harding, the Menendez brothers, to name a few), the television industry has brought information from the irrefutable world of fact into the ever-relative world of fiction. They even demonstrate how these bits of footage can be manipulated to tell many different stories. The Rodney King tape has been analyzed and reanalyzed to the point where it both proves the cops' guilt *and* their innocence. Most daunting to those who hope to use fictional media as a means of top-down control is the way Americans, particularly younger ones, interpret the images presented to them: with *irony*. Seeing the American versus Arab conflict portrayed as a wrestling match between two rhetoric-spouting idiots changes the way kids understand the news, if they even watch it. Sure, they may even boo the enemy wrestler, but with smiles on their faces. They know this is just a game. When Saddam Hussein shows up on the evening news, this sense of irony slips in again. The attempts to engineer opinion have backfired. Any appeal to the emotions will fail.

In fact, each of the methods of public relations have been undermined by their very implementation in the media. Americans have either stopped believing what their media tells them or stopped caring. If nothing else, irony provides distance. With emotional distance from the material, the audience gains protection from the techniques of mind control. As playwright Bertolt Brecht discovered, alienating devices give audiences room to think. When Amy Fisher or Lorena Bobbitt is seen framed by six TV monitors-within-monitors, their stories become distanced enough for us to experience the irony of media's fixation with them rather than the emotional "reality" of their plights.

So the distancing effects—intentional and unintentional—of the media have infused the viewing public with aesthetic and emotional safety. Similarly, the fictionalization of world events into caricatured conflicts adds a sense of irony, further removing potential propaganda victims from the realm of passion.

Another of the now defunct techniques for media domination is control of technology. In World War II Hitler confounded U.S. intelligence by making himself appear to be in more than one place at a time. Hitler's technicians, it turned out, had developed magnetic recording tape—an innovation the allied forces could not even imagine yet. In this very direct way, Hitler used exclusive media technology to create an image of the world that was untrue. Now that citizens have access to and a basic understanding of formerly exclusive technology, they cannot be fooled as easily as U.S. intelligence was in World War II. The advances in home video coupled with media's fixation on itself have fundamentally altered our relationship with the images coming to us through television. We know that an aggressive news show might plant explosives on a GM truck to make sure it explodes on impact and that witty editing—like the kind done originally on HBO's *Not Necessarily the News*—can make events that never happened appear as real as history. Deconstructionalist media satire, like the mock commercial satires done on "Saturday Night Live," expose the "secret" techniques of marketing, disabling some of the most current advertising trends, sometimes just days after they have been implemented.

Perhaps the real downfall of propaganda can be attributed to the co-option of public relations techniques by big business. Although originally brought in by government opinion engineers to pay for media campaigns that marketers were convinced would serve their own interests as well—like union busting in the 1930s—by the forties and fifties businesses saw the tremendous value in using public relations to market their own products. Techniques that were previously reserved for creating the spectator democracy became the province of big-business interests and were used instead for development of a *consumer* democracy designed to take advantage of postwar "disposable" incomes. Television advertisements, programs, and even movies came to promote a world-view in which happiness can be purchased.

In allowing this to happen, however, big business created something even bigger than itself. The datasphere was born, and it had developed a few agendas of its own. We will consider two models for the emergence of the datasphere as a true, social landscape. One—perhaps the more extreme—involves accepting the development of the mediaspace as the creation of a natural world. In this model the threads and strands of the media network are akin to the fibers, roots, or dendrites of any biological being and seek to expand, get more complex, and mate with others. Invested with the emotional responsibilities of a living creature, media rises to the occasion.

A less radical approach would be to see the development of the mediaspace as the unintentional implementation of what mathematicians now call a "complex system." A fairly new branch of mathematics, made possible by the advent of the computer, applies a new set of rules once a system—like the weather, the waves of the ocean, or the planetary population—becomes too complex to handle with simple, linear equations. Once a system has graduated to this level of complexity, it is considered a "chaotic" system and begins to exhibit an entirely new set of qualities; these qualities generally work toward the destruction of any imposed order or control, just like the intense force of the ocean eventually crashes through retaining walls and dikes. But either way you look at the upscaling of the media into a datasphere, it becomes clear that this technology got out of hand. It got too big and too complex for any one group to control and has worked against its original aims by empowering the population it was designed to direct.

IT'S ALIVE

Since World War II the media's purpose was to whet viewers' appetites for new products. By the 1950s the world behind the TV screen had become a fantasy showroom of cars, appliances, lifestyles, and attitudes that fueled the consumerist bonfire. The establishment of this national media universe worked better than the marketers expected. By the sixties, the media had become a world of its own. Kids could grow up spending more time in the media world than the real world. The datasphere became our new natural environment. We projected onto it, or into it, a great intrinsic value. We compared our own lives to those of Marcia Brady on "The Brady Bunch" or Will Robinson on "Lost in Space." Television characters filled our discussions, our fantasies, even our dreams. Social engagements were structured around television schedules. Our cultural references had more to do with what cartoons we admired than which sport we played or which church we belonged to. We treated the mediaspace as if it were a real place, and it rose to the occasion.

The datasphere began to behave like a living organism—a system with behavior as complex, far-reaching, and self-sustaining as nature herself. Like any biological entity, it sought to grow. With the help of dollars from those who still thought they were hard-wiring consumer culture, the media expanded into the tremendous worldwide web we enjoy today. Networks and independents spawned satellite linkups, cable television, telephone marketing, computer networks, video players, and home shopping clubs. More extensive than our endless ribbon of rails, roadways, and skyways, our media networks could reach out and touch anyone.

By the 1970s an otherwise disconnected culture employed television as a surrogate parent for the latchkey child and radio as a bedtime companion for the lonely divorcé. Porn videos emerged in the 1980s as a voyeuristic substitute for the socially disinclined, and by the 1990s "976" phone numbers became the preferred form of safe sex for the disease-fearing. Marketers saw how engaged people were becoming with the media and began marketing the media itself as their biggest product. The newest and best products were TVs and media tools. (How ironic it is that news footage of the L.A. riots, which were ignited by a camcorder tape, showed people looting mostly televisions and VCRs.) Television commercials for nonmedia products like cars and deodorant could only compete by incorporating televisions within televisions in their commercials. Marketers began to seduce viewers by making commercials in which people watch television commercials and then comment on them.

The emphasis in media became the media itself. This is what led to the moment where the balance of power in media shifted forever.

The marketers themselves became pawns of the media's own purpose. Like any living organism, the media sought to communicate with the rest of the natural world—all those people who were treating it like a companion, parent, or lover. A company called Odyssey, as its name suggests, allowed media to circle back and touch its creators for the first time. In the 1970s Odyssey released a game called Pong, the first video game that could be played on a home television screen. Dr. Timothy Leary, who, if classifiable in any manner, can be considered an expert on the way new technologies impact on human consciousness, lauds the invention of Pong as a major turning point in modern culture. I interviewed him in late 1993 about the video-game revolution:

"Pong was the first kids' game that you could move things on a screen yourself. The pong paddle is almost like a cursor, so, of course, the PC [personal computer] came along after that. The importance of the Nintendo phenomenon is about equal to that of the Gutenberg printing press. Here you had a new generation of kids who grew up knowing that they could change what's on the screen. Upstairs, Mom and Dad are in the living room—they're baby boomers—passively watching the news or prime time the way they passively watched Disney back when they were kids. And down in the kids' room, the kids are changing the screen. 'What are they doing?' 'They're doing that damn Nintendo! They should be up here watching educational television!' Well, there's no such thing as educational television! That's the ultimate oxymoron. The ability to change what's on the screen is the tremendous empowerment."

It was in catering to the kids' market that the engineers of consumer culture inadvertently empowered the masses they were attempting to manipulate. The marketers sought only to sell products and adopted the philosophy of "Give the kids what they want." By creating a kids' market, they created a kids' culture, with its own needs and demands.

They created what we now call "Generation X"—the first generation of Americans fully engaged in a symbiotic relationship with media.

Born after 1960 GenXers got their name from a Doug Coupland novel—*Generation X**—about kids whose lives did not quite live up to the promises of "The Brady Bunch" or even "The Partridge Family." They were forced to develop new attitudes toward media depictions of the world around them. While they've been called many things—stupid, apathetic, shallow, greedy, angry—their most important quality as far as media is concerned is a sense of irony and irreverence. The irony was developed through an emotional distance from the subjects of media. The irreverence for the sanctity of popular cultural ideology came from this generation's ability to change what was on the screen. They don't just receive and digest media. They manipulate it. They play with it. The media is not a mirror—it is an "other." They are in a living relationship with it.

While their parents may condemn Nintendo as mindless and masturbatory, kids who have mastered video gaming early on stand a better chance of exploiting the real but mediated interactivity that will make itself available to them by the time they hit techno-puberty in their teens. Nintendo teaches kids how to use their equipment. Then they can graduate to computer conferencing and video production, which allow them to interact with other living human beings. Computer networks and bulletin boards have already replaced social halls and junior high dances for many young Americans who want to interact somewhere their parents can't watch them. And even family outings are incomplete without a camcorder and the possibility of an airing on "America's Funniest Home Videos." The advent of interactive technology enhances our ability to relate to the media.

The other chief critique of Generation X is that they are not creative. Their conversations—in real life and on the computer networks—as well as their own TV shows usually

*Which, in turn, got its name from a Billy Idol band.

focus on media itself. Rather than coming up with original scenarios or new material, they may instead consider and reconsider the ethical choices made in an episode of "Ren & Stimpy" or "Beavis and Butt-head," as if they were discussing advanced cultural theory. What characterizes the GenX aesthetic and its conceptual preoccupation is a regeneration of imagery already in the media. Taking their cue from postmodern artists like Andy Warhol, GenXers examine and reexamine the images from the media that formed their own world-views and do so with humor. "I wanted to screw Penelope Pitstop," one computer bulletin board conversation starts, referring to a GenXer's childhood attraction to a cartoon character.

The news, comedy, and drama produced by the current vanguard of media-wary social activists, ranging from subversive underground documentaries on public access television to mainstream movies and TV shows like "Wayne's World" and "The Critic," all share a delight in deconstructing and reexamining media. The documentaries expose the thin logic and obsequious pandering of network newspeople, while movies and sitcoms re-create and satirize famous moments in media history. The newest comic books and poster art use recognizable imagery from the mainstream press and comment on it with sarcastic dialogue or witty slogans that expose the inner meanings or faulty logic in the original images.

Giving in to the strengths of the tools at hand—like Xeroxes, Macintoshes, and Sonys—which more easily cut and paste audio and visual samples than they generate original ones, today's media activists engage in the techniques of recycling, juxtaposing, and recontextualizing existing imagery and doing so with ironic distance. We have developed a new language of references and self-references that identify media as a real thing and media history as an actual social history.

The dance partnering of GenX and their media initiated a living interplay between human beings and the datasphere herself. Through viewers' choices and contributions, we gained the ability to feed back into the datasphere the images with which we resonate the most and in this way modify the overall quality of the mediaspace.

The media became a natural world. As such, it came to promote the agendas of nature and the assertions of chaos.

RODNEY THE BUTTERFLY

The increasingly unfathomable complexity of the datasphere looks amazingly simple once its chaotic properties are reckoned with. The bizarre new effects of media on our culture must be seen as the influence of chaos on a system that was originally intended to instill order, but got too complex to manage.

Today chaos means a whole lot more than random happenings. Chaos is the way that nature reasserts herself into our attempts at organization and control, especially when those efforts are intentionally oppressive.

What makes a system change from an orderly one into a chaotic one is—in simplest terms—its complexity. A small stream of water can be understood as an orderly system, and its motion can be predicted using simple equations. The ocean, on the other hand, is influenced by too many factors for its motion to be reduced to one or two neat, linear equations. Still, the motion and properties of systems as complex as the ocean (or even the datasphere) can be predicted or even harnessed once their essentially chaotic nature is accepted. Remember, chaos does not mean random; chaotic systems have an underlying order to them.

The main principles of chaos, as described by today's mathematics community, are called "feedback" and "iteration." If a system exhibits these two qualities, it is behaving in a "chaotic" way. Feedback is the ability for something to interact with its environmental conditions. A heater's thermostat is the simplest example of a feedback device. When the room gets too cold, the thermostat turns the heat on, changing the environment in the room. When the room gets too hot, the thermostat shuts the heat off, regulating the temperature in its environment by feeding back information through the heating system. There are also many such feedback loops in nature. When the population of rats in a field gets too high, the population of its predators, say, hawks, also increases. The world gets more dangerous for the rats, fewer survive, and then the rat population decreases again. The remaining hawk overpopulation will be corrected by the decrease in available food, and soon this population will decrease back to normal levels. All chaotic systems—including the media—have many channels for feedback.

The principle of iteration is related to feedback. When a microphone is placed too close to the speaker into which it is being amplified, it can make a loud screech. We call this "feedback" because the microphone is "listening" to its own amplified sound and then feeding that sound back into the speaker. But in the case of the microphone, this process repeats itself again and again. The microphone hears its own sound, feeds it back into the speaker, hears that sound, feeds it back, and so on, thousands of times a second. This feedback reiterates so many times that it develops into a terribly loud sound. The same principle can be observed in economics. If the government, say, miscalculated the pay rate of all its employees by one-half cent an hour, when this tiny error is multiplied to reflect all the hours every employee works in a year, it "iterates" into an error of millions of dollars.

It is easy to see how the datasphere and interactive media provide culture with a way to initiate feedback and iteration. While these media systems were put in place to reduce independent thinking and activity, they have served to give private citizens unparalleled access to the screens and speakers of their fellows. Every wire leading into a home from what was "central control" is also a wire leading out from a home back into central control or, better, out to the rest of the world. The most obvious channels for feedback are forums such as call-in radio or audience participation talk shows like "Donahue" ("How many of you agree with our guest?" The audience applauds its approval). But this is sanctioned feedback, almost on the order of a focus group or market survey. The unexpected feedback provided by local cable access, home video, computer networks, and even satellite transmission have proved much more devastating to those who wish to hold the reigns of control over public opinion.

Just like the butterfly in China who can flap his wings and make a hurricane in New York, a tiny media event, when fully iterated throughout the datasphere, can foment a cultural storm. Rodney King was such a butterfly. The two-minute, grainy home video recording of his arrest fed back and iterated throughout the mediaspace and led to one of the most violent events in our nation's modern history.

The freedom to iterate has been secured by photocopy and fax machines, computer bulletin boards, electronic mail lists, tape duplication, and even successful self-promotion. Feeding a thought or feeling back into the media network is easy—almost impossible to avoid doing once in a while. The datasphere is hungry. If an ingested idea excites others, it will probably duplicate itself and spread through the datasphere without any further effort on the part of the individual who initiated it.

It no longer matters if the datasphere is "alive" or not. Like the ocean, the weather, or a coral reef, it behaves as if it is.

VIRUSES TO THE RESCUE

The concept of viruses developed naturally from the effective exploitation of the properties of feedback and iteration. Viruses are the promoters of chaos and uniquely structured to take advantage of these chaotic and organic qualities of the datasphere. As such they also fight the techniques developed by public relations firms to create a passive, manipulable population. Viruses neutralize these techniques in the modern datasphere, one by one.

Viruses combat oversimplification and distraction. "Just say no," for example, is a public relations effort to simplify and thus distract us from the real issues involved in drug use. The phrase is designed to ignore the complex reality of life in the ghetto, peer pressure, the legality of certain drugs and the possible benefits of others. Similarly "the war on drugs" appeals to the emotions and couches other issues—racism, fear, and class issues—in a blanket statement against an enemy we can agree on. The issue here is not whether or not drug use should be sanctioned, but rather the specific tactics used by the public relations experts to dominate public opinion.

The countercultural groups involved in the drug issue create viruses that explode these simple slogans. The viruses provoke more questions, not pat answers. The smart drugs virus, for one, is a seemingly oxymoronic phrase that makes us go "Huh?" We do not raise our fists in anger against a named enemy, but instead are forced to make sense, or at least try. Viruses open up issues for discussion rather than give us an excuse to ignore our ambivalence. They make our conceptual world a more confusing, chaotic place. Anything is possible.

The easy way to tell the difference between a media virus and an old-fashioned public relations ploy is to determine whether it makes an issue simple and emotional or dauntingly complex. A virus will always make the system it is attacking appear as confusing and unresolvable as it really is. The technique of oversimplification and distraction is rendered obsolete by the media virus.

Media viruses also disable the technique of marginalization. The first response of public relations to a countercultural idea is to marginalize it. If you are against the war, then you are labeled "against our troops." If you are promoting gay rights, then you are labeled "against family values" or even "pro-AIDS and pro-pederasty." But the shell of a well-constructed virus allows its memes to spread before they can be marginalized into obscurity. The shell hides the agenda.

What allows media viruses to spread often has little to do with the dangerous ideas within them—the shell can serve as a decoy. Even better, public relations forces often wage war against the shell of a virus before they understand its inner nature. Their attempts to marginalize the shell only allow the virus to spread further. Ice-T's fiery "Cop Killer" lyrics, for example, became famous only because of efforts to extinguish them. The memes within the media virus defied sidelining because the "censorship of rock" issue had legs of its own.

Usually what allows a virus to multiply in our immensely self-referential mediaspace is its ability to comment on the media itself. The shell of a virus can be considered its "media identity." The Murphy Brown/Dan Quayle charade gained momentum because it commented on the relationship between real and fictional newsmedia. The issues within it—single parenthood, the cultural elite—were secondary reasons for the iteration of this virus. The viral shell permits the memes to spread before they have a chance to be marginalized. They take advantage of our current media's tendency to replicate anything that mirrors or promotes its own functioning and cut off yet another public relations tactic at the knees.

Also, viruses prevent the "manufacturers of consent" from exploiting "representation as reality." Viruses couch themselves in irony and appeal to the objective sensibilities of their viewers. Viral shells can be understood as framing devices that force us to distance ourselves from the issues within them. This objectification of the issues allows us to understand the symbols in our media as symbols and not reality. Again, we are made aware of the complexities beneath apparently simple representations of our world.

This complexity promotes the media and culture's more chaotic tendencies. Viruses and the datasphere exhibit what chaos mathematicians call "self-similarity," a new explanation for many of the forms in nature. A fern plant, for example, has roots whose structure is similar to the branches, which are similar to the veins in the leaves, which are similar to the structure of the cells. The shape of the whole plant reflects the pattern of plants on the forest ground, which reflect the pattern of forest terrain in the countryside, and so on. The datasphere exhibits this same self-similarity, with the structure of television cable networks reflecting the structure of individual TV sets, themselves reflecting the structure of the optic networks in the people who view them.

Countercultural media generally exploits this self-similarity and works in complementary ways on many levels at once. The music video for Jesus Jones's *Right Here, Right Now*, for example, is about how our culture is experiencing a moment where it may have an opportunity to break from its historical cycles. "Right here, right now," the lyrics say, "there is no place I'd rather be. Right here right now, watching the world wake up from history." Behind the band as they perform is a movie screen of rapidly cut news imagery: scenes like the felling of the Berlin Wall or the fall of communism. The video is a rapidly edited series of discontinuous cuts, disrespectful of the linear, orderly rules of traditional narrative filmmaking. It appears on MTV, which plays video after video, linked together only by disorienting discontinuous graphics. Finally the MTV network is only one of the many channels available now through cable television, which the viewer flips through with his remote, watching CNN images on one channel, music images on another, and both pasted together in this video. As if to recognize their own place in this giant self-similar latticework, the performers in the band allow the news footage to be projected directly onto their bodies. Jesus Jones sings about the discontinuous nature of modern social history, while its video, the station it's broadcast on, and medium through which it is broadcast all exhibit this same discontinuity.

The last of the public relations ploys that viruses obliterate is the maintenance of a sidelined, spectator democracy. Participatory, feedback media keeps dissident individuals from feeling that they are alone. News shows that attempt to demonstrate American support of a given war are undermined by alternative news coverage of protests and demonstrations. Any individual who watches network news can voice her discontent with the way a story has been presented by calling a talk-radio show or posting an opinion on a computer bulletin board. The dissident opinion iterates onto every radio tuned to the same station or computer screen that accesses the same bulletin board. Fax transmission and pirate radio in cultures as repressive as prerevolutionary Romania permitted the masses of discontents to realize they were not alone. No, they may not have been allowed to assemble in public legally, but their alternative media allowed them to network, organize, and find other people who felt equally marginalized by their leaders. Meanwhile, here in the United States, these technologies have permitted our citizenry to graduate from passive, ignorant spectators to active, informed participants.

Participation can range from simply watching TV to designing global networks. What constitutes activity in the datasphere is only limited by the number of ways a person can be exposed to or iterate viruses. As the datasphere grows, each of us come into contact with more of our viral culture. The media promotes a new kind of intimacy, and no one can escape the flood.

THE NEW EDEN

For the media is like water. It conducts social electricity. Wherever it spreads, its contents are carried, too. This is a very frightening premise to many of us and cuts to the root of our current cultural paranoia, spiritual discontent, and global friction.

Many people fear the mediaspace. Traditionally it has been the so-called left wing, environmentalist, and New Age communities who have opposed the rampant expansion of these technologies. Many of the activists in these groups are still unwilling or unable to recognize that the datasphere provides the ability to mount real grassroots countercultural campaigns. Many environmentalists refuse to distinguish between dirty technologies (burning coal, driving cars, making paper) and "clean" technologies (television, computers) and cling instead to the Luddite notion that all technology is unnatural and destructive to the planet's ecosystems.

Perhaps the loudest battle cry against the media comes from the New Age community, where media is still associated with the consumerist ideologies they so often promoted in the past. In a bizarre act of cultural self-loathing, New Age leaders look to everything American—and especially our media iconography—as somehow false and fabricated.

Social theorist and respected New Age lecturer William Irwin Thompson, who is about fifty, is most famous for his book *The American Replacement of Nature*, in which he warns that the development of the mediaspace is an "unnatural" thing. He even explores how the implementation of the media networks in America might best be understood as "a collectivization that can be mythologically identified as the incarnation of the demon Ahriman."[5] The media machine, in other words, is the province of Satan and the coming of the Apocalypse.

Where Thompson is correct is that America, and perhaps all of Western culture, is based on a fear of nature. Our own central biblical myths concern our original and unnecessary separation from God, the opposite sex, and nature herself. Cast out of the "oneness" in Eden, we instead developed a world of duality and morality. We have traditionally associated the female, the chaotic, and the natural with evil. The original iconography developed by public relations firms and carried by the media supported these dualistic notions of right and wrong, good and evil. It's no small wonder that the development of the datasphere, which breaks down these dualistic notions while promoting an atmosphere of chaos, would be called "evil."

Further, the development of technology, for the most part, had always served to insulate us from natural elements as we strove to master the forces of nature from which we had been banished. Now technology serves to link us all to nature and to one another. An irreversibly chaotic system in its own right, the datasphere reinstates a natural order where it had previously been structured hierarchically. Of course people will see this as the coming of Satan!

We can insulate ourselves from the germs other people breathe, but—if we still watch TV or read newspapers—not from the memes they conceptualize and launch into the datasphere. We are all swimming in the same data ocean.

That technology now appears to be promoting nature's agendas rather than protecting us from them is, perhaps, the most frightening but essential aspect of the media revolution. Artificial distinctions between people, classes, and even religions are annihilated as the "specialness" that was formerly required for a person to access information loses its significance.

"Electronic communication is totally destroying literate civilization," Thompson argued when he first heard about the premise of this book. "Your generation doesn't read!" Eventually, however, he admitted that "there're some good aspects by which we are forcefully being imploded into one another. There's no longer a private space. The idea of literate culture is basically a middle-class notion—it's the gentleman in his book-lined study with the privacy for reflection. That's a very elitist notion."

Indeed it is. And it is a notion that a nondiscriminatory mediaspace destroys. The media shrinks the world, bringing the reality of remote regions into the living rooms of everyone else. Thompson agrees that there is no escape: "In our culture, we're constantly being invaded and seeing horrors, such as those in Bosnia, right away. Between newspapers and television, there's this whole sense of the planet as the public space. And this makes moral escape really hard."

And far from seeking escape, Americans want more.

The only real resistance to the spread of the datasphere appears to come from fundamentalist nations and groups. Fundamentalism, after all, is the maintenance of a distinct cultural or religious identity. The datasphere tends to make the whole globe into one place. The more media incursions into a nation or even a cult compound, the harder it is for its leaders to preserve its conceptual boundaries. This is why the Ayatollah chose to react to Salman Rushdie's *Satanic Verses* with an assassination edict. A state based in fundamentalist order cannot survive in the data ocean.

Ironically, if New York's *Seven Days* magazine[6] is correct, Rushdie's whole saga turns out to be the result of an extremely successful (so to speak) media virus. Rushdie's agent, the magazine suggests, concerned about initially poor sales, himself sent the Ayatollah a copy of the book, hoping to stir something up.

Needless to say, the virus worked.

PART 2
THE
MAINSTREAM

CHAPTER 2

TV FORUMS

What we want out of television has changed. Just as painting became more abstract at the beginning of this century when photography appropriated portraiture, broadcast television appears to have become more realistic since movies on video filled the need for dramatic fare on the home tube.

TV has always been naturally suited to covering news and topical events, and it quickly replaced movie-house newsreels as America's source of current events information. TV production was faster, cheaper, and more rapidly disseminated. Now that television news is shot on video, we do not even have to wait for "film at eleven"; stations just cut to a live feed. Anything that occurs almost anywhere in the world can blaze across our TV screens immediately. Even those of us who hope to avoid the news cannot escape updates and promos slipped into the commercial breaks of the evening movie. We learn, even against our will, that somewhere something is happening to someone—be it Michael Jackson or the nation of Bosnia—and many feel compelled to stay tuned.

The social, moral, and ideological intimacy this box fosters and foists is addictive. Now that our awareness as individuals has expanded to include the entire global neighborhood, the picture tube serves as the only fully functional window in our homes. We now demand it serve a purpose other than entertainment. We want information, ideas, and issues. We want to know what's going on.

Television has risen to the occasion—so much so that it is difficult to tell if our needs are shaping the programming or if the changes in programming are shaping our concerns. In either case our TV has developed into a set of forums ideally suited to the growth and spread of media viruses.

. . . AND JUSTICE FOR ALL

For baby boomers growing up in the fifties and early sixties, TV was meant to play the role of a parent, and its dramatic messages were decidedly patriarchal. The tube taught us, as our parents did, the difference between good guys and bad guys. Cop shows filled the airwaves, and audiences anxiously awaited the capture of characters who were defined by their badness. Good and evil were givens. Capture and punishment were the audience's rewards. These shows were not even as complex as ancient morality plays.

The detectives on "Dragnet" rarely displayed any emotion. They made no decisions or judgments. They were just doing a dirty job. The musical refrain (dum de dum dum) at each episode's end signaled that justice, quite simply, had been done. After the final commercial, we even got to learn the jail sentences. By the series' end, many issues—drugs, peace, love—of the late sixties had pushed their way into the the stories of "Dragnet," but the police officers maintained a completely hard-line stance. In one episode, the detectives attend a "group therapy" session and listen to a halfhearted defense of hippie values before slapping cuffs on the group participant and booking him for marijuana possession. There was no room for a reconsideration of values—yet. Law and order still ruled unchallenged by the complexities of modern culture.

By the late sixties, Americans began to question our war effort, our National Guard, and even our cops; television—

still struggling to maintain its parental role—attempted to reassure us with new images for our police. McGarrett ("Hawaii Five-O's" protagonist) presented a cooler image for law enforcement. His well-dressed and windswept team did not have to make any decisions, either, but their job was a little more difficult. They had to act "cool" at the same time as they were being good guys. In one episode Danno, the faithful assistant, goes undercover to a hippie pot party and successfully portrays himself as part of the "turned-on" crowd. The countercultural activities are still plainly wrong, but the cop must be able to incorporate any of the social hipness associated with them. The "Mod Squad's" sexy, interracial trio (a black guy, a white guy, and a white girl) worked the same strategy, except they could not just act cool, they had to *be* cool while enforcing the law. These were three hippies who had themselves been busted—Julie was the runaway daughter of a San Francisco prostitute, Linc had been arrested for his participation in the Watts riots, and Pete had gotten caught stealing a car after his ultrarich Beverly Hills folks kicked him out of the house. Literally co-opted by the law enforcement establishment, the kids making up the Mod Squad emblemized a desperate effort to shanghai the counterculture back into the mainstream. Leather jackets, long hair, and love beads camouflaged, for a time, a truth about the ambiguity of righteously justified law enforcement in an increasingly unstructured and free-thinking society.

"Adam 12" marked the last gasp of this righteous style of cop TV. Malloy and Reed were a spin-off of "Dragnet," actually and, as cops on the beat, were forced to deal with the reality of a transformed world much more directly than their detective superiors. Their set was not a squad room or an office. Their desk was a dashboard. Reed and Malloy—from different generations—watched the changes in American culture through the windshield of their squad car. We watched the Los Angeles landscape roll by right along with them—one bracketing device further removed—through our television screens. Reed, the younger "probationary rookie," may have had a slightly easier time relating to drugged-out hippies than his senior partner, but not much. They both held a world-view that righteously justified law enforcement; the real world was just too crazy to fit into the linear reports the cops were forced to file near the end of each episode.

But Reed and Malloy added a necessary ingredient to the reality of TV law enforcement: irony. Sure, there were always clear-cut criminals for the episode's finale, but most of Adam 12's calls were comedic in nature: a domestic dispute where a husband gets his head stuck in the toilet or a girl who is too stoned to understand the dangers of highway driving. Rarely did people get hurt on "Adam 12." It was as if the world was laughing at the "straight" roles these cops had to play in an increasingly un-straight world. The officers' defense? A sense of humor. They learned to approach the growing chaos around them with irony and always got back into the black-and-white with a sideways glance at each other. The world was no longer as simple as the dualistic color scheme of their patrol car, and "to protect and serve" meant to acknowledge and permit a certain amount of bizarre activity in early seventies Los Angeles. They also helped their viewers realize that, protected and distanced by the bracketing device of a windshield within our television screen, we were safe to enjoy the irony of our cultural and legal inconsistencies rather than dress them up.

By the early to mid-eighties of the popular "Hill Street Blues," a cop's job had become an exercise in existential philosophy. This was a world in which every action had both a righteous intention and a moral ambiguity. It's not easy to be an awakened and tolerant twentieth-century sensitive man and a fighter of inner-city gang crime at the same time. This show—following other popular efforts in cop self-awareness like "Baretta" and "The Streets of San Francisco"—made the final transition in justice television from crime and punishment toward equivocation and deliberation. The shift occurred because "Hill Street" focused on its cops' lives instead of the activities of its now "alleged" perpetrators. These officers were as screwed up as any crook.

Compulsive gambling, uncontrollable violence, attempted suicide, corruption, racism, and political ambition plagued members of this modern precinct. This show did not merely say that "cops are people, too." It showed that they—just like the bad guys—can be psychologically depraved.

If TV cops are more susceptible than most people to popping an emotional gasket, maybe this is because of the role they are forced to play: Blind allegiance to the values of law enforcement doesn't work in the modern urban schema. The city is a complex system, and there are just too many channels of feedback and iteration for it to be ordered by simple, straight legal lines. Whenever Captain Furillo does nab a suspect, Joyce Davenport, his second wife and the public defender, holds a press conference on the precinct steps announcing which statute or civil rights regulation his boys have violated. Even if he and his district attorney sneak around the law, there will be hell to pay when Furillo gets home and Joyce makes him sleep on the couch.

The episode that put their whole relationship in jeopardy was based on a media fiasco. Furillo knew one of his prisoners was guilty, but did not have sufficient evidence to hold him. The media, hungry for a suspect, had already condemned the man, and a huge angry mob was gathered around the station house. Furillo told the man if he did not confess, he would simply set him free. To stay within the protective confines of the police jail, the suspect gladly confessed to his crimes, but Davenport was not so quick to forgive her fiancé his shameful tactics. Their courtship was on shaky ground for three or four episodes, as the first signs of media about media peeked through "Hill Street's" dramatic veneer. Cop TV was breaking down.

But "Hill Street Blues" also served as a bridge to the kind of show that replaced it: court TV. In a chaotic and relative universe, punishment for crime is no longer the issue. Now television begins to tackle the question of whether or not justice is even possible. "L.A. Law," (1986), the show that began this trend, was created by "Hill Street Blues" producer Steven Bochco. Here, it is lawyers who have a platform to openly debate the issues around crime, punishment, and human conflict. The closest thing we have to a cop is Susan Dey—the actress who played Laurie on "The Partridge Family" in the seventies—as an assistant D.A. whose sense of justice is only matched by her conscience. The legal and moral arguments, rather than being relegated to side discussions, take center stage as the courtroom deliberates how to cope with issues that are anything but black and white.

"L.A. Law" took its scripts from the front pages of the newspaper, and many episodes even dealt with the relationship of media to reality. This was a Los Angeles perspective on legality, after all. Recognizable media icons were represented as plaintiffs and defendants. A Morton Downey, Jr., character is tried for inciting a neo-Nazi riot on one of his shows, just months after a similar occurrence on the real "Morton Downey, Jr. Show" and another on "Geraldo." Here, in the language and milieu of courtroom television, the real-life issues of this media travesty could be discussed for the benefit of viewers everywhere. In another media-reflective episode, Arnie, the divorce lawyer, became an on-the-air legal adviser for a local news show and learned that the substance of his legal work should mean more than the public image he adopts for his viewers.

"L.A. Law" reached its peak of media self-awareness (and probably its functionality) after the L.A. riots. The show had already re-created a version or two of the Rodney King case, but now it had an opportunity to dramatize the famous trials of the police officers and the ensuing violence in the streets. This is much more than a case of art imitating life. It is television drama catering to a societal impulse for thoughtful, after-the-fact deliberation of troubling national and world events. It is ideological instant replay in digest form. The show—here at its most viral—examines the issues behind an ambiguous case using the forum of the courtroom and the language of the lawyer. But true to its subject matter, the events of this episode spilled outside the courtroom and onto the streets. Ironically it was the harmless and endearing

Stuart Markowitz, the most self-searching, guilt-ridden liberal of the whole law firm, who wound up caught outside in
the riot and was injured by some flung debris.

This was the moment when "L.A. Law," perhaps unin-
tentionally, passed the gavel to more realistic television. Just
as in real life, the issues of the Rodney King case could not
be settled within the courtroom of "L.A. Law," which is why
one of the lawyers needed to get smacked on the street.
Courtroom TV, like cop TV, attempts to create a forum for
chaos—a place where it can be discussed rationally. Where
cop shows shot or jailed chaotic influences, courtroom television attempts to talk it out. It is a conceptual interface
between the order of our laws and the chaos of our
world. Courtroom television spawned half a dozen prime-
time lawyer shows in addition to "L.A. Law," such as
"Law and Order," daytime court dramas, including "Divorce Court" and "The Judge," and real courtroom coverage, like "The People's Court" or cable's successful "Court
TV" channel.

These "real people" courtroom shows walk the hazy
line between fact and fiction. The participants on "The People's Court" have filed real complaints in small claims court,
but drop their claims to have them settled by Judge Wapner,
a retired judge who hears their cases and pays the winners
out of a kitty provided by the show. The audience gets to
watch real people argue their cases and then make its own
choice before Wapner announces his official decision. In a
nod to interactivity, the studio audience votes for the plain-
tiff or defendant electronically.

On "Court TV" live feed or videotapes of real trials are
broadcast for a cable audience. We watch murderers, rapists,
and child molesters plead their cases and receive their ver-
dicts and sentences. During recesses viewers are invited to
call in and ask questions or share their opinions about the
cases. The American fascination with trials on television occasionally even spills over onto CNN, which broadcasted
much of the Menendez, Bobbitt, and Harding trials, as well
as the entire William Kennedy Smith rape trial, protecting

the identity of his accuser with a large blue video dot over her head.

The development of courtroom television accomplishes more than simply replacing cop TV. It is a forum designed for the consideration of memes. Like C-SPAN coverage of congressional debate, courtroom television and news coverage of famous trials—Heidi Fleiss, Baby M, Joey Buttafuoco, the Clarence Thomas hearings, Woody Allen/Mia Farrow, Mike Tyson, Rodney King, the "L.A. Four," John Gotti, "Dr. Death"—cater to our need for media to provide a testing ground for new ideas. Popular cultural forums are the place for us to evaluate our rules and customs. Instead of looking to television for spoon-fed answers or confirmation of established belief systems, today we want open discussion on difficult issues and a feeling of participation in the results. The courtroom television of the past, like "Perry Mason" and "Matlock," did not address this urge. Perry Mason did not debate issues; he merely conducted a police investigation in the courtroom. Finding the guilty party meant that justice had been preserved.

Today's realism-based courtroom television is meant to ask questions and not simply answer them. This is why it can be considered viral in nature. It explodes issues out of simplicity and into open debate. We have chosen lawyers to argue the issues because attorneys are our culture's best professional debaters. Unfortunately, though, real life has proven too complex for the courtroom intellectual and audiences have demanded more immediate feedback from the front.

Today we are witnessing the latest evolutionary step in enforcement and deliberation television as it makes its transition from courtroom television to yet another viral circus, "street" TV. "COPS," shot entirely hand-held and on the beat with real, working American police officers, begins with a reggae tune over scenes of arrests. "What you gonna do when they come for you?" the Jamaican-accented lyrics ask us, making it clear that this is a show about our own lives in the jungle. But we're not just the cops. We are also the potential criminals! In addition to presenting the realities of a police officer's job, "COPS" serves as an instructional video on how to get arrested. It is a video portrait of the very edge between order and chaos in our culture. We are meant to identify with both the police *and* the perpetrator. The show breaks dualistic notions of a simple "right and wrong," or "cop and perpetrator," and instead presents us with a relativist's multiple point of view. We are no more interested in witnessing the threat that the criminals pose to the cops than we are in scrutinizing the police for signs of brutality.

Each nightly episode gives us an opportunity to ride shotgun in a real-life police car as it makes its nightly rounds, raids, and busts. We also get, perhaps, one of the most accurate depictions of the real and complex struggles of life in the United States. Even magazines as dedicated to high culture as *The New Yorker* cannot help but notice the unique role this intentionally low-tech program plays in the Zeitgeist. As their media critic James Wolcott attests, "If President Clinton really wants to study the country's urban siege mentality (which has spread to the suburbs and even into some rural communities), he could do worse than to watch 'COPS.' As an ongoing sociology lesson, it's worth a dozen blue-ribbon commissions."[1]

If we assume that "COPS' " viewership is made up of people ignorant of the show's place in the overall mediascape, then Wolcott's astute commentary is meaningless. But America is watching "COPS" for a reason. This is "Adam 12," but it's *real*. The cops may act a little more polite and sympathetic than they do normally—they are on camera, after all—but this is reality-based television. As such it feeds back something to the viewing public they have been hungry for since the failure of courtroom television to express the reality of the L.A. riots: accurate images of life in the current cultural landscape. An unobstructed, undramatized view through the window.

"COPS" works because it is viral. Just as "L.A. Law," a courtroom show, is free to discuss openly the perplexing issues of its day within the framework of our evolving legal system, "COPS" examines the pressing issues of our time on

the level where they occur, the street. This is instant feedback from the front. The courtroom trials for the suspects
arrested on "COPS" probably occur weeks or months after
the episode is shot and deal more with procedure than they
do with what may have actually happened. Under the glare
of the camcorder light and the evaluative surveillance of an
audience, the extremely human men and women on "COPS"
make decisions that will permanently affect the lives of human beings just like us. After a stern warning, a cop takes
the cuffs off a teenage girl caught smoking pot and sends
her home with her crying mother. The issue of teenage marijuana abuse, one of the grayest areas in our current legal/
moral balancing act, and one that gets millions of dollars of
advertising and pages of editorializing from both sides, is
decided in the street late at night in the blink of an eye. Law
and order, in this case, means allowing for a little chaos.

The camcorder format of the "COPS" series also ideally
suits it to representing the self-similar quality of our chaotic
world. James Wolcott's favorite "COPS" episode, in which
five police officers struggle with and eventually cuff a huge,
naked, black man (whose genitals were distorted digitally in
post-production) stands as a tribute to the mirroring power
of guerrilla-style media.

Once the man is finally subdued, he smiles into the
camera shouting, "Put my face in the papers!"

As Wolcott recounts it, "an inmate had escaped from
the collective unconscious—a taboo figure, the Naked Black
Man with the Mad Grin. He tore a hole in reality, then returned, laughing, to the realm of the repressed, a reminder
that race is still the joker card at the bottom of the deck."[2]

By adopting the tools of a cultural surveyor, "COPS"
maps accurately the topography of our self-similar social
landscape. This is a world in which media is not just an observer of events, but an active participant. Just as scientists
developed quantum physics based on the theoretical principle that no observation can be made without affecting the
system being observed, those of us watching shows like
"COPS" are keenly aware of the impact of the camera on its

subjects and, likewise, the media on the world it is docu-
menting. The criminals are not the only ones performing for
the camera; the cops carry out exemplary arrests, reading
the Miranda warning with actorly precision. Call after call,
and on camera, the police deal with the reality of our nation's most pressing social issues, sometimes successfully and
sometimes less so.

Hoping to capitalize on "COPS' " feeling of immediacy,
Barry Levinson, a traditional filmmaker, created a show
called "Homicide," and Steven Bochco developed his own,
slicker version, "NYPD Blue." These shows—a style we
could call "hybrid cop TV"—are shot on film for big budgets, but from angles that look more like random video
camcorder positions. The editing is intentionally choppy in
order to create the illusion of a single camera's worth of
footage, from which different parts of scenes are slapped together. Even though these are fictional shows, they try to
preserve the surveillance reality of video documentary.
Levinson and Bochco understand that American viewers
now demand more than conventional realism from their
television drama. They want self-conscious realism. The reality of the media presence must be incorporated into a
scene for the issues discussed to have any impact. Because
they are scripted, though, "Homicide" and "NYPD Blue"
can intentionally launch memes about which their producers
feel passionate.

Marijuana legalization, or drug tolerance, came up as a
real choice for the officer on "COPS" who decided to let the
teenage girl off the hook. On "Homicide" scriptwriters have
the opportunity to plan and launch a full-blown virus. In
one episode several officers inside a station-house vault in-
spect a huge load of marijuana that was seized in a drug
bust. Richard Belzer, a comedian with a darkly ironic wit
who plays one of the cops, seems to have established himself
as the mouthpiece for the producers' most countercultural
sentiments. Holding a bag of pot in his hands, the detective
begins a long diatribe about the history of cannabis legislation in the United States. Practically lifted from the pages of

"High Times" (a marijuana culture and advocacy magazine), the speech explains how the Du Pont company, which was marketing nylon rope, lobbied successfully to outlaw hemp, their biggest competition in the rope fiber industry. According to Belzer, it had nothing to do with the smokable marijuana, which is harvested from a different part of the plant. He explains that hemp enjoyed a comeback during World War II, when it was used to rationalize war against the Japanese, who had seized islands on which the plant grew. *Hemp for Victory* was a motivational film shown to soldiers. Finally, when the war was over, it was publishing giant Hearst who conducted the media campaign against hemp, restoring public opinion against the plant and the drug, which was made illegal again.

"You really believe that?" asks the cop who made the drug bust.

"I do," answers Belzer flatly.

"That's why you never solve any cases," punch-lines the nonbeliever, couching a huge politically virulent speech in the cues of TV dialogue. Belzer's just a comedian, the precinct clown, and this is just a TV show. But boxed safely within our TVs and yet again in the fictional police vault, Levinson's sufficiently distanced characters are free to make dangerous suppositions. As an audience we are subjected not only to a tremendous and convincingly argued conspiracy theory, but also to a picture of our law enforcers, in a deeply secret situation, sharing their doubt in the system they are upholding. The surveillance style of photography eerily reminds us that this kind of conversation might even have been captured on a hidden camera, putting the career of ironic doubters like Belzer in jeopardy.

It is not coincidental that cop TV here developed into a forum for the antiestablishment political agendas of the sixties. The people who were rebellious kids in that decade have risen to positions of power in the nineties and use their media platforms to surreptitiously release viruses they hope will inspire some reconsideration of these issues. It was, in fact, a sixties sensibility that was responsible for restructuring the forums for debate in mainstream media.

Although both shows debuted in 1993, "NYPD Blue" immediately emerged as a much bigger commercial success than "Homicide"—not because its memes were more relevant or its style more virulent, but because the experience of the show is more about media than it is about law enforcement. The datasphere rewards self-similarity and proves again and again that the best way to infect the entire datasphere is with media about media.

Ostensibly, "NYPD Blue" presents the same kinds of issues as "COPS" or "Homicide"—police brutality, corruption, ambivalence toward law enforcement—but the most significant memes of the show have little to do with cops. To experience "NYPD Blue" is to observe the expanding boundaries of what is considered permissible television. Creator Bochco takes less pride in tackling real social issues than he does in airing the first totally nude hind-shot on network TV. (But he has spent his entire professional life in the television industry. It is no small wonder that these are the issues that matter to him.) Characters use foul language, make obscene gestures, have racist thoughts, and do all sorts of stuff characters are not "allowed to do on television." All this, of course, gets the show lots of attention from the newsmedia and tabloids, who have iterated clips of series star David Caruso's unclothed buttocks about as widely as news commentators said the word "penis" during the Bobbitt trials.

The first scene of the first episode of "NYPD Blue" made its media-based agenda amply clear. A female D.A. questions an alcoholic cop. "I'd say *res ipsa loquitur* if I thought you knew what it meant," she says. "Hey," the cop answers, giving her the finger, "ipsa *this*, you pissy little bitch!" Despite the fact that by 1994 forty-four network affiliates still refuse to air the show on the basis of its violent and sexual content, it regularly rates in the top fifteen on the Nielsen chart.[3] The week that the show premiered several real

New York cops were confessing to outrageous acts of corruption and brutality on a nationally televised hearing, but these are not the only memes propelling "NYPD Blue" to success. It was also in this same week that Congress began holding hearings on violence in the media and whether shows like "NYPD Blue"—which Bochco heralded as the first "R-rated show on broadcast television"—should be permitted at all. Publicizing the show better than its producers could have predicted, nearly all television reportage on the congressional hearings included clips of "NYPD's" proposed sexy and violent content. And the premiere was just days away.

While "NYPD Blue's" producers' tactics amount to little more than crass commercialism (getting attention by saying naughty words and showing sexy body parts that haven't been said or shown on TV before), the series' cheap thrills probably reveal more about our real cultural obsessions—voyeurism, sex, and violence—than does the more progressively political and well-researched meme content of "Homicide." Most critics, including me, agree that "NYPD Blue" does not match the artistic achievement or level of cultural commentary of "Homicide," but the show has tapped into a more virulent cultural vein. America's fascination with issues is only surpassed by its preoccupation with the forums that mediate them.

HOT TUB TUBE

"We set out to create an open forum," says Michael Murphy, creator of the Esalen Institute, the original meme factory of the late sixties and early seventies. Located at the site of a natural hot spring in Big Sur, California, Esalen couldn't really be called a true media outlet, but it has inspired an entirely new range of media forums, all dedicated to direct participation, feedback, and iteration.

The sixties psychedelic era led to a great interest in Eastern philosophies, shamanism, witchcraft, and consciousness. The major universities at the time were teaching these subjects from an academic stance, but not from an experiential or participatory one. As Murphy, now a respected author on spirituality and humanities, explains from his San Rafael home, "If you're gonna suddenly start meditating, God forbid, and have a mystical experience and then change your whole lifestyle, that's not what Stanford or any respectable University has in mind. So we wanted to create a place where people could explore these things. We were willing to spawn things."

So Esalen had two major purposes: to launch new ideas and techniques and to do so in a participatory fashion—an idea in itself. They created the practice of "confluent education," what Murphy calls "the marriage of the cognitive and the affected, the emotional, spiritual and sensuous. It has by now spread to universities in more than twenty nations." Esalen also launched the first bill ever introduced to the U.S. Congress for humanistic medicine. Esalen brought Boris Yeltsin to the United States for his first visit. It hosted the work of Arthur Koestler, Fritz Perls, Buckminster Fuller, Timothy Leary, Carlos Castanada, and hundreds of other teachers, scientists, politicians, and mystics who hadn't yet gained public recognition. But its ideas were not presented in a standard, academic lecture-hall fashion. These were seminars conducted for a participatory audience. For the first time the students were as involved in the discussions as the "teachers." Microphones were passed around to audience members, who were encouraged to feed back their own ideas to the main lecturer, who accepted the fact that he, too, could benefit from the interaction.

When the official talks and forums were over for the day, the same conversations continued in the famous hot tubs. A beautiful sunset, a little marijuana or acid, bubbling hot water, and nudity brought some of the world's greatest minds together in startling new ways. This was the counter-culture's Bohemian Grove, where new ideas could be born and their creators could network with each other.

Soon the more formal events began to exude this same

spirit of interconnectivity. "It was like running a theater," re-members Murphy. "We brought unlikely characters together. We had a get-together with Fritz Perls and the Maharishi. You could not believe what was happening. Fritz Perls would ask, 'Vy, Maharishi, do you always fidget with your beads? Vy do you tuck your foot into your crotch like that?' And the Maharishi would answer, 'Oh, the Brahman is one with the Atman.' It made little sense, but it was incredible theater."

The Esalen Institute grew famous fast. "It was one of the most visible places where such stuff was discussed, explored, and disseminated. By 1967 there were two or three hundred centers like Esalen in America." The nature-retreat style of these forums was something that had previously been the domain of the wealthiest businessmen and politicians. Now it was serving the counterculture: "It was the physical setting, it was the magic—you can call it cultural magic," Murphy muses.

Esalen served, in this way, to bring the darkness and passion of the anima—the feminine life force—back into the intellect. As this concept spread, the memes discussed inside Esalen spread, too. Today even the operating principles of the Clinton administration are based on the Esalen forum. "Whatever Clinton was doing with his cabinet at Camp David the very first weekend of his administration, all of that work was flowing in through Esalen in the sixties," Murphy finally admits, humbly. "They had these organizational development process groups like we've been doing for thirty years, and they had to come out and tell the media, 'No, no, this is not encounter-group therapy.' Donna Shalala, the new head of Health and Human Services explained, 'We've all been to five thousand retreats.' That really marked a generational change. The generation of the sixties is really in power now."

The interactive forum had even more of an impact on culture as it manifested in the media. Esalen-style workshops first spread through the New Age movement to groups like EST (Werner Erhard's Seminar Training) and NLP (Neuro-Linguistic Programming and fire-walking seminars), which conducted weekend transformational workshops. A teacher would lecture, or "program," a group of several hundred paying attendees, who would sit in chairs in front of a stage. Throughout the participants would have the opportunity to talk to the teacher, or feed back, through a microphone that was passed around.

It seems only natural that a new kind of television show based on the passing microphone would be next. Phil Donahue rose to the occasion with the first truly participatory interview show.

In the early seventies this sort of television show was a revolutionary concept. No longer was it educated professional journalists interviewing the politician, author, or celebrity; it was the audience. Topics like nuclear proliferation, abortion, hunger strikes, and homosexuality were now not the exclusive province of Walter Cronkite and David Brinkley, if they dared discuss these issues. A show like "Donahue" did not have to worry about which news was "fit to print," but instead depended upon the ratings to decide which issues were fit for public consumption. These shows were very different from the so-called talk radio of the sixties and seventies, which simply pitted their call-in audiences against an extremely opinionated host. "Donahue," at least in spirit, attempted to create an open forum between an audience representative of the viewing public and a direct participant in the issue at hand.

By the early eighties, "Donahue" had become a national phenomenon and spawned the dozens of open-forum formatted shows we see today. As they became more popular, the shows deteriorated, perhaps, in subject matter. By the time Oprah, Geraldo, Sally Jessy Raphael, Jerry Springer, and their countless clones hit the airwaves, we were much more likely to find transvestites on a forum show than we were Henry Kissinger. Lamentable, perhaps, but these are the issues people would rather watch. A "Donahue" show featuring Egypt's participant in the Middle East peace conference will not fare well against a "Geraldo" panel of rapists who clean the kitchen afterward or "Oprah's" of women whose ex-husbands married their sisters. The pitfall of mainstream media, of course, is that it generally caters toward the least common denominator. But at least the media has provided a new kind of participatory forum, where the subjects people care about are discussed by people just like them.

Murphy sees this sort of television as a bastardization of the Esalen concept. "It's the opposite of what our impulse was at Esalen, which was to show our common humanity. Donahue and Oprah Winfrey are voyeuristic. You watch someone else make a spectacle of himself. You don't have to disclose yourself. It's a tremendous corruption of what's going on. The media trivializes modern life. It's a distancing, a fragmenting, and it's not community-making. When I watch, my heart goes out to these people, these transvestites, but most people look down upon the people on there."

If Murphy were to follow the first rule of media activism, though, maybe he would see these shows in a different light. It is elitist and ultimately incorrect to assume that only "stupid" people are watching these shows or that their audiences have a different relationship to the media than those of us who condemn these programs' sensationalist subject matter. Even in cases where the participatory audience, in typical mob fashion, gets riled up against the guest, those of us watching at home, in the distanced, fragmented space Murphy criticizes, are at least objective enough to see that the guest on the show may not be getting a fair shake. The viewing audience is free to think, "If I were in the television audience, I'd ask the guest this question instead of that one." It is easy to criticize a sensationalist talk show for, say, giving a neo-Nazi a platform to voice hateful rhetoric. But by exposing these sorts of people rather than censoring them, these shows reveal the underlying inconsistencies in their doctrines. Instead of appearing frightening, these people's platitudes appear as inane as they really are.

In participatory talk shows, we are at once distanced and made more involved. Unlike a drama or even a news story, which challenges us to sympathize with the subject's

plight, we are instead made to identify with a somewhat critical studio audience. While we may or may not be brought
into communion with Donahue's guest, we are brought into
a greater awareness of our own, real relationship to the show
we are watching and the role we can play as private citizens
to effect change or at least voice our opinions through the
media. This is a citizen's forum, and the public opinion
voiced here has begun to matter.

Esalen, the original interactive forum model, also generated many memes of its own, ranging from Buddhist practices to quantum physics. The most important ideas coming
out of the institute were not specific subjects, though, but
ways of disseminating these subjects, meta-memes, so to
speak, dealing with the notion of public participation and
open forums. Murphy is proud of this, even if he does not
like how these meta-memes were co-opted later by mainstream TV. "We had a real catalytic effect with these Soviet-
American exchange programs. Not only did we spawn a
bunch of citizen exchanges, but the term itself 'track two
diplomacy,' was invented at Esalen by Joseph Montville."

Like many who are involved in spreading meme technology, Murphy uses words like "spawn" and "catalyze" as if
idealogies were replicating in a chemical or biological manner. The meme he's speaking about, track two diplomacy,
led to dozens of citizen-sponsored international forums
where scientists, businessmen, computer professionals, and
even schoolchildren could discuss issues such as nuclear
proliferation, monetary standards, and the spread of AIDS.
As we have witnessed, this intercitizen communication has
led to sweeping social and political changes throughout the
world.

But so has the American media's increased focus on
participatory forums for ideas over spoon-fed news. The issues that have long stayed in the closet or as the exclusive
territory of lawmakers and their friends or colleagues are
now competing for attention on afternoon television. It is
nearly impossible for the courts to quietly outlaw homosexuality or euthanasia when home viewers who may have felt

marginalized before now see that audiences agree with their feelings. Similarly activists who may have had a hard time getting their agendas publicized over traditional channels have no trouble finding producers hungry for material with which to fill their daily hours of programming. Almost any issue, if it finds sexy packaging, can at least have its day in court on one of the many idea forums on mainstream media. A clever viral shell might even guarantee that the issue is received favorably.

Most of these forums take for granted the fact that media representations are false, or at least deserving of dissection. "The McLaughlin Group," for one, a show on which journalists engage in a spirited round-table discussion of the week's issues, hardly takes the media machinations of our politicians seriously. These journalists talk about every news leak as if it were intentional and every press conference as theatrical event more than information exchange. They joke about each politician's futile attempts to create an image for himself and debate whether or not the public will believe the charade. Even more self-consciously, the journalists on shows like "Mediawatch" discuss political advertisements or news treatment of political issues in order to evaluate just how truthful and accurate are the media's depictions of reality. "Mediawatch" makes people aware of more than the potential artifice of media—everyone already knows about that. The show calls our attention to the ongoing interaction between media, public opinion, and social and political activity. Typical topics on the show include debates on whether the media's coverage of the Rodney King case incited the L.A. riots or whether Perot's talk-show presidential campaign brought the viewing public more information or merely better disguised propaganda.

Amazingly even tabloid media has begun to encourage participation. Several of these shows offer 900-number call-in response lines for the audience to voice its own opinions on key stories. Viewers pay for the chance to feed back, and a sampling of responses are played over the closing credits. This feedback has a chance to iterate, too. "A Current Affair," for one, uses this information to gauge public opinion, and then producers alter their coverage of a particular story to reflect the audience's point of view.[4]

However tired we may be of forum media or even forum media about media, we cannot deny that this is the current focus of television and that it presents us with an opportunity to experience some measure of participation and to consume an astonishing number of memes per day. Whether we watch issues discussed by lawyers in fictional or real courtrooms, audiences on forum shows, or journalists on shows about the media, we are more immersed in ideologies and agendas than we ever were before. This is the new television bias, and its features are common to nearly all of our other media outlets. MTV and CNN are twenty-four-hour viral conduits. The Internet, Usenet, and computer-bulletin-board services are dedicated almost exclusively to the spread and discussion of ideas. The do-it-yourself and home media industries are based on the need of consumers to document their own experiences and points of view. Current political activism means being able to penetrate media forums with ideas that elicit discussion and replication in other forums.

Forum media has catered itself to our culture's need for open debate and participation. It is a way for media to address the complex, chaotic nature of the postmodern experience and liberate itself from the obligation of providing simple answers or confirmations of already-held beliefs. It opens our mainstream and alternative media to viruses of all kinds and permits natural self-regulatory mechanisms to operate relatively unfettered by the control of any select group. Forum media also calls upon the intelligence of its viewers and participants. To enjoy a courtroom drama, a computer debate, or even a rowdy battle on "Geraldo," the audience must evaluate the arguments in relationship to its own developing awareness about a particular issue. Forum media, however sensationalized or tabloid it may get, depends upon the interpretive and evaluative skills of its audiences, even if it does not demand knowledge of facts or history.

Forum media loosens the grip of public relations experts on the opinions of the greater population. It demands that an entirely new set of tools be utilized for waging a media campaign of any kind. Moreover, these are tools that depend less on money or an established base of power than they do on a sensibility about how the public and the media will react to certain ideas when they are expressed in any of our forum media. Even presidential politicians are learning that the only way to win the votes of Americans is to step into the kinds of forums that the public trusts and address citizens in the manner to which they have become accustomed. As equals.

Politics will never be the same.

CHAPTER 3

PRESIDENTIAL CAMPAIGNING

THE UNSUNG, MUD-SLUNG, AND WELL-HUNG

In the 1992 presidential campaign, all bets were off. The rules by which candidates had learned to construct their media identities and attract voters no longer functioned, and presidential aspirants needed to create new ways to appeal to a media-savvy public in a much more complex datasphere. The four major candidates, as far as the media was concerned, were George Bush, Bill Clinton, Ross Perot, and Jerry Brown, and each of these men engaged in campaigns that told as much about their attitudes toward media as they did about their political ideologies. By 1992, the media emerged as more than a conduit for the candidates' expression; it became an active partner in the campaign. A candidate's relationship to the datasphere emblematized his relationship to the country he wished to lead.

Political campaigns have traditionally involved convincing newspeople to cover candidates in a favorable light. The public got their information about candidates from the group of journalists who travel on the bus with the candidates as they make their campaign tours. Since these reporters spend all day with the candidate, surely they understand what makes him tick. We trusted the boys on the bus to accurately summarize and communicate their designated candidate's views, style, and agenda—and to do so in fifteen seconds or less. The emphasis was always to catch the candidate exemplifying whatever image the reporters already held of him. In 1991, for example, media insiders had decided that Bob Kerrey was an unfocused candidate.[1] When he whispered a joke about Jerry Brown over what turned out to be a live microphone, reporters seized the opportunity to use this mistake to emblematize Kerrey's lack of his own clear goals.

Like any other in American history, the political campaign of 1992 was full of well-publicized gaffes—maybe even more. Mainstream news' fixation with the gaffe was a large part of what led to America's dissatisfaction with media middlemen, paving the way for the new style of participatory campaign media that was to come. For example, Clinton's alleged affair with Gennifer Flowers brought the tabloid press onto the same level as more formal journalism. *National Star* and "A Current Affair" were as likely to break these stories as any "legitimate" network news show. The CNN coverage of the Gennifer Flowers press conference included a question from Howard Stern's "Stuttering John," who asked her, "Do you plan to sleep with any other presidential candidates?" The distinction between tabloid, network, and even satirical reportage had disappeared. As the reporters on the bus stooped to gather material as mediaworthy as the tabloids, they undermined their own ability to convince their viewers that they were the singularly worthy translators of the candidates' messages.

The growing dissatisfaction of the public with the job that its reporters were doing, coupled with the growth of the datasphere and the increasing opportunity to circumvent the established media channels, drastically changed the face of political campaigning. Initially the construction of the datasphere enabled candidates to continue their traditional media tactics with greater ease. Forcing reporters to accept prepackaged press releases, a disinformation tactic perfected by James Baker during the Reagan years, reached an altogether new level once candidates began to package their own video footage. By 1991 local news shows, hungry for good visuals, began to broadcast campaign-produced imagery as its own. Now media strategists could do more than stage photo opportunities; they could shoot and edit them as well. Broadcasters did not generally tell their audiences that this footage had been packaged by the campaigns. Satellite technology also aided a campaigner's propaganda efforts. Once local television stations began to rent access to satellites on their own, candidates started conducting interviews directly with local anchorpeople who, so honored to be granted an interview with such an important person, were easily manipulated by candidates used to a much tougher crowd of journalists.

These factors seemed to tip the scales in favor of incumbents and wealthy candidates. Anyone who could afford to produce high-quality footage could get the news to carry it. An incumbent could also get easy airtime by granting an interview to a small station on a topical or local subject and then use the local affiliate's precious satellite time as a platform for his own campaign. These qualities of the developing datasphere, along with the power of traditional advertising and marketing methods, looked as if they were going to make it even harder for newcomers or alternative candidates to get their messages across. Luckily for democracy the scales were soon to tip the other way.

The public was ripe for a change. As Ken Auletta explains in his *Esquire* magazine review of the 1992 campaign, "The diminution of the media's importance is linked to a broader trend toward the elimination of elites and middlemen. . . . It happened when candidates and citizens alike rebelled against the media middleman. This year they decoded—perhaps forever—the insider game once dominated by the boys on the bus."[2]

Americans were fed up with being told about candidates by purported experts and desperately wished to hear them speak directly through the forums they had come to trust. These forums were not network news, television commercials, or traditional debate. They were talk shows, forum shows, call-in radio, and other participatory media. The success of each of the candidates in this election was dependent on his willingness and ability to navigate the new terrain of interactive-style media.

STICKS AND STONES

George Bush, the incumbent, refused to acknowledge these new tactics and forums. To their credit Bush and his campaign manager, Baker, were masters of the old style of media control. They knew how to market themselves to the press and exhibited tremendous skill in their public relations campaign for the Gulf War. But by the time the election came around, there were too many players on the field for Bush to control the ball. Media coverage could not be dictated through videos released by the Pentagon. The very boundaries of the battlefield were being redefined. Bush's was probably the last campaign to fight in a traditional fashion, and it betrayed his inability to take advantage of the new, sprawling, omnidirectional datasphere. Even the media viruses he did attempt to launch were ill conceived and short-term. Once they had time to iterate, they only served to gnaw away at the institutions and ideologies he was himself supporting.

In 1988 one of Bush's greatest media hits against his opponent, Michael Dukakis, was the "Willie Horton" virus. Bush supporters aired a television commercial that ostensibly attacked Dukakis's stance on crime and punishment. A furlough program that Governor Dukakis implemented for the State of Massachusetts allowed prisoners to take time off from jail to visit family and friends. One prisoner, Willie Horton, a convicted murderer, raped a woman while on furlough, casting grave doubts on the merits of the program. A group supporting the Bush campaign ran a series of TV ads publicizing the Horton case as evidence for their charge that Dukakis was soft on crime.

While the tactic against Dukakis may have worked in the short run, political and media analysts soon unwrapped the Horton virus and did not like what they found. One widely criticized ad emphasized the fact that Horton was black and his rape victim was white by showing cartoon silhouettes of each in the appropriate color. Articles ran in magazines and newspapers blaming the Bush campaign for inciting bigotry and shrouding an essentially racist agenda in an advertisement about crime control. Bush eventually distanced himself from the advertisement—it was not his own election committee, after all, who produced the ad—but Willie Horton soon became a symbol of racism and dirty political tactics rather than Democratic wimpiness.

By 1992 it was the Democrats who were bringing up the name Willie Horton, in order to remind voters of the excesses perpetrated by the Bush campaign supporters. In August, the *New York Times* reported that "it is not Republicans who are seizing on . . . Horton's image to frighten people out of voting for Democrats . . . Willie Horton is emerging as the Democrats' most potent rhetorical weapon, with supporters of Gov. Bill Clinton gleefully dropping his name as often as they recall President Bush's 'no new taxes' pledge."[3]

The Willie Horton ad became a full-fledged media virus once its significance in its media context became more important than its original stated purpose. Like all media viruses, it acted against the established political structure and campaign tactical system even though it was first constructed to maintain it. The Democrats clung to the virus once it had exploded as a preemptive strike against potentially damaging mudslinging. Clinton knew his greatest liabilities were a questionable personal life and liberal value system. His admission of smoking pot, his draft status, the Gennifer Flowers scandal, and his own independent-thinking wife stood as ripe targets for Republican attack. In the face of Bush's all-out assault on these fronts at the Republican Convention, Clinton retorted, "They're running against Hillary, basically trying to make it kind of a Willie Horton–like thing against all independent, working women, trying to run against them in a way that I think is really lamentable."[4] (Interestingly enough, it was actually Al Gore who first brought up the issue of Dukakis's prison furloughs in one of his debates with the governor during the 1988 Democratic primary!)

This new use of the Willie Horton virus caught on throughout the anti-Republican media. The term "Hortonization" was coined to label the Bush campaign's attitudes toward abortion rights, homosexuality, the decline of family values, Ice-T, and Murphy Brown. David Nyhan, a Boston *Globe* columnist, even called Bush's enemy Saddam Hussein "the gold medal winner of the First Quadrennial Willie Horton Talent Search." While Bush may not have been directly responsible for the original Willie Horton ad, he would be made to pay for it. A technique that incumbents had relied on—casting stones out of the tower down at approaching challengers—had been exposed as a dirty tactic. The stones themselves could be used to examine the thrower's own prejudices.

In Bush's case, nowhere was this more clear than in his campaign's attempts to cast Clinton and the Democrats as homosexuals. The strategy was to associate the challengers with qualities upon which all Americans could—wink wink—look down. But the Republicans, still unaware that their tactics would not work in an interactive mediaspace, were employing the techniques of the past. Unfortunately for them the laws of media war had changed. They could no longer count on gravity to keep stones falling down and away from themselves.

The attacks on Clinton's sexuality began as a way of making Bush seem more virile. Just three days before the 1992 Republican Convention, Reagan's former political operative Lyn Nofziger had said that Reagan was initially against the appointment of Bush as vice president because "he thought Bush was a wimp."[5] Meanwhile Clinton—who may indeed have had affairs with Gennifer Flowers and others—appeared more like a Jack Kennedy, with a healthy sexual appetite, especially compared with Bush. (Comedians jibed that the President was married to a woman who looked like she could be his mother.) The Republicans realized that calling Clinton a "skirtchaser" (as one party spokesperson did the night before the convention began) only added to his virile image. They needed a new approach, and homosexuality was the answer.

As with blacks, Bush could not simply state that he was "against" them while his opponent would help them. The Republicans could not openly condemn homosexuals. Instead they chose to associate Clinton with gay imagery and let their constituents do the rest. It began when Bush arrived in Houston and told his audience that congressional Democrats "give new meaning to the words closet liberal." Further, trying to associate Clinton with the stereotype of a gay interior decorator, he noted that the Democrat was so confident about winning the election that "I half expected, when I went over to the Oval Office, to find him over there measuring the drapes."

Pat Buchanan followed suit that same evening. "Like many of you last month," he said jovially, "I watched the giant masquerade ball at Madison Square Garden, where 20,000 radicals and liberals came dressed up as moderates and centrists—the greatest single exhibition of cross-dressing in American political history." As John Taylor pointed out in his article on the Republican Convention for the admittedly liberal *New York* magazine, "Pat Buchanan developed a more baroque version of what is emerging as the central Republican analogy for the Democrats—that by trying to hide their supposedly liberal agenda, they are behaving like a sexual deviant who pretends to be normal."[6] Buchanan also enjoyed calling Al Gore "Prince Albert," as if to evoke a sense of sexual deviancy.

The Republican strategy was a bit too obvious. Gay Republicans began to speak out against these sorts of character attacks, and media analysts delighted in dissecting the oblique jabs at Democratic values. In an effort to distance Bush from the rebound of stone throwing while preserving its effect on his opponents, Republican strategists let others do the President's dirty work for him. Rather than inventing their own images, the Republicans chose to co-opt viruses that were already circulating in the mediastream. This was a clever scheme in that it freed them from the charge of mud-slinging. The virus was "already out there." They were simply articulating its memes.

The Woody Allen/Mia Farrow scandal was one virus ripe for manipulation. New York's most envied couple, who had always demonstrated state-of-the-art postmodern relationship skills, were now revealed to be less than exemplary. Woody had not only engaged in an affair with and taken nude photographs of Mia's adopted nineteen-year-old daughter, but he was also accused of molesting his own seven-year-old daughter, Dylan. Mia, meanwhile, was portrayed as an obsessive, vindictive child gatherer, whose own psychosis was only surpassed by the accusations she made about Woody. As this scandal unfolded, Bill Clinton and Al Gore were staging their celebrated Democratic Convention in New York. The Republicans seized the opportunity to associate the candidates and their host city with the sexual deviancy of Woody Allen and Mia Farrow.

This was a much more complex and effective media virus than Willie Horton or simple homosexual innuendoes. Woody and Mia were already media entities. The public was familiar with the couple from the kinds of roles they played in Allen's films and already knew that these scenarios were at least partly autobiographical. Allen had an affair with a teenager in *Manhattan* and another in *Husbands and Wives*. His self-perceived distance from his children and his confusion about family relationships was explored in *Hannah and Her Sisters*. Even as the Soon-Yi scandal broke, the press kept us aware that the events in Allen's real life should be interpreted as the further development of an overall film/media persona. The *New York Times* mused, "For decades, Mr. Allen has fashioned a compelling alter ego in his films as a nebishy, nervous New Yorker in constant psychic distress. His experience in the courtroom will allow him to refine that character even further."[7] Moreover, as an audience, we had come to be on intimate terms with Allen and his characters. We could relate to his neurosis as well as his agendas. Allen's films invited us to identify with him, and, whether he meant

us to or not, we identified with the Woody Allen we could infer from the composite character of the parts he wrote and
played. As *Time* magazine put it, "In life as in art, Allen
seemed the perfect New York lover: successful in a creative
field, earnest and funny, qualities that in New York carry the
same cachet as 'rich' in, say, Dallas."[8] In real life Woody and
Mia were not married, but their relationship typified an enlightened cosmopolitan approach to love and parenting.
Journalist Eric Lax, who spent time with the couple, wrote
admiringly, "Few married couples seem more married."[9]

The shock of learning that a media personality whom
we had grown to know and love intimately could have sex
with his lover's daughter was just too much. All of the neuroses and behaviors that were rationalized to us in his films
and made to seem so endearing now looked like sickness.
We learned that a media identity—and an attractive one at
that—was false. Now we detested these once sweetly neurotic
behaviors and no longer trusted the man who seemed to embody them. In a campaign in which Bush was attempting to
focus on trust and one in which Clinton was developing
close ties to mainstream media, these were useful qualities in
a virus. By associating Clinton and the Democrats with the
Woody/Mia virus, the Republicans could cast doubt on
Clinton's own media representations, his popularity in New
York, his family values, his show-business pals, and his sexual promiscuity.

The Woody/Mia virus was easy to co-opt because of its
remarkably self-similar structure and dissemination. This
was a story about people in stories, whose own personal photos, tapes, and videos provided a dark underbelly to the
body of films with which we were already familiar. Mia
learned of Woody's affair when she discovered nude photographs of her daughter in Woody's apartment. When she
wished to charge Allen with child molestation, Mia immediately videotaped Dylan recounting the events. The tape soon
"found itself" in the hands of a television journalist, who
(amazingly) chose not to air it, but only to relate its contents.
Later Woody produced his own tape-recorded evidence, too:

a phone call in which Farrow's housekeeper made "disparaging remarks about Ms. Farrow's abilities as a mother."[10] Meanwhile Farrow herself used her son's recording equipment to tape several phone calls between herself and Woody, just before and after her public accusations against him.

The entire war between Allen and Farrow was conducted through media—not just home recordings, but the mainstream media. It was a battle for public opinion. Woody's interview in *Time* was countered by Mia's story in *Vanity Fair*. Woody appeared on "60 Minutes," displaying a Valentine card sent to him by Mia with pins stabbed through the hearts of her family. Mia signed a book deal; Woody held daily press conferences. "I see now that I have spent long years with a man who had no respect for everything that I hold sacred. Not for my family, not for my soul, not for my God or my goals," wrote Mia in a "letter to a friend" that served more as an intentional press release of her feelings. This couple was experienced at playing the media.

And this is what made them such easy pawns for others to use. Their story had its own identity as a media event, so it could be used for any purpose, and without the participants' consent. The *New York Times* understood Woody's self-created predicament: "As a film maker, he has made a brilliant career of analyzing his faults and putting his neuroses on public display. The trial was a highly unwelcome surrender of artistic control over the Allen persona."[11] At first the press joked that the whole affair was a Democratic plot "staged to draw attention away from the Republican convention," jibed the *Village Voice*. "For Pete's sake, the *Post* ran the convention on page four."[12] Even if it were true that the Woody/Mia story was distracting New Yorkers from the Bush campaign, the Republicans were quick to capitalize on memes that were potentially damaging to Clinton.

Newt Gingrich, Republican House minority whip, understood that this was an extraordinary opportunity for an extraordinary election year. In a memo to the White House, which he leaked (Mia Farrow–style) to the Washington *Post* just to make sure it got noticed, Gingrich announced, "Normal, traditional consultants keep applying their knowledge of the normal in a year that is unique." Gingrich knew that simply espousing "family values" was not enough to win an election and took on the personal responsibility of voicing the Republican agenda through a new-style, high-profile media virus. In August of 1992, just after the tremendously successful Democratic Convention in New York, Gingrich told an audience in Georgia, "Woody Allen is currently having nonincest with a nondaughter for whom he is a nonfather because they have no concept of families . . . it's a weird environment out there."

Time, quick to dissemble the virus, wondered who was the "they" in the sentence—New Yorkers, Democrats, deviants in general? But the message was clear. The same New York that so enthusiastically supported Bill Clinton also deified a character like Woody Allen. Just as Woody Allen's soft, intellectual neurotic admissions were revealed to be masking a much deeper psychopathology, so did Clinton's support of gays, lawyers, New Yorkers, and liberal values reveal his own moral deviancy.

Attorney General William Barr picked up on the Gingrich theme and modified it further to make it a much more pure media virus. Rather than attacking Allen or his actions directly, Barr chose to deconstruct the movie director's relationship to the media. "Seeming genuinely puzzled by all the fuss," he said to a Roman Catholic group, "Mr. Allen explained to *Time* magazine that he was in love with the girl. And having fallen in love, Mr. Allen implied, it must follow as night follows day that the two of them would consummate their love in sexual intimacy. After all, he said, 'The heart wants what the heart wants.' " Barr is acting as a media analyst more than a sexual moralist. By deconstructing the *Time* interview as a postmodern media construction, he gains the necessary distance and freedom for a scathing assault on Allen and Clinton.

"There you have it," he continued as he explained the iconic significance of Allen's statement to the press. "In seven words Mr. Allen epigrammatically captures the essence of contemporary moral philosophy. The heart is presented as an unreasoning tyrant over which reason, and therefore morality, has no influence. Try that as an instruction for your children when they ask you if a particular course of conduct is good or bad." Barr's statement created just the media stir he might have hoped for. His own comments spawned a media virus about an existing media virus. When Barr's words were analyzed and regurgitated by the press the next day (on the front page of most newspapers), he used the follow-up interviews as an opportunity to spread the memes he had wrapped within them. "This was not a media event," he declared, but a reaction against Woody's "pithy summary of contemporary moral philosophy." Barr was not taking a personal stand against Allen, but against "twenty-five years of permissiveness, sexual revolution and the drug culture ... the guiding principle behind our moral decline—the rallying cry of the long binge that began in the mid-60s."[13] The battle lines between the counterculture and conservativism had been drawn.

Given that the media itself was already seen as part of the countercultural "rallying cry," the Republicans' strategy was to attack media iconography as a way of affirming their own virtues. Dan Quayle, who by most estimates had nothing to lose, declared war on lax family values by pitting himself against fictional media icons, who, he believed, would be in no position to fight back. As he soon learned, he had miscalculated the boomerang effect.

The bizarre episode began shortly after the L.A. riots of 1991, when Quayle blamed the uprising on what he called, "a poverty of values. It doesn't help matters," he said, "when prime-time TV has Murphy Brown—a character who supposedly epitomizes today's intelligent, highly paid, professional woman—mocking the importance of fathers by bearing a child alone and calling it just another lifestyle choice." This was the breach birth of the terms "cultural elite" and "family values," viruses meant to blame Hollywood and the media for the decline in traditional morals and the associated rise in violence and discontent.

In some ways the press appreciated this as a clever ma-
neuver. *USA Today* understood that not only had Republicans developed a "short hand" for "everything you hate
about Hollywood," but that Dan Quayle had "tapped a
source that would carry his message faster and more effectively than anything he might have done on his own."[14] The
press recognized that by attacking a major television figure,
Quayle had launched a true media virus. Further, by choosing a fictional newswoman, he was also taking a swipe at the
newsmedia as a whole, without targeting any real newspeople. Was it a mere coincidence that candidate Clinton
was himself raised by a single parent? The Quayle virus implied that this would make for a questionable moral leader.

The brilliance behind this virus, at least in its original
incarnation, was that it appealed to the right-wing American
ambivalence about the women's rights movement. To many
Murphy Brown symbolizes what has gone wrong with America. Conservative viewers are still far more comfortable with
the image of Mary (Tyler Moore) Richards in the newsroom
than Murphy (Candice Bergen) Brown. Mary's comedy was
based on her innocence and pathos. She sweetly and un-
threateningly changed big, old, mean producer Mr. Grant's
mind about office issues or Murray's next raise. Two decades
later it is Murphy Brown who occupies the imposing office
on the left of the TV set, and it is her little, young, timid
producer Miles Silverberg who must sweetly and unthreaten-
ingly voice his disagreements with *her*. The roles have been
reversed, and Americans are still worried enough about it
for this tension to be the basis of a hit comedy.

For the virus to benefit Quayle, he needed to tag Hollywood as the force accelerating this moral discomfort. But
Quayle attacked the cultural elite, if we can call them that,
on their own turf, and they fought back hard. The first wave
of self-vindication came on Emmy night, when celebrities
ranging from the show's producers to comedian Dennis
Miller seized their moments on the podium as opportunities
to reframe Quayle's anti-Hollywood sentiments. They succeeded in cracking open Quayle's media virus and revealed

the agendas they believed were hidden within it. As Diane English, the show's producer and good friend of the Clintons (another not so coincidental fact that, unfortunately for Bush, the press was not so quick to pick up on), said, "I would like to thank in particular all the single parents out there, who, either by choice or by necessity, are raising their kids alone. Don't let anybody tell you you're not a family."

So now the issue was Dan Quayle versus single mothers. "Last night they said I attacked single mothers," responded Quayle in a speech the next morning. "They said that I believe single mothers and their children are not families. That is a lie. Winning an Emmy is not a license to lie. Hollywood doesn't like our values. Hollywood doesn't like our beliefs." But it was too late. True or not, Hollywood had infected Quayle with his own virus, and the mutation it would cause had only begun. Quayle had locked horns with a fictional foe, and the more he fought, the less real he became.

The hype and hoopla leading up to Murphy Brown's big fall 1992 season opener rivaled the presidential debates themselves. Murphy Brown, the character, was going to respond to Dan Quayle's attacks as if he were talking about her in real life, which, well, which he was. In the episode single mother Murphy, albeit fictional, directly tackles the reality of solo parenting. Meanwhile, as she attempts to calm her crying infant, she overhears the vice president blast her on TV. Within the world of the TV program, she is turned into a helpless, real victim, while Quayle seems like a disconnected media icon, totally unaware of her humanity. "I'm glamourizing single motherhood?" she yells back to the disembodied voice of Quayle. "What planet is he on? I agonized over that decision!" Other characters read real copies of the real New York *Daily News* from the day of Quayle's original speech that carry the headline DAN QUAYLE TO MURPHY BROWN: YOU TRAMP. (Still shots from the episode, with characters holding up the newspaper, appeared in the next day's *Daily News*, of course, capping off an episode even more self-similar than the Amy Fisher TV movie.)

But America tuned in to Murphy Brown that night

mostly for her well-publicized direct response to Quayle through an editorial on her fictional TV show, "FYI." The character addressed the audience directly: "In searching for the causes of our social ills we could choose to blame the media or the Congress or an administration that's been in power for twelve years, or we could blame me. . . . But tonight's program should not simply be about blame. The vice president says he felt it was important to open a dialogue about family values. Unfortunately, it seems that for him the only acceptable definition of a family is a mother, a father, and children. . . . Perhaps it's time for the vice president to expand his definition and recognize that whether by choice or circumstance, families come in all shapes and sizes."[15] From the show within the show, the doubly encased memes written by the Clintons' best friend hit their target.

Quayle's defense grew into a surreal effort at appeasement. The morning before the show broadcast, he sent a stuffed elephant to Murphy Brown's fictional baby, with a handwritten note promising "President Bush and I will do everything possible to make sure you and all children—no matter what their family situation—have the opportunity to grow up in prosperity." The producers of the show thanked Quayle for his thoughtful gift, but mocked him gently at the same time, informing him that they would send the toy to a homeless shelter "for a *real* child to enjoy." Quayle was put into a precarious position. The fictional characters could attack him freely (he drew first blood, after all), but for him to fight back, he needed to reduce himself to a cartoon reality totally unbecoming of a national leader. More than one newspaper cited *Who Framed Roger Rabbit?* as the closest cultural reference to Quayle's willing self-immersion into a fictional world.

To soften the blow of what was sure to be a devastating attack from the estranged cultural elite, Quayle chose to watch the episode that evening protected by a Benetton colors–like assortment of single mothers. The news journalists showed up to photograph Quayle sitting good-humoredly amidst the women and their babies, but the media circus surrounding Quayle and Brown was much too sophisticated for an old-style photo-op session. No static image of Quayle sitting on couches with African-American and Hispanic women would suffice in a media war as complex as this one had become. Quayle was still using the clunky weapons of the past, and his tactics appeared obvious, especially in the context of a worlds-within-worlds self-mirroring media battle.

"In the struggle of the stories," asked *Time* journalist Lance Morrow, "whose is the authentic American voice?" Indeed, is it Murphy Brown, daughter of ventriloquist Edgar Bergen, and now, herself, the puppet mouthpiece of producers who happen to be Hillary Clinton's activist friends? Or maybe it is Dan Quayle, who, having no puppet, "has become a moral symbol and performer himself: statesman and toon." Morrow chided the vice president for "wagging his finger at hallucinations of the popular culture" and for doing something "confused and vaguely degrading. Something unworthy and a little stupid."[16]

The Republicans' technique stood revealed. They had hoped to cast stones down onto the groups they wanted to blame and marginalize—unwed mothers, gays, New Yorkers, cultural elitists—but managed only to get themselves dragged down into battle. They had attacked a show that was already used to interweaving real news events and world issues into its fictional stories. Real-world newscasters and clips from current events were regularly incorporated into the show. "Murphy Brown" had established itself as a political and cultural iterator and one that ignored the normal top-down flow of news information. Once Quayle demonstrated his own immunodeficiency to the media viruses in the culture surrounding him, he was quickly dismantled and destroyed by them.

It is possible that the sacrifice of Quayle to the media by the Republican Party was a calculated risk in a desperate campaign. He was made into a media virus so that his very person could be injected into the datasphere as a weapon against the liberal and countercultural establishment. His credibility was already in question; he may even have been considered dispensable. In any case, consciously or not, Quayle was used to pinpoint and attack enemies in the media. Because these were media attacks rather than personal ones, they veiled the more controversial conservative ideologies in a war against ideas and icons rather than real people.

Most of Quayle's activity can be reduced to this simple strategy. The Murphy Brown virus was an argument against abortion, women's rights, educated people, and the news-media itself. It attempted to assert that the rich and educated in our society glamourize immorality and that this immorality leads to social woes like teen pregnancy, poverty, and race riots. In addition, because Clinton's campaign had so endeared itself to the entertainment community, the Republicans hoped to reverse the effect of Clinton's popularity in Hollywood by equating show business with antifamily values. Many, but not all, of Quayle's attacks on the cultural elite focused on the entertainment industry.

The *New York Times* began to keep a tally of Quayle's enemies. In one piece, headlined ON QUAYLE'S LIST: A RAPPER AND A RECORD COMPANY, the *Times* reported, "Vice President Dan Quayle has set his family-values sights on what he sees as a new demon in the entertainment world . . . he is now targeting a rap performer, Tupac Amaru Shakur, and his record company, Interscope Records of Los Angeles."[17] It seems one of Shakur's albums, *2Pacalypse Now*, had some lyrics about "droppin' the cop," and a Houston state trooper was shot and killed by a man who said he was listening to the song at the time. What Quayle did not say (directly, at least) to his Houston audience after visiting with the officer's mourning daughter, was that Frederick W. Field, the man who runs Interscope Records, had just hosted a Hollywood fund-raiser for Clinton the week before. While Quayle consoled a poor, fatherless child, Clinton was partying with the people who influenced black people to commit murder.

Bush picked up the theme of a deviated criminal Democratic agenda, if also indirectly, by targeting lawyers, whom he hoped to associate with the same kinds of faulty values—in this case, homosexuality, New Yorkers, and greed. In his speech at the Republican Convention, Bush said that sharp lawyers were running wild in "tasseled loafers," terrorizing Little League coaches with personal-injury suits. The imagery is clear, especially in the context of a convention where "gay" and "New York" have already been equated with a decline in the nation's moral fiber. The tassels are a cue for understanding that these men are not "real men." Meanwhile, left to their own devices, these shyster pansies prevent real men from engaging in their macho male-to-male activities, like Little League baseball.

But while these thrown stones may have garnered applause at the convention, the media and most Americans seemed aware of the technique Bush was employing. "The President's aides have found something they think is even scarier to voters than Willie Horton: lawyers,"[18] the *Times* snapped on its front page the next day. The paper got down to the core of the virus, citing that "recent public-opinion surveys suggest that Americans viscerally dislike lawyers and feel that society is, in the words of one Bush campaign focus-group participant, 'sue happy,' [and that this] can be made a partisan campaign issue." It goes on—and this was an article, not an editorial—to comment sarcastically, "On the political stage, however, the Bush campaign has developed an election year syllogism worthy of Ionesco: Mr. Clinton is a lawyer. Lawyers are bad. Mr. Clinton is bad."[19]

While the *Times* did not support the Bush campaign, more interesting than its distaste for his views was its willingness to dissect his tactics. This was an article about a media virus, written for an audience that has become more concerned about the way media works than its particular content. The *Times* was teaching its readers how to see through incompetently formulated media viruses, which tend to simplify issues rather than demonstrate their complexity. The real media virus here was that the Bush campaign was using focus groups to find an issue it could highlight the way it did

Willie Horton in 1988. But this was not 1988, and the playing field had changed.

The Republican campaign was based on obsolete public relations tactics. Bush's planners were used to waging their attacks against more progressive opponents by equating liberal agendas with immorality and cloaking hate campaigns in the overcoat of higher virtues. The Russians, Manuel Noriega, and Saddam Hussein were no longer viable campaign enemies, so new threats had to be created. As the *Village Voice* explained, an army of dangerous enemies was drummed up: "the GOP now hopes to make up in quantity what it lacks in quality . . . the media elite . . . cultural elite . . . Hollywood elite, pornography, drug kingpins, Murphy Brown, Woody Allen, Hillary Clinton and the whole 'radical liberal Democrat Party,' gays, lesbians, welfare mothers, coddlers of criminals, criminals, urban dwellers, and . . . change itself."[20]

A campaign of many enemies served to disenfranchise many previously loyal Republicans. Gay Republicans felt forced to leave the party, and so did many women. Many of those who even secretly supported members of Bush's blacklist left in droves. Worse for Bush, Americans who saw through this way of playing the media resented the Republican tactics and looked toward candidates who got more directly involved with the voting public instead of simply firing media missiles down at their underdog enemies.

TALK-SHOW CANDIDACIES

It was Ross Perot who initiated the greatest change in the way candidates relate to their media and probably Clinton who best capitalized on the new relationship. On "Larry King Live," in February 1992, Ross Perot became the first major candidate to announce his bid for the White House on a television talk show. He took phone calls from viewers, spoke in plain English, and established himself as a man who was willing to make a direct, unmediated appeal to the

American public. The other candidates were forced to follow
suit in the presidential bridge game. Bush became the
dummy, while Clinton played trump.

Clinton, who that same month was being accused of
draft dodging and adultery, was at his weakest in his own
battle against the media. As he put it, "During the first primary [New Hampshire] in February, I started getting bad
press and nobody wanted to talk about the issues anymore.
I wondered if the voters felt the same. So I started having
town-hall meetings where I'd just show up, talk for ten minutes, then answer questions for an hour."[21] That Clinton's
"town halls" immediately followed Perot's "Larry King"
appearance is more than coincidence, but not enough to account for his whole campaign strategy. Clinton's crew, anxious to get him away from the press's questions about his
personal life, gambled that the public cared more about social and economic issues (for example, James Carville's heralded strategy slogan: "It's the economy, stupid") than they
did about the candidate's sex life. Luckily they were right.

Clinton explained his circumvention of the press in—of
all places—a *TV Guide* interview: "I think the watchdog
function is fine. But it's often carried to extremes in a search
for headlines. For instance, the missing pages from my State
Department file—here was a deal where *Newsweek* bit on a
rumor. So you had these serious reporters who just wanted
to grill me about that—when the economy is in the tubes,
when 100,000 people a month are losing their health insur-
ance . . . And I'm supposed to take these people seriously as
our sole intermediaries to the voters of this country? . . .
Anyone who lets himself be interpreted to the American
people through these intermediaries alone is nuts."[22]

Clinton communicated directly to his American viewing
audience through some very unlikely forums. He appeared
on "Arsenio Hall" wearing dark shades and playing his saxophone and conducted a forum with teenagers on MTV.
"When people look back at this year and ask, 'What really
happened?' " Clinton said after the campaign, "I think two-
way communication on TV between the candidate and the

people will be the story. Arsenio and MTV give me a chance to directly communicate with younger voters—who might or might not watch news shows or read newspapers. When people talk to me about Arsenio, they don't talk about what they read or heard about it; they talk to me about what they *saw* on it."[23]

Clinton made two important points about his candidacy through his unorthodox media campaign. First, that by going on forum TV, he was willing to interact directly with a public more concerned with real issues, a public dissatisfied with a media that had been spoon-feeding it scandals for the past few decades. While "Arsenio Hall" can hardly be considered representative of all Americans, his audiences probably identify with him more closely than Dan Rather's do with *him*. Second, Clinton knew he was dealing with a post literate culture. There were many voters out there who no longer looked to the print media or even network news for their information about what was going on in the world. Clinton chose to appeal to these younger voters by appearing within the media they already respected. Simply by acknowledging MTV and its viewers' political concerns seriously, Clinton demonstrated his willingness to address issues that other candidates were ignoring.

He also demonstrated a willingness to appear human. One of us. He admitted being an Elvis Presley fan, and after the press corps privately dubbed him "Elvis" (for the way he sneered like the singer), the candidate agreed to sing a verse of "Don't Be Cruel" during a CNN interview. Bush tried to use this against Clinton. "He's been spotted in more places than Elvis Presley," said Bush. "America will be checking into Heartbreak Hotel. Now I know why they say he's like Elvis. The minute he takes a stand on something, he starts wiggling."[24] But Bush only hurt himself with these comments. No one speaks badly about The King and gets away with it . . . or the votes of white American Southerners. His comments made him once again into a reactive, impotent candidate whose only alternative was to attack the virility of his challenger.

From a viral standpoint, this battle was no contest. Clinton created media viruses with his actions, while Bush and Quayle used words to neutralize or co-opt the viruses of others. Clinton, originally following Perot's lead, realized he had both to circumvent traditional media channels that focused the campaign on his personal weaknesses and to reinvent himself not so much with words—people look at television more than listen to it—but with actions. Unlike the photo opportunities exploited by his Democrat predecessors (Dukakis posed in a war tank, Carter in his peanut fields), Clinton's media *tactics* were themselves his statements. His message was embodied in the kinds of TV appearances he made. Here was a candidate who was not afraid to go head-to-head with the audience on a "Phil Donahue Show," the callers on "Larry King," or the kids from MTV. He also demonstrated his faith in the intelligence of the public at large. He asked voters to rise above the middlemen of the media—not by attacking the press as partisan, as Bush did—but by making a direct appeal to the people through interactive-style media.

Bush eventually made his own appearance on "Larry King Live" and the right-friendly "Rush Limbaugh" radio show, but only after the two other candidates had worn out the uniqueness of the forum. He was obviously desperate to catch up. In a last-ditch effort to inject himself into the modern media, Bush appeared in a strange commercial reminiscent of the TV show "Max Headroom." "Virtual Bush," participants on computer bulletin boards called the spot, which was a quick-cut video nightmare of Gulf War scenes, computer screens, and TV monitors on which Bush's pixilated image slowly came into full resolution. The commercial ended with the word "BUSH" being typed onto a computer screen, as if the President had infiltrated the datasphere itself in the form of a pure, disembodied consciousness. And the last thing Bush needed to accomplish in his quest toward state-of-the-art media manipulation was to appear so unnatural and removed in the sphere that had replaced the political world to which he was accustomed. This campaign was won by the people who could call the new datasphere "home."

The moment Clinton clinched the election, in fact, was pinpointed by *Time* magazine as the evening of the second presidential debate, when the candidates were forced to abandon traditional debate tactics and appear instead on a "Donahue"-style forum show. The moderator cum host Carole Simpson—more than one media outlet made reference to the similarities between this CNN newswoman's style and Oprah Winfrey's—served as an intermediary between a Gallup-selected "undecided" studio audience and the three main candidates from which they were to pick. She marched about the audience with a microphone, encouraging questions and inserting a few of her own when the candidates failed to respond satisfactorily. Particularly damaging to Bush, who hoped to rely on the tactic of stone-throwing character assault on Clinton, was Simpson's immediately coaxing her audience members to share how they felt about mudslinging. "The amount of time candidates have spent on this campaign trashing their opponents' character and their programs is depressingly large," one audience member declared into the microphone held before her. "Why can't your discussions and proposals reflect the genuine complexity and the difficulty of the issues to try to build a consensus around the best aspects of all proposals?" A pretty enlightened viewpoint.

Bush's response attempted to defend the tactic, rather than respond to the audience's need. "You can call it mud wrestling, but I think it's fair to put it in focus," the President said. Clinton, on the other hand, delighted in the question and tried to make it clear that this open forum was his preferred setting. He hoped to establish that he was truly at home in an interactive datasphere:

"I believe so strongly in the question you ask that I suggested this format tonight. I started doing these formats a year ago in New Hampshire [only after Perot appeared on "Larry King," of course]. And I found that we had huge crowds because all I did was let people ask questions and I tried to give very specific answers. . . . I hope the rest of the night belongs to you." Clinton's answer was strong because it acknowledged the underlying need voiced by the audience: to find a candidate willing to address the complexity of real issues in a modern, participatory mediaspace.

This divide between Clinton and Bush further widened later that same night when a black woman stood up and asked plainly, "How has the national debt personally affected each of your lives?" The President was floored. He began to answer the question three times, stumbled, and finally admitted, "I'm not sure I get it. Help me with the question, and I'll try to answer it." Bush was panicking.

"Bush just lost the election," James Carville, Clinton's campaign manager, announced as he watched Bush scramble.[25] But Clinton had prepared for just this kind of moment. This was his turf. He moved away from his podium and came out so far into the audience in order to approach the woman directly that the television cameras were forced to shoot him from behind. He had broken the invisible "fourth wall" between the performers and the spectators. He was redefining media with his own footsteps. "Clinton connected," announced *Time*. What he said about "personally understanding" the plight of "real people" was much less important than the staging he employed to deliver it. He communicated not through the media, but *with* media. Bush ended the debate by nervously looking at his watch, obviously wishing for the torture to end and commenting jokingly but pathetically that Barbara Bush would probably make a better President than himself. His glance toward his wristwatch was replayed on every news show, emblematizing that the time had come for him to leave the political-media stage. He was as out of place as a silent movie actor in the high-tech world of talkies.

Clinton, on the other hand, knew how to navigate the new media ocean, even if he was not one of the men responsible for pioneering it.

DIAL-A-PRESIDENT:
THE PEROT/BROWN VIRUS

Jerry Brown began his campaign for the presidency with a straight and simple media virus: 1-800-426-1112. The announcement of his candidacy—made on the steps of Independence Hall in Philadelphia in October of 1991—was itself a declaration of independence from traditional campaign funding, which he believed was the root of nearly all political evil. Through Brown's direct-dial pledge line, private citizens could respond instantly, from a grassroots level, to a candidate who stood for the rights of individuals and not corporations or lobbying groups. Contributions would be limited to $100. Brown's campaign was an act of defiance.

"I run for President," he told us, "because I believe that this country deserves a real political choice. This election must be about something more than Democratic 'insiders' against Republican 'insiders' debating over incremental change. It is time to choose. The entrenched political establishment and their media allies believe that our country is on the right track and that its problems can be met with incremental efforts. If you believe that, please do not vote for me. However, if you search your heart and if my message rings true to you—then I tell you, it is not enough to vote for me. If you share my vision, then you must join me in this candidacy. It is time to choose: stand with them or join with us . . . I don't question the right of the Washington establishment to criticize, to scrutinize or to form opinions on substance or political viability. It is their privilege to believe that only card-carrying members of the Incumbent Party are worthy of election. However, when they assume the power to confer legitimacy, and thus determine who will be heard and who will not, then they steal what belongs to the voters—the right to choose."*

Brown's message was viral in its concept and deploy-

---

*Edmund G. Brown, Jr.'s announcement speech, Independence Hall, Philadelphia, October 21, 1994.

ment. Like any full-fledged viral attack, its deployment *was* its message. When he spoke of the difference between traditional, "incremental" change and his own plan for change, he was outlining a paradigm shift. His candidacy demanded a change in the way we view the political process. It was a movement away from incremental, or linear, step-by-step thinking and toward a more transformational or even chaotic urge. He capitalized on the weaknesses of the established political system—that people felt left out—by offering the opportunity for citizens to feed back through their own telephones. He spoke of reclaiming the right to "confer legitimacy," which had been usurped by media and established corporate and political bodies.

When Brown appeared at the first Democratic Party debate, he defied the official ground rules by holding up a sign with his 800 number and asking supporters to call in. On the surface this was a plea for funds. But the memes within this virus were much further reaching. They were emblematic of Brown's entire campaign message, "Speaking truth to power." As a media virus, it worked. The day following the debates, most newspapers carried the television picture of Brown holding up his sign. He—and his brilliant adviser Pat Cadell—knew that media had become a self-reflexive forum and that those watching and making it were most interested in the way it worked and changed than in its informational content. Again this campaign was about changing the way campaigns are run. It was a meta-campaign, so it was able to spread its memes through the media in a very chaotic way.

Brown's young campaign manager, Jodie Evans, reported that their 800 number drew in about 120,000 contributors. When she was interviewed in October 1992 by *Campaign* magazine, the editors were clearly impressed and even baffled by the success of this simple tactic. "The effort by all standards of modern political logic should have gone nowhere. The 'bang-for-the-buck' it achieved is unparalleled in modern presidential history," the magazine glowed. What *Campaign* did not understand was that modern political history had undergone a basic shift. The development of a two-way mediaspace had changed the way people perceived their ability to speak back to the tube and the politicians inside it.

As Evans put it, "Instead of buying votes through paid media—using special interest dollars—he [Brown] was speaking to a need for commitment, providing a voice for the great mass of people that was not being heard. That became the great source of power for a campaign that seemed to come from nowhere: the power of people trying to take back control of their own destiny."[26] Something as tiny as the flap of a butterfly's wings had the chance to iterate toward systemwide changes.

Brown's aide-de-camp, a gurulike philosophic presence named Jacques Barzhagi, understood how the laws of chaos could be harnessed to reshape the political campaign paradigm. He defended the Brown organization's apparent lack of cohesiveness by calling on the laws of systems math. "What appears to you as utter chaos in our campaign," he told one reporter, "is actually carefully strategized, dynamic chaos." The campaign self-consciously utilized many of the emerging new datasphere technologies, as much to spread their message as to demonstrate the ability of individuals to participate directly in the media. As part of an overall program called "We Are the Press," the campaign encouraged letters to the editor, public-access video, fax messages, Internet, Compuserve, and computer bulletin board forums.

Brown's campaign was based on satisfying people's urge to participate in the electoral process. It felt good to play, too, and not just watch from the sidelines. Likewise it was more exciting to instigate change by re-creating the rules by which the game was played. The campaign labeled the other candidates' mandates as "incremental change" because they were seeking to work from within the system. Jerry, as his fans called him, would change the very level of the playing field. This was absolute change. If Jerry's candidacy accomplished anything, it was proving that, in the words of Jodie Evans, "The status quo is a losing proposition."

Unfortunately for Brown, people just did not believe

that the kind of change he called for could be implemented by a politician from within an established political party. Although he sought to change the system, he had already held the office of Democratic Party chairman and still hoped to reclaim the party to serve his new goals for the nation. The party resisted him; it was an establishment just like any other. Brown's campaign seemed to want to burn down the castle while at the same time becoming its new resident monarch. A virus with such an inconsistent code can never hope to survive. The proponents of an antimedical establishment media virus like smart drugs cannot simultaneously hope to become the CEOs of Burroughs Wellcome pharmaceuticals.

Brown's campaign also lacked internal organization. However positively or even dynamically chaotic, "We the People" lacked leadership. While this can be seen as a positive sign—there was no repressive authority, and supporters were free to create self-organizing substructures ad infinitum—it also made the campaign diffused and unfocused. Brown was great at getting his virus to spread, but its memes were weak and ill defined. Worse, the basic operations of his campaign were poorly managed. Even newspapers that wanted to interview Brown had trouble getting through to the candidate, making firm appointments, or receiving campaign materials. Brown is a handsome, charismatic guy whose followers sometimes seemed more like groupies than responsible planners. He ran his office out of a charming old firehouse in San Francisco, where workers felt more like part of a cool new recording company than a presidential campaign. Most of them were in it to follow Brown, but Brown's philosophy was to let them create the campaign without top-down management. As a result, no one was in control.

If people are going to make a commitment to crash the system, they need to feel as if there's something safe to replace it, or at least someone who knows how to tinker with the engine. Enter Ross Perot, the 1992 campaign's best virus, even if not its best candidate. Perot stood for the most sweeping kinds of change, but was packaged as a common-sensical and nonthreateningly sweet old Texan. His reassuring age and manner perfectly balanced his radical call for a paradigm shift.

Perot's campaign worked so well because it was not staged as an act of defiance. Where Brown seemed angry, Perot seemed simply amused. "Let's just pop the hood," he'd say, "and see what's wrong under there and fix it." Perot's media appearances were revolutionary tactics, but they were expressed as matter-of-fact, utilitarian strategies. He announced his candidacy on "Larry King Live" only after more than forty-five minutes of prodding from the host, almost as if it had been decided on the spot. Unlike Brown, Perot was not bucking the established politics of media; he was simply stepping in and reinventing it as he went along.

For the most part, this made Perot appear like a capable leader. If he could run a revolutionary campaign as effort-lessly as this, he might be able to change some of the in-grained patterns in Washington, too. This appearance was somewhat deceiving. Perot's campaign was far from effortless or casually designed. Besides being a billionaire, Perot had run a huge computer company and understood the complex and evolving relationship between people, their technology, and the media. It was fitting for Perot to announce his can-didacy on CNN, the first international cable television net-work, and on an interactive call-in show, too. This was also the platform from which Perot could symbolically launch his most overarching virus: teledemocracy.

While the idea of electronic "town meetings" began with Buckminster Fuller (who may even have come up with the idea at the Esalen Institute), Perot's knowledge of com-puter systems software and the capabilities of communica-tions technology allowed him to present the idea as a concrete alternative to our present system of representation in Washington. The first hint of his intentions for rede-signing the nation's feedback loops came in the way he pre-sented himself as a candidate. He would only run, he told

Larry King, if people from all fifty states put him on the ballot. He would only act on America's collective will. Like Brown he set up an 800 number that within days boasted ninety-six separate lines. When this was not enough, he made a deal with the Home Shopping Club to lease 1,200 more lines that received up to 250,000 calls in a single day. State-of-the-art consumer culture technology had been transformed overnight into an interactive forum for an independent political candidate.

Like Bucky Fuller, who was criticized for his optimistic view of the role of technology and media in creating our future, Perot had a history of deep faith in the positive power of media. As early as 1970, Perot told Ted Koppel on ABC's "Issues and Answers," "We want to use television, which we consider to be the most powerful social instrument ever developed, to arouse and inform the American people, to give the American people a voice again on individual issues." By 1992 the technology had arrived. Perot sought to set up live, interactive forums—electronic town halls—where citizens could debate via satellite television about the issues affecting them. Congresspeople from each district could watch and participate, too, and more accurately represent the opinions of their constituents. "We'll have a way for the people to respond, and we'll be able to display it by congressional district," Perot explained.

The proposition even got praise from magazines like *The Atlantic*, which saw Perot's participatory-style electronic government as a way to reinvolve an American public that felt alienated by the techniques of public relations. Electronic town meetings could prevent issues from being oversimplified or emotionalized, the magazine argued, because, "such meetings expose people to conflicting arguments and make them think about their preferences before they vote. The last thing a democracy needs is for people to vote their raw feelings, their first impulses, before they have had a chance to reflect on them and discuss them with others."[27]

Perot's idea was to dismantle the current political system and to reorient the media machine around it. Rather than attacking those in power, he acted sympathetically to their problems. He shielded himself with simple talk. "Good, wonderful people come to Washington and are surrounded by the Beltway special interests. And over a period of time, those people become their constituents because you've got to have their money to have enough money to run your next campaign. And the reason you need so much money for that next campaign is you have to buy television time. And suddenly, we, the voters, are just sitting out here like pawns in the game, and they try to program us like robots over television. I think that's over," he told Larry King, "and I think your method of communicating with people on television is one of the reasons it's over. People like to have a voice. That's a magic thing there, where people call in and talk. The radio talk shows are really magic things, where people call in and have a [voice]. People really really care about this kind of thing. Our voice."

Perot's strategy was to symbolize this high-tech interactive forum concept in every facet of his campaign. Instead of traveling around the country in an airplane and conducting press conferences on the tarmac, he preferred to talk to the public through the call-in radio and TV shows, often over the telephone or via satellite. As *Time* put it, "Ross Perot had been transformed overnight into a kind of shaman for the television age, a faith healer who proposed to cure the ills of a nation with sound business sense and plain Texas talk."[28] The week before the election, he staged three half-hour infomercials over network television, where he used charts and a pointer to outline his economic plans for the nation. Again he was employing the media forums we had become familiar with as marketing programming to, quite literally, sell his ideas to the viewing public.

Meanwhile it was his job to warm up his high-tech media persona with good, old-fashioned Texan logic and phraseology. The two tones are not incompatible. Viruses are meant to stir a do-it-yourself passion. They do not simply attack the established system of doing things; they offer a way for regular people to take charge. A camcorder tape of the Rodney King beating demonstrates the power of consumer-grade video to fight police oppression. A book on smart drugs encourages people to take charge of their own pharmaceutical intake. Likewise Ross Perot encouraged a "pop the hood and fix it" participatory attitude toward government that appealed to voters' basic intuition. It seemed as if the only problem was the existing organizational structure. Once that was removed, we could all just get together and work this thing out using do-it-yourself technology and a little American ingenuity.

So why didn't Perot win? He fell into the same trap that captures many of the most aggressive virus launchers: paranoia. Viruses exist to infiltrate an existing organizational structure. Their enemy is the host organism. To create a virulent strain of memes, one needs to understand where the target organizational structure functions and where it doesn't. But this sort of world-view is susceptible to a conspiracy mentality. It is easy to see the workings of the repressive top-down authority everywhere you look. The creators of the smart drugs virus, for example, often see the link between the FDA and the pharmaceutical industry as a conspiracy designed to prevent Americans from getting the potentially inexpensive health care they need. Many such paranoid activists feel that the AIDS virus was concocted in a CIA laboratory in Africa. The most radical rap musicians believe the white race is a satanic one, created by the devil himself to repress black expression. Given the obstacles these activists face, it is not surprising that they adopt such extremist views. But paranoia and presidential aspiration don't mix.

Perot had a history of championing somewhat paranoid causes. His greatest efforts in Washington were spent lobbying for more investigation of MIAs and POWs who he believed had been held captive in Vietnam long after the war. His ability to analyze and critique the Bush regime inspired many, but his fear of the power of this regime ultimately stymied his own efforts. He dropped out of the presidential race for several months because he was afraid, he said, of actions that the Bush campaign was planning to take against his family. When Perot reentered the campaign, it took him quite a while to refocus the media's attention on his agenda rather than his paranoia.

This is why personal and interactive forums served him so much better than more formal media interviews. Perot's ratings skyrocketed after his infomercial campaign and his scene-stealing straight talk at the debates—so much so that the Clinton camp had gotten worried about maintaining its own lead. Perot's crucial error was accepting an opportunity to be interviewed on "60 Minutes," the preeminent investigative paranoia forum. Perot believed he would be part of a story about Republican dirty tricks; when he realized the interview was meant to challenge him on his paranoid beliefs, he took off his microphone and started to leave. He should have trusted his media instincts and kept going. By continuing the interview and defending himself, he came off like "Inspector Perot in a world infested by plotters, wiretappers and saboteurs,"[29] as *Time* later analyzed the gaffe. Perot described in vivid detail a plan supposedly hatched by the Republicans to leak dirty photos of his daughter to the tabloid press on the eve of her wedding, and then to disrupt the ceremony the next day. But, as *Time* pointed out, "All he had had were 'red flares,' not facts, he conceded. . . . The interview alone was wounding enough, the portrait of a would-be president so credulous as to take drastic action on unsubstantiated rumors."[30]

The rest of the media, still resenting the Perot style of avoiding their questions and speaking to the public directly, seized on the opportunity to discredit him. The virus was blown.

CHAPTER 4

KIDS' TV

SLIP IT IN THEIR MILK

H. Ross Perot's next major media presence was in the form of a "Sesame Street" puppet named H. Ross Parrot, who taught the alphabet, complete with a Texan drawl and common-sense style: "What we've got here is a great big alphabet just sitting here and nobody saying it!" This incarnation of Perot as kid TV icon has not been developed in order to get the candidate support from six-year-olds. Most children watching the program probably do not even realize the bird is based on a popular politician. But their parents who are watching with them do.

Children's television is as innovative as any programming being done today. Kids learn from and are entertained by puppets, animation, elaborately costumed characters, special effects, and popular music. The most imaginative of kids' shows, though, appeal to the parents, too. In the tradition of "The Soupy Sales Show" and "Rocky and His Friends," most kids' shows are directed at the child on one level and at the parent on another. There is a subtle, usually satirical or ironic communication going on between the makers of kids' TV and the parents who are watching alongside their children. This communication almost always has an irreverent tone, as if to counterbalance the surface sweetness or moral uprightness of the show's main message.

This is why kids' television has become, perhaps, the media's best conduit for controversial memes. The shows, their styles, and their characters serve as innocuous veneers for the hidden agendas of their creators. The Rocky and Bullwinkle cartoons, made in the sixties, were a tongue-in-cheek satire of America's cold war paranoia. Boris Badenov and his partner, Natasha, were sinister Russian spies, out to capture and kill "Moose and Squirrel" at any cost. Viewers were encouraged to laugh along at this glaring satire of patriotic fervor, as embodied by the all-too-serious flying squirrel. Soupy Sales was a bitingly funny intellectual comedian whose own kids' show served more as a platform for higher comedy and media satire than it did as an entertainment for children. Even his infamous downfall—when he asked each of the children watching to send him little green pieces of paper—was really a comment on the ruthless merchandising exercised by shows like "Romper Room" and "Bozo the Clown" on their young viewers, selling do-bee hats or promoting contests. The joke, of course, backfired, but Soupy had launched a prototypical media virus and developed a new mutation of the kids' show host that was to evolve much further in the coming decades.

We have come to expect hidden messages in our kids' TV. Today parents are more suspicious of shows *without* satirical subtexts. Programs like "Barney," which are huge hits with children under ten, are despised by parents and college-age students, who can find no entertainment value in them at all. Barney is just a purple dinosaur who sings songs with kids. The show is absolutely straight. But his straightness has led to anti-Barney rallies on college campuses, where giant effigies of the kiddie-hero are thrown into bonfires. In similar quests for irony, news shows jumped at the opportunity to appeal to the anti-Barney sentiment by covering, in great detail, the story of a boy who started a tragic fire by setting his Barney doll ablaze.

Meanwhile, more sophisticated "kids'" programming like the cartoon "Ren & Stimpy" find a receptive audience among teenagers, college students, and adventurous adults.

By following in the tradition of children's TV with satirical subtexts aimed at adults, new kids' TV, produced and written mostly by late baby boomers and Generation X members, are testing the limits of the tube's ability to spread counter-cultural messages.

PEE-WEE'S BIGGEST ADVENTURE

"I'm still in shock," announced Howard Rheingold, author of *Virtual Reality* and *Virtual Communities*, on an electronic bulletin board after his first experience of Pee-Wee Herman. "I tuned in to Pee-Wee this morning. I don't think the term 'acid flashback' is strong enough to describe my reaction. I think I'll watch this show a LOT. It makes me feel, well, *normal*."

Most impressions of Pee-Wee's television show were equally strange. The comedian/performance artist had tapped into something both entertaining and unsettling at the same time. The show—banned from the airwaves after the actor's embarrassing arrest in 1991—stands as one of the most viral creations of all time. It is media at its most self-referential, meme-dense, and psychedelic. Pee-Wee's own background accounts for much of the show's peculiar adoration of six-ties and seventies cultural insurgency and media iconog-raphy.

Paul Reubens, the young man who plays Pee-Wee, born to parents Milton and Judy Rubenfeld, was obsessed with media from the time he was a child. At six he was sent to his school psychologist for what his teacher considered to be an abnormal fixation with television and the "I Love Lucy" show. He attended California Institute of the Arts, a school created by Walt Disney in the late sixties and staffed by a very alternative and psychedelic array of professionals. One teacher at the school remembers Reubens as a wild and cre-ative performance art student who sometimes could be spot-ted running down the halls in a dress. At the time, though,

Reubens still hoped to become a serious actor and looked down on comedians who, he said, "are all crazy and neurotic, and display absurd behavior."[1]

Nevertheless, in 1977, he gave in to what he believes were the expectations of others and joined the Groundlings, a "Saturday Night Live"–like improvisational group in Los Angeles. His characterizations for the troupe seemed to embody his attitude about comedy in general: crazy and neurotic personalities, all of whom displayed absurd behavior. His most successful character, of course, was Pee-Wee Herman. Eventually he appeared as Pee-Wee in an HBO special, complete with greased crew cut, outgrown plaid suit, bow tie, and white socks and shoes and performed a sketch about indecent exposure in which he asked a character with an unzipped fly if he had a license to sell hot dogs. Ironically Pee-Wee's career ended when the same charge was made against him.

After appearances on other adult shows, like "David Letterman," Reubens had a hit with his first film, *Pee-Wee's Big Adventure* (1985), directed by *Batman* and *Beetlejuice*'s Tim Burton, and was immediately offered a spot on CBS's Saturday-morning children's lineup. So the origins of "Pee-Wee's Playhouse" were anything but child-oriented. While the character was a witty, sarcastic nerd-boy somewhere between ten and fifteen, the audience he played to was "Late Night," HBO, and alternative theater. At least a third of his viewers were over eighteen. Pee-Wee was not a Saturday-morning character, but a performance art piece—mostly intentional—that used a kids' television slot as merely one canvas in a giant, multimedia event.

Reubens refused to appear in public as anyone but Pee-Wee. All of his interviews were conducted "in character," and he turned down roles in other films—most notably one in John Waters's *Cry-Baby*—because they would have compromised the unique position of the Pee-Wee icon in the overall mediascape. Reubens was in total control of Pee-Wee and made sure all of his appearances were intentional viral eruptions. By maintaining the seamless integrity of the Pee-Wee character, he became a true-to-life Max Headroom: He was not a human being, but a media icon. He only existed when he was being broadcast. This gave him tremendous freedom to satirize our media and our culture. Like a media guerrilla, he could appear on the set, make his devilish commentary totally protected by his childlike veneer, and then disappear. There was no "actor" to comment on Pee-Wee's intentions. He existed only as a totally spontaneous, immature, and irreverent media presence. "Pee-Wee seems to have been born in the funny papers, where many characters have no family or domestic context," noted *The Atlantic*.

As in "Mister Rogers' Neighborhood"—which many believe "Pee-Wee's Playhouse" was satirizing—Pee-Wee would only come into existence as he entered his playhouse. Once there he and his friends moved from idea to idea, game to game, with no more connective scripting than Pee-Wee's sudden "Hey! I know!" When he left on his flying scooter at the end of the show, he would disappear into a Claymation universe the same way Mr. Rogers would disappear into a scale model of his little town. Pee-Wee's playhouse was filled with pop-art-influenced props and furniture and, even more notably, TV screens of all shapes and sizes. One screen played cartoons, while another manifested the telepresence of an apparently cross-dressing genie. "Pee-Wee's Playhouse" was a joyous romp through a world of media, technology, fantasy, and discontinuity. Pee-Wee owned a talking, tickling chair, an animated ant farm, and a freezer with loud Claymation food. Holding it all together was the consistency of the Pee-Wee persona: smart, witty, snotty, and, most of all, playful.

The best media analysis acknowledged that there was more going on here than met the eye. *The Nation* pegged Pee-Wee for what he intended to be: "As TV's first postmodern kiddie icon, Pee-Wee Herman carried a lot of cultural luggage. His Saturday morning hit show was a campy commentary on gender, authority and the television industry itself. Full of sexual innuendo, double entendre and autoreferential visual puns (Pee-Wee once 'went camping' on the set, complete with flaming campfire), 'Pee-Wee's Playhouse' played house in the wreckage of American innocence."[2]

Amazingly the alternative media seemed almost oblivious to the Pee-Wee subtext. The *Whole Earth Review* critic praised blankly, "No violence, no conflicts, no guns, no preaching, no sex. Just a decidedly weird house and cast of characters doing nothing more wacky than making ice cream soup or watching a travelogue of Hawaii."[3] Maybe it was only the mainstream media, threatened by Pee-Wee's agenda and his agility, who were able to recognize the potency of the virus.

Time understood that the Pee-Wee virus was more than wacky weirdness, and that in the anarchic world of childhood, television can serve as "the baby-sitter of a spoiled kid's dreams: it promises everything, never says no and lets you change the channel if you don't get what you want . . . In this kingdom, Pee-Wee Herman is the prince of prepuberty. . . . The spectacle is both corny and hip, retrograde and avant-garde."[4]

As some were beginning to suspect, Pee-Wee's campiness tested the boundaries of what is permissible in mainstream media. His gay innuendos were glaring. Pee-Wee's weekly playmates looked like members of the Village People. One was a hunk lifeguard, and another, "Cowboy Curtis," admitted to sleeping in the nude. On one episode Curtis receives a pair of new, size-fourteen boots from another playmate, Jombie. "You know what they say about big feet," asks the Cowboy of Pee-Wee. "What?" responds Pee-Wee. "Big feet, big boots." The show's main female character, Miss Yvonne, served more to distance Pee-Wee from any heterosexual aspirations than to entice him into standard American romance. While Pee-Wee might ask to watch her change into her pajamas, whenever she tried to kiss him, he announced angrily, "Game over!" She was a caricature of an overweight "fag hag" who admired Pee-Wee from afar but knew her only association with him would be in the company of his other male friends, and distanced through campy satire.

Gay camp reached a peak on "Pee-Wee's Playhouse Christmas Special," an evening show on which guests included Grace Jones dressed in a plastic bustier singing "The Little Drummer Boy," Oprah Winfrey, Annette Funicello, Charo, Zsa Zsa Gabor, Cher, and Dinah Shore. "Cher was right there in the same room as my chair," Pee-Wee punned after she left the playhouse. This special marked a turning point in Pee-Wee's career. It was as if he were now out of the closet or at least openly pushing the limits of his medium a little further. It was important to the larger design of the Pee-Wee virus that his unique relationship to the media be exploited. To grow, the virus needed to break more and more boundaries. But to stay safe and undetected by the cultural immune system, it needed to remain shrouded as kiddie fare.

Pee-Wee's comedy and commentary were more about media itself than they were about sexuality. Even the sexual innuendo had the quality of "Can we get away with this on TV?" It is too simplistic to see Pee-Wee as a promoter of gay values or lifestyle to kids. He was, much more importantly, testing our media and our culture's ability to play. He approached an issue like homosexuality with the mentality of a child to see how it looked in a new context. His comedy was utterly dependent on cultural references from the sixties and seventies, which made him the first genuine Generation X hero.

The assumptions of these post-baby boomers all depend on finding deep meaning and resonance in pop cultural iconography. A bond with another human being can be established based on mutual admiration for a cult TV show like "The Brady Bunch." Rather than praising their common media identifications, GenXers share ironic distance from the shows, toys, and emblems of their youth. What excuses their current fascination with their own past childhoods is the clever spin they can put on it through alienation, recontextualization, or satire. This is where Pee-

Wee was most masterful. He exploited our cultural confusion about what it means to grow up. As *The Atlantic* explains, Reuben's work "draws from . . . the first fifteen years of life and of the past thirty years of American culture as though they were somehow coextensive . . . his evocations of the past are weirdly affecting . . . their present impact depends on Reubens' ability to gauge precisely his audience's appreciation of their original social context."[5]

It also depends on his ability to remember the exact details of the cultural references of his own childhood—an ability that GenXers value highly. Silly Putty, psychedelic sixties cartoons, magic decoder rings, and TV sitcom characters are all appreciated and then challenged by Pee-Wee, who, from the safety of his childhood veneer, can pick apart a mythology that appeared so seamless to us when we were growing up. He deconstructed the media representations of the past by dislocating them in screens within screens and scrutinizing them with both the arrogant glee of a ten-year-old brat and the craft of a thirty-five-year-old performance artist.

"Now Pee-Wee's human animator, Paul Reubens, has been permanently deconstructed by the very forces he targeted," mourned *The Nation* after the actor's arrest in the summer of 1991. "The industry that makes big bucks exposing sexual fantasies to millions and selling mutilation toys to tots has declared Pee-Wee a nonperson for getting caught in a position of self-abuse inside a darkened 'adult' movie theater." Although Reubens had already decided to cancel the show before the arrest, CBS pulled the series out of its repeat schedule, his star was removed from the Hollywood Boulevard Walk of Fame, his doll was taken off toy-store shelves, and newspapers began running articles for parents about how to explain to their children what happened to Pee-Wee Herman. A new Pee-Wee media virus had been spontaneously launched, and it exposed as much about our culture as did Pee-Wee's intentional machinations.

The story quickly spawned media about media about

media: Pee-Wee, a media star, watching a porn movie and, allegedly, masturbating, was in turn watched by a cop who arrested him for public exposure of his genitals. Forty-eight hours later his mug shot appeared in the papers, side by side with his Pee-Wee face. So many articles appeared instructing parents on how to tell their children about Pee-Wee's downfall that the Boston *Globe* ran a satire column instructing parents on how to tell their children about the Boston Red Sox failure in the pennant race! As the media inquiry grew, conspiracy-style allegations were made by Pee-Wee's supporters. *The Nation* warned, "The moral? Orgies can go awry, and don't go camping in the wrong playhouse. And don't think you can survive as a rebel, however hilarious, in TV's well-fortified cultural garrison." It was as if Pee-Wee's media provocations had brought this wrath upon himself. Other bizarre media icons, like Cyndi Lauper and Joan Rivers, came to Reubens's defense against CBS, but the majority of media reacted against him.

The suspicions that "well-meaning" cultural guardians secretly held all along about Pee-Wee had been proven true. He was some kind of sexual deviant and a poor role model for the children of America. These critics may have wanted to call attention to Pee-Wee's moral ambivalence all along, but Reubens was so subtle and campy that to accuse his work of homosexuality or psychedelia was to admit familiarity or even a preoccupation with taboo cultural iconography. Who dared accuse little Pee-Wee of espousing gay lifestyles just for having Grace Jones as a guest on his show? Who would admit that some of those Claymation scenes looked acid-inspired? In the new context of Reubens's arrest, however, moralists were liberated to label the actor a deviant and review his work as dangerous in retrospect. Now our cultural immune system was free to recognize the dangerous viral construct and respond to it accordingly. Meanwhile America's eternal prepubescent had come of age. He got busted for whacking off.

BART SIMPSON:
PRINCE OF IRREVERENCE

Pee-Wee Herman did not exit from the media before he spread his infectious kiddie laugh to the tube's next child antihero, Bart Simpson. But where Pee-Wee's "Heh heh heh" seemed to communicate a sense of knowing, Bart's is gleefully destructive. His name intended as an anagram for "brat," Bart embodies youth culture's ironic distance from media and its willingness to dissemble and resplice even the most sacred meme constructs. As an animated character, Bart can do more than just watch and comment on media iconography. Once a media figure has entered his animated world, Bart can interact with it, satirize it, or even become it.

"The Simpsons" marks another evolutionary leap in the development of kids' TV. Its origins were also adult television; the cartoon first served as transition material for "The Tracey Ullman Show" in 1987 to bridge the gap between Ullman's comedy sketches and the commercial breaks. Soon these animated tidbits became more popular than the live-action portion of the show and Fox Television decided to give the Simpson family their own series. It is not coincidental that what began as a bridging device between a show and its commercials—a media paste—developed into a self-similar media pastiche.

"The Simpsons' " creator, comic-strip artist Matt Groening (rhymes with "raining"), has long understood the way to mask his countercultural agenda. "I find you can get away with all sorts of unusual ideas if you present them with a smile on your face,"[6] he said. In fact the show's mischievous ten-year-old protagonist is really just the screen presence of Groening's true inner nature. For his self-portrait in a *Spin* magazine article, Groening simply drew a picture of Bart and then scribbled the likeness of his own glasses and beard over it. Bart functions as Matt Groening's "smile," and the child permits him—and the show's young, Harvard-educated writing staff—to get away with a hell of a lot.

"The Simpsons" takes place in a town called Springfield, named after the fictional location of "Father Knows Best," making it clear that the Simpson family is meant as a nineties answer to the media reality presented to us in the fifties and sixties. This is the American media family turned on its head, told from the point of view of not the smartest member of the family, but the most ironic. Audiences delight in watching Bart effortlessly outwit his parents, teachers, and local institutions. This show is so irreverent that it provoked an attack from George Bush, who pleaded for the American family to be more like the Waltons than the Simpsons. The show's writers, as had those for "Murphy Brown," quickly responded, letting Bart say during one episode, "Hey, man, we're just like the Waltons. Both families are praying for an end to the depression."

The show shares many of the viral features of other nineties programs. Murphy Brown's office dartboard, for example, is used as a meme slot; in each episode it has a different satirical note pinned to it. The "Simpsons' " writers also create little slots for the most attentive viewers to glean extra memes. The opening credits always begin with Bart writing a different message on his classroom bulletin board and contain a different saxophone solo from his sister, Lisa. Every episode has at least one film reenactment, usually from Hitchcock or Kubrick, to satirize an aspect of the modern cultural experience. In a spoof of modern American child care, writers re-created a scene from *The Birds*, except here, Homer Simpson rescued his baby daughter from a day-care center by passing through a playground of menacingly perched babies.

The show's current supervisors, Mike Reiss and Al Jean, are both *Harvard Lampoon* veterans who delight in animation's ability to serve as a platform for sophisticated social and media satire. "About two thirds of the writers have been Harvard graduates," says the thirtyish Jean from the office he shares with Reiss on the Twentieth Century lot, "so it's one of the most literate shows in TV."

"We take subjects on the show," adds Reiss, who was Jean's classmate, "that we can parody. Homer goes to college or onto a game show. We'll take Super Bowl Sunday, and the parody the Bud Bowl, and how merchants capitalize on the event." Having been raised on media themselves, the Diet Coke–drinking, baseball-jacketed pair gravitate toward parodying the media aspects of the subjects they pick. They do not comment on social issues as much as they do the media imagery around a particular social issue.

"These days television in general seems to be feeding on itself. Parodying itself," Jean believes. "Some of the most creative stuff we write comes from just having the Simpsons watch TV." Which they do often. Many episodes are *about* what happens on their TV set, allowing the characters to feed off television, which itself is feeding off other television. In this self-reflexive circus, it is only Bart who refuses to be fooled by anything. His father, Homer, represents an earlier generation and can easily be manipulated by TV commercials and publicity stunts like clear beer. "Homer certainly falls for every trick," admits Reiss, "even believing the Publishers Clearing House mailing that he is a winner." When Homer acquired an illegal cable TV hookup, he became so addicted to the tube that he almost died. Lisa, the brilliant member of the family, maintains a faith in the social institutions of her world, works hard to get good grades in school, and even entered and won a *Reader's Digest* essay contest about patriotism.

"But Lisa feels completely alienated by the media around her," warns Jean. "The writers empathize with her more than any other character. She has a more intellectual reaction to how disquieting her life has become. When Homer believes he may die from a heart attack, he tells the children, 'I have some terrible news.' Lisa answers, 'Oh, we can take anything. We're the MTV generation. We feel neither highs nor lows.' Homer asks what it's like, and she just goes 'Eh.' It was right out there."

Bart's reaction to his cultural alienation is much more of a lesson in GenX strategy. Bart is a ten-year-old media strategist—or at least an unconscious media manipulator—and his exploits reveal the complexity of the current pop media from the inside out. In one episode—the show that earned Reiss and Jean their Emmy nomination—Homer sees a TV commercial for a product he feels will make a great birthday gift for Bart: a microphone that can be used to broadcast to a special radio from many feet away (a parody of a toy called Mr. Microphone). At first Bart is bored with the gift and plays with a labeler he also received instead. Bart has fun renaming things and leaving messages like "property of Bart Simpson" on every object in his home; one such label on a beer in the fridge convinces Homer that the can is off limits. Bart's joy, clearly, is media . . . and subversive disinformation.

Homer plays with the radio instead, trying to get Bart's interest, but the boy knows the toy does not really send messages into the mediaspace; it only broadcasts to one little radio. Bart finally takes interest in the toy when he realizes its subversive value. After playing several smaller-scale pranks, he accidentally drops the radio down a well and gets the idea for his master plan. Co-opting a media event out of real history, when a little girl struggled for life at the bottom of a well as rescuers worked to save her and the world listened via radio, Bart uses his toy radio to fool the world and launch his own media virus. He creates a little boy named Timmy O'Toole, who cries for help from the bottom of the well. When police and rescuers prove too fat to get into the well to rescue the boy, a tremendous media event develops. When newscasters interview Timmy, Bart makes political progress against his mean school principal by instinctively co-opting his own virus to personal ends. In Timmy's voice he tells reporters the story of how he came to fall into the well: He is an orphan, new to the neighborhood, and was rejected for admission to the local school by the principal because his clothes were too shabby. The next day front-page stories calling for the principal's dismissal appear. Eventually the virus grows to the point where real-world pop musician Sting and Crusty the Clown, a TV personality from within the world of "The Simpsons," record an aid song and video to raise money for the Timmy O'Toole cause called

"We're Sending Our Love Down the Well." The song hits number one on the charts.

So Bart, by unconsciously exploiting a do-it-yourself media toy to launch viruses, feeds back to mainstream culture. He does this both as a character in Springfield, USA, and as a media icon in our datasphere, satirizing the real Sting's charity recordings. The character Bart gets revenge against his principal and enjoys a terrific prank. The icon Bart conducts a lesson in advanced media activism. But through Bart the writers of "The Simpsons" are enabled to voice their own, more self-conscious comments on the media. Finally, in the story, Bart remembers that he has put a label on his radio toy, earmarking it "property of Bart Simpson." In attempting to get the radio out from the bottom of the well, Bart falls in. Once there is a real child in the well—and one who had attempted to play a prank on the media—everyone loses interest in the tragedy. The virus is blown. The Sting song plummets on the charts, and the TV crews pack up and leave. It is left to Bart's mom and dad to dig him out by hand. In our current self-fed media, according to the writers of "The Simpsons," a real event can have much less impact than a constructed virus, especially when its intention is revealed.

No matter how activist the show appears, its creators insist that they have no particular agenda. Reiss says he promotes no point of view on any issue. In fact he claims to pick the show's subjects and targets almost randomly: "The show eats up so much material that we're constantly just stoking it like a furnace when we parody a lot of movies and TV. And now so many of our writers are themselves the children of TV writers. There's already a second generation rolling in of people who not only watched TV but watched tons of it. And this is our mass culture. Where everyone used to know the catechism, now they all know episodes of 'The Twilight Zone,' our common frame of reference."

Reiss is deceptively casual. Even if he and the other writers claim to have no particular agenda—which is debatable—they readily admit to serving the media machine as a whole. As writers, they see themselves as "feeding" the show and using other media references as the fodder. It is as if the show is a living thing, consuming media culture, recombining it, and spitting it out as second-generation media. With a spin. Even Bart is in on the gag. In one episode, when Homer is in the hospital, the family stands around his hospital bed recalling incidents from the past, leading to a satire of the flashback format used by shows to create a new episode out of "greatest hit" scenes from old ones. Bart refers to a past show, and his mother asks him, "Why did you bring that up?"

"It was an amusing episode," says Bart, half looking at the camera, before he quickly adds ". . . of our . . . lives." Bart knows he's on a TV show and knows the kinds of tricks his writers use to fill up time. In this sense "The Simpsons" is a lesson in modern media discontinuity. Bart skateboards through each episode, demonstrating the necessary ironic detachment needed to move through increasingly disorienting edits. "It's animation," explains Jean. "It's very segmented, so we just lift things in and out. If you watch an old episode of 'I Love Lucy,' you'll find it laborious because they take so long to set something up. The thesis of 'The Simpsons' is nihilism. There's nothing to believe in anymore once you assume that organized structures and institutions are out to get you."

"Right," chimes in Reiss, finally admitting to an agenda. "The overarching point is that the media's stupid and manipulative, TV is a narcotic, and all big institutions are corrupt and evil." These writers make their points both in the plots of the particular episodes and in the cut-and-paste style of the show. By deconstructing and reframing the images in our media, they allow us to see them more objectively, or at least with more ironic distance. They encourage us to question the ways institutional forces are presented to us through the media and urge us to see the fickle nature of our own responses. Figures from the television world are represented as cartoon characters not just to accentuate certain features, but to allow for total recontextualization of their identities. These are not simple caricatures, but pop cultural samples, juxtaposed in order to illuminate the way they effect us.

As writers and producers, Reiss and Jean serve almost as "channels" for the media, as received through their own attitudinal filters. While they feel their only function is to "stoke the furnace," the media images they choose to dissemble are the ones they perceive need to be exposed and criticized. Reiss admits, "I feel that in this way 'The Simpsons' is the ultimate of what you call a media virus. It sounds a little insidious because I have kids of my own, and the reason we're a hit is because so many kids watch us and make us a huge enterprise. But we're feeding them a lot of ideas and notions that they didn't sign on for. That's not what they're watching for. We all come from this background of comedy that has never been big and popular—it's this Letterman school or 'Saturday Night Live,' *Harvard Lampoon, National Lampoon.* We used to be there, too."

In "The Simpsons" Reiss has found a thicker shell for his irreverent memes: "It's as though we finally found a vehicle for this sensibility, where we can do the kind of humor and the attitudes, yet in a package that more people are willing to embrace. I think if it were a live-action show, it wouldn't be a hit."

Reiss is correct. Currently in the mainstream media, it is only kids' TV that has a sufficiently innocuous appearance to permit its irreverence. The audience interested in its subversive attitudes is not large enough to keep the show in business, but the millions of kids who tune in every week to watch Bart are. A popular animated children's show is the perfect virus. It spreads for one reason, then releases potent memes that do not seem evident on the surface. "The Simpsons" works as a true media virus because its functioning is dependent on its media context. It exhibits self-similarity in that its episodes are media about media, and it promotes an interactive spirit because its main character is a self-styled media activist. As long as its memes stay shrouded in "kids' " comedy, the cultural immune apparatus remains unprovoked and the virus is free to run rampant. But if the show gets too obviously provocative, heads roll.

"REN & STIMPY": PLAYING IN THE CLOSET

"Ren & Stimpy" is a lesson in media activism, too—not as played out by cartoon characters but by their animator, John Kricfalusi, who personally tests the limits of his medium's ability to carry countercultural messages. Kricfalusi comes from another adult entertainment tradition, that of Ralph Bakshi and his 1972 X-rated cartoon feature, *Fritz the Cat*. Kricfalusi's own directing debut came in 1987 on Bakshi's Saturday-morning cartoon, a modernization of "Mighty Mouse" that, not surprisingly, aired on CBS in the half-hour slot after "Pee-Wee's Playhouse."

"The New Adventures of Mighty Mouse" was a much more blatant display of adult humor and hidden agendas than "Pee-Wee's Playhouse," and the network's censors were correspondingly more paranoid. Eventually, believing they saw Mighty Mouse snort cocaine in one episode (no one knows for sure exactly what he was really doing), they canceled the whole series. Kricfalusi went out on his own and soon gained the interest of the Nickelodeon cable channel (owned by MTV), which was looking for alternative "personal" styles of animation to compete with network, mainstream cartoon programming. With Kricfalusi they got more than they bargained for. His unlikely cartoon duo, Ren, an emaciated, hypertense Mexican "asthma-hound" Chihuahua, and Stimpy, a fat, lovable, dim-witted cat, embody a psychedelic, postmodern, homosexual, antiestablishment set of memes. Kricfalusi's dedication to lacing his cartoons with these agendas ultimately cost him his job and his rights to the material. Episodes were deemed unfit for children by Nickelodeon's executives, who decided to do further seasons of "Ren & Stimpy" without their creator. (Nickelodeon claims the dismissal was due to Kricfalusi's inability to meet production schedules, and its current producers—in an obvious attempt to keep its older viewers—still try to lace episodes with provocatively subversive content, although not with the success of the original creator.)

Kricfalusi's dismissal notwithstanding, "Ren & Stimpy" may be the most direct hit by subversive children's TV on the mainstream media that houses it. Unlike "The Simpsons," which satirizes media through sampling and guest appearances, "Ren & Stimpy" makes a frontal assault on our expectations about media. Such outrageous events occur in this cartoon, and so explicitly, that viewers almost feel the need to shake themselves awake, as if to say, "Is this really happening on television?" The specific ways "The Ren & Stimpy Show" accomplished this high naughtiness quotient reveal a lot about our current cultural immune deficiencies.

Most important to the success of "Ren & Stimpy" was Kricfalusi's convincing target viewers that his show was, indeed, intended for them. His "wink wink" came, as it usually does, in the form of obvious bracketing devices like fake commercials, direct address, and shows within the show. Many episodes begin with a commercial for Log, a toy from fictional toy manufacturer Blammo (meant to rhyme with Whammo). Log is just what it says it is: a log. The advertisement's lyrics immediately recall "Everyone wants a Slinky" or "Another fluffer nutter": "What's great for a snack and fits on your back? It's log, log, log." Log is nothing more than a wooden log, but, as we learn in later ads, it can be used in any number of ways or even purchased in one of dozens of costumes. The commercial appeals to the childhood mind-set specific to GenX, in which industrial waste products like springs, plastic rings, or gummy rubber became multimillion-dollar products like Slinky, Hula Hoop, and Silly Putty. But Kricfalusi regenerates and celebrates the imagery without the cynicism of "The Simpsons." GenXers enjoy the ironic distance they have as adults, but do not condemn the experiences of their youth. Slinky and Silly Putty may have been overpriced scams, but they were fun. Log is exaggeratedly silly, allowing GenX viewers to laugh at the aspirations they or their boomer parents had as kids, but also giving them permission to enjoy, with ironic distance, what it was like to grow up in a postmodern junk culture. This sets the tone for the whole show. Meanwhile kids can watch, too, and simply enjoy the characters and silly songs.

"Ren & Stimpy" also winks to its older audience in the form of shows within the show. Like "The Simpsons," who watch "Itchy and Scratchy," Stimpy is a fan of "The Muddy Mudskipper Show," a cartoon about a rather abusive little fish. The characters' relationship to the cartoon comments on the nature of their own animated reality. Ren, the realist, scolds Stimpy for believing in Muddy's existence. "Cartoons aren't real!" he screams. "They're not flesh and blood like *us*!" Stimpy simply looks through the camera at us, confused. His fanaticism about Muddy is no worse than the cult following for "The Ren & Stimpy Show." By calling attention to this, we are both distanced from and rewarded for our own relationship to the cartoon. This is a celebration of the GenX ethic: We can acknowledge the need to relive the media of our past and are allowed to do so as long as we wink along in recognition of our own silliness.

"Ren & Stimpy" is a kids' experience from the past, but pushed so far stylistically and subtextually that adults can appreciate the nuances and techniques they may have missed the first time around. To analyze it this way is not beyond the intent of the show or the experience people have watching it. "Rocky and His Friends" and "Underdog" are enjoying comebacks, but "Ren & Stimpy" is so tremendously successful because it is directed at an audience that enjoys a self-conscious awareness of their relationship to media. The show gives us exactly what we wanted when we were kids and then some. It tests the limits of allowable grossness, weirdness, and naughtiness.

The original Kricfalusi episodes of the show were fraught with some of the most humorously disgusting images in television. Stimpy had a collection of "nose goblins" he kept stuck to the bottom of a chair; they are green, talking pieces of dried mucus. Fantastically exaggerated magnifications of tooth decay, ear wax, ticks, nose hairs, eye veins, and underarm stubble abound. One episode was about harvesting Stimpy's coughed-up hairballs, and another focused on his Kitty Litter, which he also eats. This passion for the grotesque is a tribute to repressed childhood fixations. Kids love gross, slimy stuff. Some psychologists even believe that the fascination with slime and intimate body parts is an aspect of the child's developing sense of intimacy and sexuality and an important stage in the development of physical affection. But children are usually scolded for what are thought to be disgusting preoccupations. They are told that growing up means learning to be clean and are encouraged to repress messier urges. "Ren & Stimpy," by freeing its viewers to enjoy all the grotesqueness they can tolerate, is a statement against this sort of repression. It is an invitation to reawaken the child's world-view and, more than that, to overthrow societal restrictions and possibly arbitrary barriers to self-expression.

The original version of the show also daringly opened other locked closets of our social psyche. Homosexuality, perhaps our deepest, darkest cultural dust bunny, was the issue that got "The Ren & Stimpy Show" in the most trouble. Ren and Stimpy are not necessarily gay, but there are many suggestions even in current episodes that they are more than just friends. The dog and cat live together, sleep in the same bed, bathe together, and assume the roles of a husband and wife. Theirs is a domestic American life, and their relationship is often depicted as overly codependent. If anything, by not explicitly mentioning the boys' sexuality, the show is telling us that their sexuality is just a part of their lives and no big deal. But as a meme within the cultural virus of the show, their gayness has been exploited quite deliberately.

In the original pilot, Stimpy was supposed to have been pregnant with Ren's love child. This, like many other direct references to their homosexuality, was cut, but Kricfalusi managed to sneak in other more oblique references. In one episode Stimpy wins a contest and leaves home to become a TV star. Ren cries by his bedside photo of Stimpy—especially because he had a fight with him before he left—and misses his pal so much that his pillow turns into Stimpy and embraces him. In the end Stimpy gives up his fame and $43 million to come home to his true love. In another show Stimpy gives birth to a child who turns out to be a fart named Stinky. Ren is disgusted with Stimpy's stretch marks and even more disturbed when Stimpy goes through tremendous postpartum depression. When Ren tries to get Stimpy to kiss him under the mistletoe, little hearts emerge from his chest and his eyelashes grow. Another time Ren kisses Stimpy's forehead, causing his tongue to slowly uncurl and erect.

The most blatantly gay episode, and the most meaningful one, too, was called "Sven Hoek" and concerned the visit of Ren's brother, Sven. Ren, who has gotten fed up with Stimpy's stupidity, is anxious for the visit of his brother, who should be smart, like him. Sven turns out to be a near clone of Stimpy, and the two bond very fast. First they share their disgusting collections of nose goblins and spit with each other. Then, after a game of "seek and hide," the two end up in the closet together, sitting in Stimpy's cat box. As Stimpy relieves himself in the litter, we watch Sven smile as he realizes he is sitting in Stimpy's pee. As if aware of our own emerging realization about his sexuality, Stimpy turns to us and says, "Hey! This is private!" and shuts the closet door. Then, in the original script but cut by Nickelodeon from this scene, were lines through the closed closet door about playing "circus." Stimpy volunteered, "I'm a sword swallower," after which we were to hear a gulping sound.

If there was any doubt at that point about what was happening, it was made even clearer by Ren's jealous reaction on returning home to find "Sven Loves Stimpy" scrawled on the living-room wall. He goes mad with jealous rage and decides to urinate on Stimpy and Sven's favorite board game,

"Don't Whizz on the Electric Fence." When he does all three are electrocuted and die. Besides the obvious metaphorical value in the dangers of "sitting on the fence" when it comes to sexuality, the episode made clear, once and for all, that the hints at Ren and Stimpy's sexuality were absolutely intentional.

Esquire picked up on the cue and commented, "Kids won't even find out how much their values have been perverted until they hit high school!"[7] What *Esquire* considered a perversion, other, less mainstream media outlets praised as culturally progressive. *Reactor*, a Chicago alternative music and club-life magazine, conducted a spoof interview with Ren and Stimpy about coming out of the closet called "Happy Happy Queer Queer!" The piece jokingly concluded, "Now, there's no doubt that in the future, we will be forced to witness arranged dates, vehement denials from the network, along with probably a well-publicized marriage for one of them and of course the macabre speculation every time one of them takes ill."[8] The writers at *Reactor* obviously have a sense of how Ren and Stimpy function as media entities, so their mock analysis concerns ways in which gay people have their lives fashioned and adjusted for media representation.

It is surprising that so many gay references were left in the show while its seemingly less virulent political memes were more often cut by network censors. Maybe this is because political satire is easier and less embarrassing to recognize. Kricfalusi managed to offend both right-wing traditionalists and "politically correct" liberals by daring to consider all such thought obsolete. The most famously banned episode, titled after its superhero protagonist "Powdered Toast Man," cast Frank Zappa (a notorious rock and roll media viralist in his own right) as the pope, who at one point shoves his face deep into the superhero's buttocks. Later in the episode, Powdered Toast Man crumples what he calls "dusty old papers"—the Constitution and the Bill of Rights—and burns them in the Oval Office fireplace in order to roast marshmallows, an action he says will "relieve U.S. citizens of their constitutional rights." Righteous viewers complained to the Federal Communications Commission and the episode was shelved.

Another of Kricfalusi's characters, staunch conservative George Liquor, infuriated feminists on the Nickelodeon staff, who thought the name was meant as a pun on "lick her" (which is why Kricfalusi went through the pains to spell out the name "Liquor" on the screen so many times). According to Kricfalusi, his critics have lost the ability to distinguish between cartoons and reality, and consider characters like Liquor a genuine threat to their value systems. Nickelodeon executives rejected one episode, "Man's Best Friend," in which George Liquor physically "disciplines" Ren and Stimpy. Kricfalusi is angered but almost amused by these na- ively harsh reactions to his brand of comedy and cites an overfelt sense of political correctness for the misinterpreta- tion of his humor. "Somebody . . . used the word 'vile' to de- scribe 'Man's Best Friend,' " Kricfalusi argues, "but it's not violent. It's slapstick. I had to keep explaining to them that it's a cartoon! . . . Our biggest mistake is that we do our risqué material cleverly. They notice it more because our show is a hit."[9]

In all fairness, though, "Ren & Stimpy" draws more attention than, say, MTV's "Liquid Television" cartoons be- cause it is more ostensibly directed at children. The dis- sociated style and meme-rich content of a TV show is no crime in itself. Foisting these ideologies on growing minds is considered a far greater cultural crime. Kricfalusi himself admitted in an early *Spin* magazine interview, "I think we are destroying the minds of America, and that's been one of my lifelong ambitions."

Kricfalusi's formula for accomplishing this is based in postmodernism and chaos. More than challenging specific moral constructs, his cartoons eat away at the current model of reality, replacing the notions of linearity and continuity with a discontinuous, almost existential collage of pictures and ideas. "Ren & Stimpy" is a postpsychedelic cartoon. Its characters and plots do not follow the normal order set out by dramatic convention. In one episode they may reside in a trailer, and in the next they live in a house. Sometimes it is Ren who has a job, other times it's Stimpy. Sometimes they are astronauts, and sometimes they even die, then reanimate for the next show.

This sense of discontinuity is amplified by the style of the show, which uses a disconnected sort of animation in which psychedelic and quick-changing images move in front of 1950s-style backgrounds of stars and paint splatters. The sound track of the show uses quick samples of classical music or sound effects over a satirically monotonous wash of 1950s Muzaky background tracks, reminiscent of old public school instructional films or "Leave It to Beaver" television-era vacuum cleaner advertisements. The juxtaposition of old seamless imagery with the popping veins and sudden mood shifts of the characters only makes this discontinuity more pronounced. In one episode, clearly meant to evoke the feeling of a sixties LSD-flashback movie, the boys, distanced as astronauts on a show within the show, get stuck on a planet where they physically mutate dozens of times and lose their language skills and many parts of their bodies. With no rational way out, they just embrace each other for the last time, push a button, and disappear.

In Kricfalusi's new world disorder, the only alternative in an increasingly discontinuous and alien reality is to embrace the fundamental humanity we all share in the form of love. Before we dismiss this argument as reading too deep into the show, let us remember even *Esquire* mused that " 'Ren & Stimpy' is ultimately about friendship, need, and other timeless values. Who can say no to love? . . . We see in Ren a projection of our own repressed psychotic tendencies. His scream, complete with eyeballs that detach from their sockets, taps into the shared primordial well of our societal alienation."[10] Ren plays Vladimir to Stimpy's Estragon. While Ren recognizes the futility of his attempts to impose order and rationality on his world, Stimpy is too simple to care. Ren must learn to live in the "happy joy" manner of his pal Stimpy, even though he is so much more intelligent. At least on the surface.

It is actually Stimpy, in all his dim-witted glee, who has developed the coping mechanisms necessary for smooth sailing on the waves of an unfathomable postmodern sea. In the episode called "Marooned," the boys are stranded on an alien planet. It is Stimpy who takes time to appreciate the beauty of the planet's moon, while Ren is so stuck in his expectations of where a moon should be that he hits his head against it. When Ren panics—"We're marooned!"—Stimpy is self-conscious enough of his media identity—he is only playing the part of Stimpy—to smile and realize: "Just like the title of this cartoon!"

Stimpy, as dull and TV-addicted as he may be, is also equipped to survive in a discontinuous reality. He intuitively understands the nature of media and its accompanying alienation and knows that the way to endure is to espouse the ancient virtues of joy and friendship. Like GenXers, who pride themselves on their ability to hold on to the merriment of their youth, Stimpy maintains his simple but grounded sanity by seeing his life as a free-form and joyous adventure. Because he has no expectations, he can adapt spontaneously to the ever-changing conditions around him. "Ren & Stimpy" does "destroy the minds of America," as Kricfalusi intended, by posing an alternative, albeit mindless, strategy for moving through life in the media era.

While the post-Kricfalusi "Ren & Stimpy" maintains its reputation for provocative and disgusting moments, it has lost its greatest value as a viral conduit: At its core, like all of the best kids' TV, the show was a primer on living in a discontinuous, cut-and-paste reality. Whether it is Pee-Wee Herman re-creating a childhood through the antics of an adult or a kid like Bart Simpson deconstructing and subverting the media messages from the adult world around him, kids' TV manipulates adult culture by doing more than one thing with media at the same time.

CHAPTER 5

THE MTV REVOLUTION

WARFARE IN THE SIMULACRE

Crown jewel of the Viacom media empire, the MTV network began as a twenty-four-hour music video outlet—TV "does" radio—but it ignited a revolution in television's ability to impart attitude, style, data, and meaning. "I want my MTV" has come to mean a lot more than "turn up the bass," and the network can take credit for restructuring the music and media industries, as well as influencing filmmaking and news-gathering techniques, public opinion, social issues, and even, more recently, presidential and world politics. It has given a powerful voice to a previously unheard, or, at least, unheeded and underestimated segment of society.

The MTV invasion was fostered by the spread of cable TV (and, in turn, helped sell cable subscriptions to millions of households with kids). As a seemingly endless number of channels became available to American homes, it was only a matter of time before an all-music station would establish itself. Rock videos had already been playing in some of the hipper English and New York clubs since the mid-seventies—Max's Kansas City in Manhattan called itself a "video club" and played black-and-white videotapes of concert and club footage to its crowds between live sets years before music videos as we know them now existed. A few late-night rock-and-roll TV shows began to broadcast visuals along with

the hits, and several bands shot videos of their stage per-
formances intercut with graphics and scenes depicting the
narrative of the song or the tone of the music. When cable
became a reality for most American homes, MTV emerged as
the first channel dedicated exclusively to rock videos. Although it was denounced as a further commercialization of
an already too commercialized music industry, before long
MTV was as important a factor in an album's popularity as
the music itself.

MTV gave musicians a way to express themselves and
their style visually in a format much broader than a record
jacket. Record promoters saw MTV as an opportunity to advertise their artists for the cost of producing a short-subject
film, and seized on the opportunity to sell music by packaging bands in visual imagery. Since the purpose of these videos, unlike traditional television, was not to tell stories but to
market a band, MTV videos came to resemble commercials
more than they did short-subject films and took the form of
a series of images that augmented the experience of a song.
The aim of a good rock video is to establish a set of symbols,
totems, or even memes that together reflect the world of the
performer's music—or at least the world-view being sold.

THE TIME MACHINE

MTV works differently from traditional media: It creates an
aesthetic world rather than a narrative one. We do not generally follow the choices of a character made over time; instead we view a succession of images—a flow. While some
viewers find themselves absolutely lost watching programming with no plot, others—particularly younger viewers—
have developed a whole new way of absorbing visual
information. Pat Aufderheide, a media critic and cultural editor of the progressive newspaper *In These Times*, was one of
the first to realize just how categorically different the experience of music videos is from traditional television:

"One of music video's distinctive features as a social expression is its open-ended quality, aiming to engulf the viewer in its communication with itself, its fashioning of an alternative world where image is reality. [It is] an abolition of traditional boundaries between an image and its real-life referent, between past and present, between character and performance, between mannered art and stylized life."[1]

Music videos are, indeed, open-ended. Most video-makers reject any obligation to interpret a song's lyrics or story literally. Besides saving on budgets, filming imagery rather than the explicit narrative of the song gives the videos their open-ended quality. Most rock videos do not aspire to tell stories with beginnings, middles, and ends, but instead impart meaning through visual collage. They only need to create a mood or define an aesthetic that communicates the intention of the song or the style of the artist. What makes a video and, in turn, its artist memorable is not what happens during a video, but what it looks like. Peter Gabriel's famous "Sledgehammer" video invented a visual style by Claymating and mutating the artist's face as he sings his song, which creates an ambience for the song more than a story. It is a textural experience—a moment to moment appeal to the senses.

Any meaning from a video like "Sledgehammer" is derived from the relationship of the audience to the world of the video. We do not watch videos as much as we are engulfed by them. The most successful videos invite audiences into a new world order. A band called A-Ha hit the top of the charts only after its video for "Take On Me" aired on MTV. Making use of yet another new animation technique, this video involves a girl reading a comic book who gets invited into the story by one of the drawn characters, an animated version of the band's singer. She goes on a motorcycle ride with him inside the comic. Again the video functions by pulling viewers into a new textural environment. This video used a kind of pencil-scratched animation to create the effect of something between a real photograph and a drawing. The effect, at the time, was hypnotic.

Videos in the tradition of "Take On Me" also invite interactivity. We are promised that if we have enough faith in the imagery of our media, it can become real for us. Like Bruce Springsteen, who in his "Dancing in the Dark" video invites a random teenage girl from the audience to dance with him onstage at a concert, the lead singer of A-Ha brings a young girl into an animated wonderland.

On a more subtle level, the overall success of these videos can be attributed to the ability of their animation or other special-effects techniques to impart meaning. Peter Gabriel's video stunned us because its Claymation so effectively mutated the singer's face. The implication is that, at least within the MTV world, anything is possible—the human being is pliable.

A decade later Michael Jackson's 1992 "Black or White" video brought us a new computer-animation technique— morphing—and a new set of associated thematic implications for a more socially aware MTV audience. By seemingly transforming one face into another, Jackson's animators let us experience a world where the lines between the races— and even the sexes—have no meaning. The video animation technique imparts the meaning.

The best videos exploit the fact that the world inside one's MTV is not bound by the same laws as consensus reality. A girl can suddenly find herself dancing with a superstar, or a person's face can mutate into someone else's. On an even more fundamental level, rock videos are essentially unreal. They exist in no-time. Singers only move their lips to songs recorded months earlier. Scenes are cut so discontinuously that the vocalist may appear on three different continents within a single lyrical phrase. No attempt is made to convey a reality consistent with the laws of nature as we know them. Instead, admitting the inherent inconsistencies of their worlds, videos are liberated into a timeless dreamworld, where discontinuities are exploited as opportunities.

MTV was developed to be discontinuous experience. Unlike traditional programming where each show falls into its own half-hour or hour-long slot, MTV is almost without schedule. Although more recently MTV has initiated a

number of regularly scheduled features, for the most part
MTV is music videos on tap—a constant flow of music and
images available at the flick of a switch, just like timeless air-
port or elevator music. Executives at the channel capitalized
on this quality early on. Some of the first promos asked,
"What if time had never been invented?" Another announced that MTV is on "twenty-four hours every day . . . so
you'll be able to live forever." The VJs, as they are called, occasionally make segues between the videos from a studio,
backed by filmed images of fish or clocks, reminiscent of
screen-saver programs for personal computers. Like the idle
computer, MTV is in suspended animation and thus in suspended time.

The videos also adhere to this principle. MTV is dominated by quick-cut videos, which disallow any attempt by
the viewer to create a continuous experience over time. The
fact that these videos do not linger on an image for long is
not simply to cater to the short attention spans of its young
viewers. In fact, what may seem like a muddle of random images for viewers unaccustomed to the MTV style is quite
comprehensible to those who have been raised on a more
discontinuously styled media. Until MTV the shortest edit
duration considered permissible by filmmakers was two seconds. Anything shorter was thought to be too quick for an
audience to make sense of. Today videos regularly use edits
as short as one-third second or even "flash frames" that
might last a tenth of a second or less. The increase in images
per second corresponds directly to an increase in the
amount of visual information younger viewers are capable of
gleaning off the monitor. MTV can be seen as a form of educational television in that it trains eyes and brains to scan
more images faster and faster.

For those hoping to sell records, faster cuts mean more
opportunities to catch attention. Each image is a potential
attractor—a potential seduction. For videomakers the quick-
cut style is an opportunity to show more images and create
a more complete set of pictures about an imaginary world.
For the performers more cuts are an opportunity to appear

as more characters or in more permutations. For the perceptive viewer, the quick-cut style communicates as much as any
of the individual images do. The discontinuity is an opportunity to interact with the medium.

The quick-cut editing of rock videos promotes a participatory involvement from their audience. The shots go by so
quickly and are so apparently discontinuous that the viewer
must make his own connections between the images. It is almost a slide show, in which the real movement occurs in the
transition from picture to picture. Regular movies work by
creating the illusion of movement between many separate
frames of film shown in rapid succession. Our eyes smooth
out the motion so that the images appear continuous, and
we easily perceive that the subject is running or jumping or
crying. Rock videos, often using choppy super 8mm film, acknowledge rather than smooth over frame-to-frame discontinuities and exploit them in order to tell different kinds of
stories—stories about a mediaworld where discontinuity is
the rule.

Still, for the viewer to comprehend the meaning or
even "meta-continuity" of the video, he must actively draw
connections between the succession of shots. While audiences less than a century ago could not understand the basic
film grammar of a reaction shot (taking the camera off the
character speaking and focusing on the listener), now a typical modern audience has the interpretive skill to find the
sense in intentionally discontinuous images. Imagine trying,
if you have never been exposed to film or media, to understand the rock video of a song used in a movie—say Whitney
Houston singing a song from the film *The Bodyguard*. Sometimes you see clips from the movie—usually greatest-hits-
style quick cuts between chase scenes and love scenes with
costar Kevin Costner. You also see shots of Whitney singing
the song, maybe in a recording studio, or on a film stage, or
even onstage in a performance within the plot of the film. So
while Whitney straddles both or even all four realities—
recording studio, soundstage, film story, and stage within the
film story—Costner is restricted to just one, the film story.

But by the end of the video, for him to do his bodyguarding, Costner runs onto a stage where Whitney's character is performing to save her from an attempted attack. The climax of the video is Costner leaping from one reality into another, which, of course, is meant to be an expression of his love for Whitney's character, above and beyond his role as her bodyguard. For the audience who does not even know that *The Bodyguard* is a movie, how can it make sense of all this? Even those who have seen the film will have trouble rationalizing the world of the video while maintaining the reality of the film.

Just where is Whitney supposed to be when she is singing the song in the studio? Is this after the shooting of the film, when she is remembering the plot of the movie as she watches scenes projected onto a screen behind her? But the song must have been recorded before the filming of the movie so that she could lip-synch during the film. Or is she lip-synching now, along with music she recorded during the film? Or is she really singing in all of these places, and if she is, how do they keep the sound so consistent? And why is she so emotional about all this? Is she remembering the plot of the movie? Is she remembering the filming of the movie? Was she really in love with Kevin Costner? Will he burst onto the soundstage out of his role as her costar because he loves her in real life?

The impact of rock videos like this one result from, as with the Stage Manager character in Thornton Wilder's *Our Town*, the ability of the performer to engage in the action on many levels at once, both participating in and commenting on the scenes at the same time. A rap singer may walk through a ghetto with his tough street friends, but he is also reciting or, rather, lip-synching his lyrics into the lens of the camera. He is both the participant in and commentator on the scene. The video may even cut to dancers in a studio, news footage of the L.A. riots, or a Soweto uprising. Like poetry, which uses images or words from multiple cultural or even mythic sources to create resonance, these videos use a visual sampling from media history in order to impact on the audience. The faster and more overlapped the sampling, the deeper the potential impact.

Without our participation in connecting the sampled images into a single whole, a rock video remains a nonsensical series of unrelated moments. Once a viewer has developed the ability to draw lines of connection—which can be done differently with each viewing—videomakers are free to increase the rapidity of the cuts so that more and more samples may be incorporated. As with digital technology (compact discs), the faster the sampling, the more accurate the "reproduction." For a video this means associating more image content with a single phrase of music. This can be accomplished by increasing the number of cuts per second or by overlapping images, splitting screens into several parts and putting screens within screens.

The implications of this technology and style are important because they go to the heart of the MTV ideology of timelessness and eternal youth. In Jesus Jones's "Right Here, Right Now" video (described in chapter one), the density of imagery is achieved by projecting images onto a screen behind the band and onto the band members themselves. We are exposed to a multiple reality: The band performs in temporal suspension onstage, while images from current history—the Berlin Wall, Tiananmen Square—flash on and around them. Implied is that modern media technology such as satellites, CNN, camcorders, rock videos, and cable TV allow for a time compression. The Romanian revolution occurs all around the world in a single moment. One event in one geographical or temporal corner, thanks to media, occurs in many different places simultaneously and repeatedly. Likewise, within a single video, the images from several years of major global events can be strung together and viewed in rapid succession. This sampling technology brings all history into a single moment. Meanwhile the lyrics of the song reiterate the theme "Right here, right now, there is no place I'd rather be. Right here, right now, watching the world wake up from history."

The discontinuous jumble of media imagery makes

sense because someone is, according to the lyric, "watching." Just as global weather systems make sense to us now with the advent of satellite technology, historical patterns can be viewed in a new perspective through media and editing. Satellites allow us to see vast regions of atmosphere on one weather map; media allows us to span vast distances of time in a single-edit point or multiple image. The band, and the MTV viewer, are liberated from the linear, sequential history of events and, according to Jesus Jones anyway, the conflict and bloodshed associated with historical struggle.

This is the "MTV Revolution." It is a break from history of all kinds: parents, school, jobs, ethnic heritage, social repression, linear stories, and even consensus reality. The revolution is fueled by a celebration of discontinuity as an opportunity for instantaneous transformation. An image from the past can be suddenly morphed into a new form. Even the pop stars themselves seem to exhibit discontinuity as they morph themselves from one cultural icon into another. As models for the designer beings of an MTV future, today's rock stars demonstrate contemporary totemization at its best: the cultivation of human media viruses.

MORPHING JACKSONS

The surgical development of the Michael Jackson persona has been no secret to his public. Outdoing rock groups of the past such as The Beatles or The Rolling Stones, who changed the style of their hair, clothes, and music to keep up with or even lead pop cultural trends, Jackson has made a point of altering his physical being. A new album means more than a new sound, a new outfit, and a new video; it means a new nose or chin. Like the most advanced of biological viruses, Jackson can alter himself in order to succeed in environments that have developed an immunity to his current incarnation. The case study of the Jackson mutations reveals a lot about meme-splicing and regenerative media techniques.

Jackson's first real mutation was to go solo—to break from the continuity of his family group, the Jackson Five. Jackson chose to tell the story of this separation by recycling comfortable old pop cultural imagery. Michael knew he needed to emblematize his emancipation from the group. This would not be accomplished by creating a brand-new image for himself, but rather by co-opting the image of someone who already had. This was a good strategy: He did not try to affect change within the mediascape by making a change to the real world and hoping that the media would cover it favorably. He made changes on the level of media imagery and let the meanings of these symbols do his work for him. The Jackson public relations strategy was to in-corporate media iconography from the past into himself in order to redefine his own place in the media. To develop an identity as solo-performer-leaving-a-successful-group-to-reach-even-greater-stardom-alone, he chose to emulate Di-ana Ross.

The emerged as a two-pronged strategy. First he made sure to be seen with her at public events. They were already associated through their label, Motown, and Ross had pro-vided the Jacksons with considerable professional and per-sonal support. But the Michael Jackson image capitalized on the Diana Ross *story*, which was also based on a career move characterized by leaving behind her successful partners and striking out as a solo performer, ultimately becoming a su-perstar. More than associating with Ross in public, Jackson began to make himself look like Ross. His first physical al-terations were to slenderize his nose and straighten his hair. His voice became wispy, and he developed the Ross habitual gesture of smiling, tipping the head to the side, and brush-ing the now relaxed hair off the forehead. If Jackson was go-ing to strike out on his own, he would do it as gently and innocuously as possible. As he probably learned from chil-dren's television, the most virulent strains are the most ap-parently harmless ones. His later association with and idolatry of Elizabeth Taylor served the same meme-associative function. Taylor remains one of the few child stars who developed into a full-fledged adult cultural icon.

Michael has also strived to make his image as mutable as any MTV visual. Each time he decides to make an adjustment to his media persona, he does so by recalling icons from media history. When he needed to revitalize his image in a music industry growing more dependent on MTV visuals, he chose the Sergeant Pepper motif and dressed himself in mock soldier outfits reminiscent of The Beatles, who had developed the look as a way of infiltrating the music television and album art of the late sixties (a look that itself was meant to recall a more historical cultural iconography). When he needed to prevent his constant makeovers from casting him as too effeminate or swishy, he selected the imagery of old werewolf movies to make facial transformation seem virile. His "Thriller" video also turned heads because it attempted to redefine the rock video by associating itself, again, with techniques from other media. Considered an epic at eleven minutes, the video recalled the styles of fifties horror pictures and ended by rolling movie credits.

His next incarnation, "Bad," worked to counter some of the sexual ambiguity of his earlier identities. Another few plastic surgeries saw Jackson, now with a more masculine and slightly cleft chin, in tough-man New York director Martin Scorsese's subway, leather-clad and crotch-grabbing with a large and angry dancing street gang. Moving into blacktop bopper territory, Michael was capitalizing on the Nike media blitz, buying and then licensing Beatles music to the sneaker company before making a deal with LA Gear to design a sport shoe of his own.

But Michael had spread himself a little too thin. He was still a superstar, but his antics made him appear more like a quick-change artist than a musical performer. His brilliant adaptive strategy was to incorporate the quick change into his media identity. His video release for "Black or White" showed him dancing with Africans, Chinese, and Russians as he moved seamlessly from country to country. Then, borrow-

ing from and mutating a socially conscious Benetton advertisement, Jackson's video morphed the faces of a racially di-
verse group of young people in a virtuous testament to the
quick change. It was as if all of Michael's media machinations had been part of a great lesson plan. To further frame
his efforts in social relevancy, the original version of the
video ended with Michael morphing himself from a panther
into a street hoodlum and smashing up a car. The sight of
gentle Michael Jackson in such a rage was too much for the
public to handle, and Jackson had that section of the video
edited out the day after its MTV premiere, leading many to
wonder whether that had been his intention all along. His
image depends on hinting at his rage, his sexuality, or even
his blackness, but never committing to it. In any case the
segment and its deletion served as a useful media propellant
for a later virus launch.

Jackson's more self-conscious representations, however
stunningly self-reflexive, did not serve his career as well as
he had hoped. His *Dangerous* album had declined on the
charts faster than expected, and the reclusive pop star realized that yet another media incarnation would be necessary
to promote himself into the nineties. Following the cue of
Clinton and Perot, Jackson took his appeal directly to the
people by agreeing to an interview with Oprah Winfrey. The
show, which garnered a whopping 56 Nielsen share (62 million viewers), was the fourth-most-watched entertainment
broadcast in television history. Michael took a new, honest
approach to his race. "I'm a black American . . . I'm proud
of my race," he declared, explaining to Oprah that his increasingly pale appearance was actually the symptom of a
rare skin disease called vitiligo. This was a different Michael.

"In a single evening of TV," announced *Entertainment
Weekly* after the interview, "the Genius Weirdo had reposi-
tioned himself as the Genius Victim—abused and melan-
choly, yet strengthened and redeemed by extraordinary
talent."[2] He explained how his father had abused him and
how he had never really tried to buy the Elephant Man's
bones. Most of all he attempted to defend his image engi-

neering: "When people make up stories that I don't want to be who I am, it hurts me." That *Entertainment Weekly* called his appearance with Oprah, as well as his Super Bowl half-time show and appearance at Clinton's inaugural gala, a "re-positioning" is telling. Jackson is a media virus more than he is a performer or songwriter. His career can only be under-stood as a series of purposeful media manipulations by an entity whose life is supported wholly by the media on which it thrives. When Oprah asked Michael about his incessant crotch-grabbing, he told her, "It happens subliminally"—an odd way to phrase human motivations or impulses. Does he mean that he holds his crotch as a subliminal message to his audience or that his own behavior is media-reactive at the core? Whatever the case may be, Michael Jackson, the pre-eminent pop media manipulator of the eighties emerges in the nineties as a product—or a victim—of the media swirl.

As if to make this point, he told Oprah that his only girlfriend is Brooke Shields—one of popular culture's shin-ing but unwilling examples of virginity, whose own problems getting taken seriously as an adult actress can only serve to highlight Michael's difficulty in getting taken seriously as an organic human. Ever the perfect virus, Jackson forces us to wonder if he is a living being with intent and direction or just a collection of memes wrapped in the shell of his media identity, looking for new, friendly hosts. Michael cloaks him-self in a wispy, mutable, lily-white package, as if to camou-flage just how "Dangerous" his memes are supposed to be to our cultural values.

Michael's eventual fall from grace was inevitable. Whether or not he truly physically molested children is irre-levant to the manner in which his viral shell was des-troyed—or destroyed itself. (Child sexual abuse is a stirring media buzzphrase as well as a heinous act, but has nothing, finally, to do with the disintegration of Jackson's public im-age.) Michael the virus was not the "victim" of his young ac-cuser or his own lascivious nature; he was the casualty of faulty code. There were two ways for the Jackson virus to provoke a cultural immune response: He could get too dangerously sexual, or he could get too impotently Disneyesque. His strategy had always been to hold on to both of these sets of imagery and use them to balance each other. Effeminate plastic surgeries become the stuff of macho horror movies; an all-too-corny Super Bowl half-time extravaganza with thousands of children is revealed as the wish fulfillment of a once beaten child; crotch-grabbing onstage is balanced by a gentlemanly "romance" with Brooke Shields. But while the cut-and-paste quality of the mediaspace can support discontinuity, it cannot leave inconsistency unchallenged.

We were fascinated for long enough by Michael's sexual and racial ambiguity. We had been teased for years. We wanted relief. When the first accusation of child sexual molestation against Jackson was made in September 1993, the tension between Michael's surface innocence and darker inner life finally snapped. That the media and his public reserved judgment on Jackson for so long is a testament to the resiliency of the media persona he had developed for himself. *Newsweek* wondered out loud, "Why has Jackson so far been spared the full Pee-Wee Herman humiliation?"[3]

It is because the media takes its cue from the public. ("A Current Affair," for one, slanted its Michael story favorably because its call-in line indicated overwhelming support for the pop hero.) Network news, newspapers, and magazines focused on things like Elizabeth Taylor's visit to Michael in Asia, Pepsi's cruel and perhaps premature dropping of him as a product endorser, and his sleeping pill addiction and treatment. Even after two young boys, who thought they were springing to Michael's defense, admitted that they had slept in the same bed with the man, the public was unready to accept the star as a molester. He was simply very, very weird. Sleeping with children can almost seem sweet— especially when the adult is only an androgynous Peter Pan and the sleepover is occurring at the "Never Land" ranch. Unlike Pee-Wee, Michael never tried to make us think. There was no decoding necessary, no hidden agenda. He demanded nothing of us—which means our relationship to his weirdness was participatory. He sang with a thousand kids at our Super Bowl! We had gone too far out on a limb with this weird young man to sacrifice him without condemning ourselves, too, along the way.

So the media gave us time to distance ourselves from the virus before it was completely dismantled. It featured Michael's revelation of his own drug addiction, at once helping him maintain his role as "victim," but giving us the chance to dissect Michael's strategies in a new light. We watched Michael's own defense infomercial, in which he maintained his innocence and attacked the mass media for blowing a false charge out of proportion. His only mistake, he claimed, was loving children so much. "Don't treat me like a criminal," he pleaded, going into detailed description of the "humiliating" body search he underwent.

But the desperation with which the public and the media representing us clung to the vestiges of Jackson's defenseless image just made us resent him more on another level. We had gotten ourselves into a bad relationship and were looking for an easy way out.

The anticlimax of Jackson's cash settlement with his accuser was a perfect finish. Although it appeared on the front page of the *New York Times*, the big news here was that the story would end with no big news. Now we could all remain uncertain about whether or not Jackson had really committed the immoral sexual act. We could defuse the ticking bomb of the Michael Jackson media virus without ever learning whether there was dynamite inside. Just as Tonya Harding admitted a limited sort of half-guilt or guilt-after-the-fact in the Nancy Kerrigan beating (she confessed to obstructing investigators after the deed was committed), Jackson now "settled" for expediency. His lawyers stated, "In short, he is an innocent man who does not intend to have his career and his life destroyed by rumors and innuendo."[4]

But what we were really watching was the dissolution of bad code—a reconciliation between the discovered virus and its frightened and angry host. Jackson had pushed the envelope too far, but to explode the virus altogether would have inflicted far too much damage on the public's own conscience. We all wanted a way out that would preserve a morsel of doubt about what happened. With both Jackson and Harding, we and the blown viruses were allowed just such an exit.

What followed from Michael's clan, "Jackson Family Honors," failed to illicit an intense response from the viewing public, but it was not designed to do so. In the self-promotional special masquerading as an awards show, the Jackson family honored Motown founder Berry Gordy, who "made" the Jacksons, and Elizabeth Taylor, who did Michael's damage control. Accepting her childlike trophy, Taylor told Michael, "You're the brightest star in the universe, and don't let them dim your light." Although fans in the audience actually booed and jeered when they realized Michael would not be singing (they were subjected instead to lesser-known family members singing about their childhood together in Indiana), for Michael to have sung would have broken his unspoken pact with the public.

If we are to maintain our belief that he, and we, are innocent, Michael must spend time "recovering" from the wounds he received in the media war. Like Tinker Bell, he can only come back to life after enough people have clapped for his return. To strut onstage and promote himself once again as "Dangerous" would have been suicide. We would have had to believe him and then destroy him.

TRUTH *AND* DARE

While Michael's survival has always depended on leaving his sexuality in doubt or at least in the imagination, Madonna has made her career out of imagining her sexuality out loud for us. A consummate media professional, Madonna regularly reinvents herself much as Jackson does, but with a more intentional agenda and carefully conceived selection of memes. While Jackson's machinations can be seen as a kind of damage control (Too black? Get a nose job. Too threaten-

ing? Act like a girl), Madonna's are based on a version of social consciousness and a desire to provoke a negative but fascinated response from the public. Madonna's career has
been more dependent on media backlash than it has on positive excitement or artistic achievement in the traditional
sense. While she bemoans the fact that her media manipulations get more attention than her work (she told *Vanity Fair,*
"I think people like to concentrate on that aspect of me so
they don't have to pay me any respect in the other categories"[5]), her fame and prominence derive from her iconographic performance more than her onstage gyrations.

By the time Madonna released her book *Sex,* the *New
York Times* recognized that her ongoing relationship with the
media stood as her most significant performance art event.
"Millions of words will be printed around the globe about
her. The controversy, the reviews, the analyses, the gossip,
and the photos of the star will complete the phenomenon.
For the significance of Madonna's work is really inseparable
from the circus of attention that surrounds it."[6]

Deconstructing this performance art event called Madonna is almost too easy. From her name to her songs to her
1991 self-promotional documentary *Truth or Dare* to *Sex,* Madonna is an assemblage of cultural provocations, all based
on the recycling of previous imagery and violation of audience expectations for that imagery. Embodying the stages of
eighties to nineties sexual evolution, she began as the tom-
boy street urchin of the song "Holiday" and developed into
a diamond-clad "Material Girl." As the Reagan/Bush era
promoted prayer and closeted sexuality, out came a brasher
Madonna, pushing "Like a Prayer," "Papa Don't Preach,"
and the famously censored "Justify My Love" video. Finally,
as AIDS recloseted sexuality, Madonna reached deep into
gay subcultures for "Vogue," actually a transvestite style, and
the bisexual partnerings in *Sex.*

But Madonna's strategy is unique in that she stakes out
a certain pop cultural niche and then bends it in order to explode calcified mythos or at least to explode her own profile.
Her "Material Girl" video borrowed its theme and its chore-

ography from Marilyn Monroe's "Diamonds Are a Girl's Best Friend." For her appearance on the 1992 Oscars ceremony, Madonna dyed her hair platinum blond and performed as if she were Marilyn; the tremendous applause from the Academy itself, in front of millions of viewers worldwide, confirmed Madonna's placement in the iconographic slot. Once dubbed "the new Marilyn," she could slowly mutate into the bold sex promoter she became, taking the cultural icon along with her. This is significant because it is more than simply a bending of self—it is a bending of the cultural territory she had already won.

For her strategy to be successful, it must meet with resistance. Rebellion is useless if no one is offended. Madonna's is a career and social movement dependent on a confused cultural response—an inadequate immune system—and this is why she employs the techniques of viral manufacture and dissemination. Witness the extraordinary self-similarity in *Truth or Dare*. Here was a film that was really about the making of itself. Its themes, if they could be called that, were the voyeuristic tendencies of the media and the public, as well as the exhibitionist tendencies of pop icons. If "Express Yourself" is really to be accepted as the anthem of this film, then its center would have to be the episode in which one of the cities on her tour tries to censor her stage act. We watch as, almost instantaneously, Madonna's reaction to the police bust changes from shock to animated delight. This is the moment she has been waiting for. At last someone is offended enough to try to stop her. Plus she is being filmed in her steadfast defiance.

Were only her later efforts received with less willingness, Madonna might be an even bigger star than she is today. Her three-pronged approach to the release of her *Erotica* album was administered to popular culture like a broad-spectrum antibiotic; she intended to dose every cell. Madonna had become a pure media entity. As such it was more important for her to dehumanize and despecify her personal relationship to the media. If she simply releases an album, she is Madonna the recording artist. If she does a movie, she is "crossing over" into films. If she publishes a book, she is taking a stab at a new industry. If she does all of these at once, she is something more—yet at the same time something less—than each of these roles: She is a media virus. By being able to spread independently of a particular context, Madonna becomes more than a virus generator. Her image *is* the shell of the virus.

Madonna's sex war had three major beachheads: her book *Sex*, her album *Erotica*, and her film *Body of Evidence.* The book was the most self-consciously viral package of the three, wrapped in a sealed Mylar pouch, as if to preserve the freshness of the dangerous memes encased inside. Like a stick of gum in a pack of baseball cards, a CD single of "Erotica" came enclosed in the $49.95 book package. Cross-splicing memes from one medium to the other, Madonna adopted the persona of a gold-toothed dominatrix named "Dita," who in Madonna's videos promotes and mediates sexual encounters and in the book embodies her sexual alter ego, writing letters about her darker desires.

The album *Erotica* received more praise from reviewers than the scorn Madonna had been anticipating. The press seemed to understand her intentions; the *New York Times* remarked insightfully that "*Erotica* zeroes in on a cultural mood and . . . bends that mood to her political purposes. Its most provocative songs filter a tabloid-television view of sex and stardom through her own brand of feminism. She reiterates the message that she has been sending out for . . . years, but in more explicit ways."[7] Even the wording of the review—"zeroes in," "filter," and "reiterates"—shows a sensitivity to Madonna as a viral construct.

Maybe it was this understanding of Madonna's intentions that diffused some of the expected negative reaction. Her film with Willem Dafoe, *Body of Evidence*, got tepid reviews despite the fact that she engaged in prolonged, slightly sadomasochistic sex scenes and masturbation on screen.

The only protest against her barrage of sex media was a demonstration by New York Roman Catholics outside a store that was offering sneak peaks at the *Sex* book for a one-dollar donation to an AIDS charity. But their protest ended once the store agreed to stop calling the viewing booth a "confessional." *Newsweek* reported the lack of media reaction to Madonna's deep thrusts: "Madonna, who throughout her career has been able to turn an exposed belly button into a major-league scandal, here couldn't parlay a legitimate publishing event into a hubbub worthy of Sinéad O'Connor's clipping file."[8]

Unfortunately for the pop star, America had begun to develop a cultural immunity to the Madonna virus. Part of the problem is that it is difficult for Madonna-the-media-empire to launch countercultural attacks. Viruses come from outside the body politic, not within it. Sinéad O'Connor can still rustle a few feathers by ripping up a picture of the pope on "Saturday Night Live." Madonna, the Media Queen, made her own recombinant meme statement a week later by ripping up Joey Buttafuoco's photo on the same show. She no longer creates real events that are covered by media; she recombines media events to comment on a wholly self-referential realm. Her media self-consciousness does not go unnoticed, which is why as soon as she adopts a new media identity, most journalists begin to ask, "What's next?"

It is hard to take Madonna's social and political pretensions seriously when she seems so blatantly opportunistic. When the pope deems birth control un-Catholic, she makes sexy videos with Catholic imagery. When abortion and teen pregnancy are in the headlines, she performs songs about a teenage girl "keeping my baby." Madonna loves to "push people's buttons," whatever they may be. However mercenary it may sound, she performs the function of a viral probe, testing our cultural immune response to the issues and images in her media expression. If she is using a "shotgun" approach, she seems to do so with surprising accuracy and reach, economizing on imagery by actually manifesting in her life the memes she promotes in her work. The most telling aspect of *Truth or Dare* was the way Madonna played the game of the title: She told the truth *and* performed the dare.

More than prompting a reconsideration of our sexual values, Madonna-the-exposed-virus has focused our attention on the power of our media iconography and given us a better understanding of the self-referential quality of the mediaspace. As a media miner, she has burrowed new tunnels and connections between media industries and expanded the influence of MTV into other markets the way *E.T.* and *Star Wars* pushed the film industry into merchandising, comic books, and electronic gaming. She also helped to define a new sort of multimedia human presence, like a Bart Simpson or Max Headroom, who is capable of penetrating the social conscience from many avenues at once. The fact that we may have gotten tired of Madonna's memes may reduce her value as a cultural instigator, but our newfound distance from her content allows us to deconstruct her media tactics and learn about something a whole lot more interesting than her sexual fantasies.

SIMULATION STIMULATION

Post-Madonna, post–Michael Jackson MTV invites much more direct speculation on the tactics used in the mediaspace. Now that these stars' viral constructs have been essentially obliterated, we in the audience are free to explore the regenerative and self-referential quality of their imagery without endangering anything. There is no longer an illusion to uphold.

Like most of the iconography generated on MTV, Madonna is not original material. She is based on pop icons from the past, and even at her most original, she co-opts imagery from well-established subcultures. The drag queen and the dominatrix have been around a long time. MTV artists define their own identities by choosing cultural symbols with which they want to be identified. On the simplest level, this might mean sporting a leather jacket to evoke James

Dean or a slicked-back haircut to resonate with Elvis Presley. On the surface, this is mere packaging: A performer or even a fan's identity is dependent on the totems he wears or the brand of motorcycle he sits on for photographs. (One would be hard-pressed to find a bike other than a Harley on an album cover.) On a subtler level, though, the appropriation of media samples and social symbols for the purpose of regenerating them is the MTV philosophy in action and constitutes a new brand of social activism.

Many media theorists now argue that because these media icons—these representations of reality—are not "real," they serve to take us out of a direct experience of reality. Jean Baudrillard, French philosopher and admired observer of American culture, argues that the increasingly self-referential quality of media (and life in general) removes us from real experience and puts us in a mediated fantasy world called the "simulacre." He believes that the self-conscious artifice and bracketing devices in our media are designed (by someone or something) to convince us that our nonmediated reality is more valid. This way of thinking would see Disneyland, for example, as a way of hiding the overall infantilism of our culture. We enter this theme park and relive childhood fantasies in order to make the infantilism in our daily lives less noticeable by comparison.

Baudrillard believes the mediaspace poses an equivalent danger to reality itself: "We are in danger of a total dissolution of TV into life, the dissolution of life into TV . . . We must think of the media as if they were, in outer orbit, a sort of genetic code which controls the mutation of the real into the hyperreal, just as the other, micromolecular code controls the passage of the signal from a representative sphere of meaning to the genetic sphere of the programmed signal."[9]

This description of the process by which we interact with our media is meant to alarm us, but it sounds almost like an MTV promotional voice-over! The network often announces itself as if it were coming from outer space (which also explains its spaceman logo) and as if it were interacting with its viewers on a genetic level. The language of genes, as Baudrillard pines, is a language of symbols. The way DNA "tells" a cell how to replicate or what color eyes a person should have is with code—not through a real, mechanical process. DNA codons are not physically related to the blueness of eyes any more than the word "blue" is. They are both pure symbols.

MTV has also reduced its reality to a set of symbols. So removed is, say, a leather jacket from the original biker who wore it that the article of clothing is reduced to a symbol of machismo or even a symbol of James Dean, who is iconic enough in his own right to be considered worthy of reference. The visual cues we get from MTV are like a series of dead metaphors ("Time is running out" means something to us today, even though we don't think of an hourglass when we hear the phrase). Madonna only needs to make a tiny visual reference to Marilyn Monroe (a skirt blowing up will do) for us to understand an entire set of associations.

By growing dependent on a language of symbols, MTV has not doomed itself to utter meaninglessness, but rather given the television medium an unprecedented potential to communicate. It hardly makes sense to mourn that we no longer sound out the words we read on a printed page. Yes, by learning how to read we dissociate, to a certain extent, from the organic origins of the sounds of the words, but we gain the ability to replicate, juxtapose, and disseminate many ideas at once. That a genre like poetry can develop to the point where a single phrase intentionally evokes the imagery of a dozen other poems is not lamentable but laudable. That the nature of the relationship between MTV and its viewers is comparable to an organism and its genes only attests to the network's ability to transmit lots and lots of memes.

For MTV is admittedly and purposefully regenerative. The network takes images from media's past and either bends them to new purposes or combines them to create new meanings. This can be called "memetic engineering," in which popular culture mutates through the conscious splicing or recombination of old memes into new ones. The mutation occurs on what might be considered a "hyperreal" plane because, like the codons in DNA, the memes on MTV are not directly or mechanically connected to the realities they represent or dictate. This hyperreality is certainly free of any logical mandates of time or place. Just as a blond African was unheard of until time and space condensed enough for a Nordic to mate with a Zulu, so was a rap video impossible before MTV could condense the "reality" of the street, the dance floor, and the recording studio. Yes, MTV is a timeless, imploded dimension, but this is precisely what makes it capable of mimetic engineering. A narrative simulation of daily life in the style of a fifties television drama cannot adequately express the multiplicity of feelings and issues that are part of the current cultural experience. The simulacre is what allows a video to communicate, exclusively through symbology, something about the reality of ghetto life, politics, homophobia, or environmental decay.

But, the sages argue, are MTV's viewers conscious of any of this? How could a stoned teenager be perceptive enough to decipher this new language of symbology? The answer is that this is *his* language and, for better or worse, this is *his* emerging reality. The icons on MTV are almost indistinguishable from the representations of reality in his daily life. A video that makes use of superimposed graffiti is no different from the subway he rides to school each morning. To see the rappers in that same video dressed in monks' robes elevates the graffiti to the sanctity of stained-glass imagery and the rap lyrics to the litany of a Gregorian chant. It is the "adults," and not the teenagers, who have so much trouble making sense of the juxtaposition of these images and complain about the illogical anachronisms and discontinuous narratives.

To maintain viewers' awareness of this system of symbology, music videos and the MTV presentation format employ intentionally alienating devices. Viewers are constantly reminded of their relationship to the media they are watching, either through screens within screens, superimposed text, rapid cuts, or VJ interruptions and commentary, as well as self-consciously distracting video editing and special effects. Entire shows are dedicated to preserving a distanced and ironically aware viewership.

MELTDOWN

You are watching a Robert Palmer video on MTV when suddenly the image gets shaky and then melts down totally. The images on the monitor dissolve into a colorful fluid, eventually finding themselves in a bottle labeled "Liquid Television." This is a typical opening to "LTV," as it's been tagged by its producers, MTV's weekly foray into the world of animation specifically designed to deconstruct and parody media and popular culture. Segments by independent animators range from "Stick Figure Theater," a comedy cartoon in which recognizable media images like a Madonna video or a Hitchcock film are primitively drawn on note cards, to "Aeon Flux," a never-ending violent futuristic fantasy in which a beautiful gun-wielding heroine kills everything in her path.

Because it has no clear through line, the show, and even its nonlinear individual segments, can be quite difficult to watch. It requires viewers to change their expectations of media and adapt to a new kind of storytelling. Executive producer Japhet Asher, a thirty-two-year-old British documentary filmmaker, saw this as his purpose in creating "LTV":

"What I'm trying to do in television relates to dreams more than to linear kinds of storytelling. And I think that is where things are going in our media." This forces his audience to participate. "There's a great deal of interactivity because the way you make connections between different segments and different ideas and how you respond is operating on a different level than a traditional drama. We're challenging people to make connections."

"LTV" is about learning to make connections in an apparently discontinuous media world. This is what turns a seemingly discreet set of symbols into liquid. As Asher expressed it in a pitch meeting to MTV execs, "Put your favorite television shows in a blender and hit puree and you'll wind up with 'Liquid Television.' " Even many of the segments within the show are about making sense of apparently random image combinations. In "Psychogram," the camera pans over a bizarre collection of picture postcards, as a British voice-over (performed by Asher himself) connects them into a paranoid spy story. The only thing linking the cards are the narrator's conspiratorial conclusions.

To Asher the kind of training "LTV" conducts on its audience is a necessary societal engineering. "Today there is such a bombardment of information in daily life that people have to evolve, get used to it, and survive it. Editing is a great function of life. People have to learn how to control their own destiny; you have to learn to think for yourself. You have to be prepared to accept that things are changing, and have fluid thought, or you'll be in trouble."

"Fluid thought" means being able to think as a person does in a dream state. The bombardment of data and imagery must be integrated into a single story. Animation provides a nonthreatening forum in which this can be practiced. Asher believes, "People are much more resistant to having new kinds of stories told to them than they are to seeing new animation styles. The ability for animation to explore the psyche is much larger, and it can map territories beyond imagination now."

Like many members of the GenX, postpsychedelic generation, Asher and his colleagues at San Francisco–based Colossal Pictures believe that there is much to be gained from exploring consciousness. As vice chairman of the company, he sees it as his responsibility to help America explore its current frontiers of mind. He is aware of how our culture began to fixate on courtroom drama and sees that as only one step in an ongoing evolution toward a media of thought. "America had gone inward and was going towards the courts and the judicial system; that America was a frontier of laws.

I believe that now we're really dealing with a frontier that goes inward—a frontier of the mind. Everybody's free in their mind if they want to look and explore."

To develop this ability, "LTV" encourages us to think in a chaotic fashion. On the simplest level, this has to do with seeing the media as a place to play with thought by deconstructing its images and learning how we have been affected by them. A mock ad for "Lee Press-on Limbs" shows a woman whose arm has fallen off just before an important evening out with a new date. The screen flashes the words "Horror! Pain! Fear! Guilt!" exposing the emotions such ads hope to exploit in order to sell their products. Another regular segment shows a fashion consultant named Lidia using a computer to come up with new looks for Sinéad O'Connor, George Michael, or Sylvester Stallone. She ends each week's segment with the slogan "The more you look, the better you'll see."

Beyond media parody and dissection, cyberpunk (gritty, computer-world science fiction) segments like "Aeon Flux" attempt to impart a new dramatic paradigm more consistent with the chaotic world-view. The heroine is engaged in a fairly plotless quest. As if in a video game, she moves or climbs from room to room, killing whoever stands in her way. One of her chief weapons is a bug that bites people and injects a fast-acting, fatal virus. She infects or shoots thousands in her journey toward a high tower, where she apparently hopes to assassinate a leader. On her way she steps on a tiny tack that becomes lodged in her heel. Just before she shoots her intended victim, the nail penetrates her foot. She loses her balance and falls off a window ledge to her death. As in a self-similar chaos equation, one single woman is able to inflict tremendous damage on an entire city using a microscopic virus, but she is herself brought down by a tiny tack that just happened to find itself in the heel of her boot. Chaos is the agressor's Achilles' heel.

Asher hopes that "LTV," too, will function as a deceptively high leverage point in our increasingly chaotic culture. "Let's hope it catches on and spreads like a virus. If there's any hope for interaction, people are going to have to open up their minds to new approaches to stories and be prepared to interact with them." Meltdown television is a disintegration of TV as a parental or dictatorial force as it worked from the fifties to the eighties. "This is television anarchy. Definitely, that's what we want."

Even though Asher is one of the first members of the post-baby boom generation to rise to a position of power in the media, he believes he will soon be followed by others. "I feel like the lunatics are running the asylum right now, and that's a good thing. We all grew up on TV, and I'm very pleased to shake it all up now." Asher offers himself and his popular show as hard evidence that his generation did not all become couch potatoes. "I've always been a great believer in our Generation X. I don't think there's any such thing as a vidiot. That's a ridiculous phrase. The fact that somebody's capable of absorbing a vast amount of visual information makes them very intelligent, not very stupid."

HATING WHAT SUCKS

Beavis and Butt-head, "Liquid Television's" most successful spin-off, hardly appear to support Asher's contentions about the intelligence of MTV fans. These animated teenage pals first showed up on "Liquid TV" as a comedy segment, but are now internationally famous for the afternoons they spend together irreverently watching MTV. On the surface "Beavis and Butt-head" satirizes stupid, middle-American heavy-metal airheads. The cartoon characters blow up frogs with firecrackers and use cats as baseballs. But their show works on a much deeper level as an instructional video on how to watch MTV with appropriate skepticism.

Like the boys in "Wayne's World," Beavis and Butt-head, clad in AC/DC and Metallica T-shirts, appear to understand the tactics of rock videos and are free with their commentary as they watch. The show is structured much like regular MTV, in which videos are aired back-to-back, but here the videos are augmented by the wisecracks and antics of two typical adolescent viewers. That "Beavis and Butt-head" is so popular attests to the audience's understanding of this sort of comedy. That "Beavis and Butt-head" has been censored and ultimately banished from daytime television (the show now only airs late at night) attests to the threat the characters pose as viral conduits.

The experience of "Beavis and Butt-head" is akin to watching MTV along with two bratty comrades. They spend most of their time giggling maniacally in recently lowered pubescent voices. Their laughter is their main form of communication with each other—a kind of agreement that they are not being taken in by the images in the videos they are watching, but rather maintaining a jaded attitude. As we watch an Aerosmith video with the boys, they voice-over their critique. The lead singer is pictured stark naked, with his hand deftly covering his genitals. "Where's his penis?" asks Butt-head. "It's in his hand," giggles Beavis. More laughter from both before Beavis adds, "where it always is." Their comments function like the graffiti on inane billboards that targets obvious sexual innuendo with arrows connecting one character's eyeline to another's breasts.

When something occurs in a video too subtle for Beavis or Butt-head to notice, the animators clue the audience in to the boys' own susceptibility to media manipulation. When the Aerosmith singer lights up a cigarette in the video, we see Beavis unconsciously light up his own cigarette. However cynical he believes he has become, he still blindly follows the examples set by his heavy-metal heroes. The show still promotes viewer awareness by allowing us to witness areas where the characters' own detachment has been compromised.

But these instances are usually limited to one or two per episode. Usually when the boys are disturbed by something they do not understand, they simply switch channels. After watching Jermaine Jackson dance and squirm in what they assume is a giant condom, Butt-head calls out, "Change it!" We cut into a Boy George video. As George sings "I'm a man," Beavis retorts, "No way, he's not even a boy." The two are clearly uncomfortable with Boy George's sexuality and change the subject of their conversation to the style of the video, in which people move about in period costume.

"Is this supposed to be the future?" Beavis asks. "It sucks. Change it." To which Butt-head responds with surprisingly advanced wit, "Beavis, I'm cool, but I can't change the future." More laughs. The boys understand that MTV prides itself on its ability to bend time and bring images from the past into the present, but they know how to take this all in stride. They change the channel, inflicting their will on the medium the only way they know how: channel surfing. In doing so they again demonstrate for us how to watch TV in the nineties. "I see them as an extension of our best promos," admits MTV creative director Judy McGrath, "which have always been irreverent."[10]

Near the end of one episode, the boys happen upon a David Byrne video from the movie *True Stories*. The "concept" video takes place in a bar, where clients, one by one, stand on a stage in front of a microphone and mouth the words to the song. The boys watch in silent confusion, as Byrne, the real vocalist, rises to the microphone. There is obviously supposed to be a message here—something about the relationship of audience to media or even a star to his own media—but the boys are not sophisticated enough or sober enough to care. "This video's over my head," complains Beavis.

"It's under my butt," answers Butt-head as the two finally giggle. Their mutual annoyance has united them once again. "I don't like videos that suck," continues Butt-head.

"Me, too," giggles Beavis in bad grammar as he switches off the TV and the episode ends. When all else fails, the show instructs, just shut the damn thing off.

But most adults do not understand the instructional agenda of "Beavis and Butt-head." They only see two ugly adolescents destroying things and millions of teenagers enjoying them do it. Unable to decipher the language of the simulacre, adult "consensus" culture has no choice but to stamp it out whenever there is an opportunity to do so. In October of 1993, a five-year-old named Austin Messner set a fire that cost his baby sister Jessica her life. The local fire chief blamed Beavis and Butt-head's antics for having inspired the child's pyromania, and Attorney General Janet Reno, already riding a wave of public distaste for violence on television, had a new example of just how dangerous the media had become. MTV ducked for cover and changed the "Beavis and Butt-head" time slot so kids couldn't watch.

"Beavis and Butt-head" was not removed from MTV's daytime schedule because its characters set fires. Dennis the Menace performed countless acts of potentially life-endangering malice per minute, yet was never threatened with censorship. Or, as the *New York Times Magazine* suggested, critics of the show, like Attorney General Janet Reno, might best look to their own televised atrocities before blaming kids' shows for desensitizing America to the dangers of handguns and pyromania. Instead of focusing on fictional television, the magazine argued, Reno should instead be reconsidering the "protracted, prurient coverage of events like the firestorm at Waco (which she co-produced). At least 'Beavis and Butt-head,' a cartoon, does not pretend to be reality. Next to the pyrophilic news spectaculars surrounding it, its jokey efforts to stimulate a viewer's imagination almost start to look like art."[11]

"Beavis and Butt-head" was not targeted for its obviously satirical depiction of teenage pranks. It was targeted for its much less obvious, and much more subversive commentary on the dangers of growing up in the simulacre. The cartoon was attacked for using a language that adults could not understand. Grown-ups got spooked by essentially activist memes shrouded in meta-media.

Now that Viacom, the parent company of MTV and Nickelodeon, has taken over Paramount, producer of such meme conduits as "Entertainment Tonight" and "A Current Affair" as well as owner of Simon & Schuster, the Beavis and Butt-head contagion is sure to spread much, much further. A book and CD have already been released, and a movie is on the way. This is the real impact of today's media empire mergers. They give virulent memes new connective pathways and breeding grounds.

MTV POLITICS: ROCKING THE VOTE

At first the principal theme espoused by MTV was rebellion for rebellion's sake. MTV meant watching stuff on TV that your parents couldn't understand or wouldn't approve of if they could. The choice to watch MTV was a statement of self-expression for the young viewer. This reflected the overall marketing strategy of cable television contractors, who were using freedom of choice as a way of convincing customers to rent a box and access to thirty or forty additional channels. Further, MTV presented itself as expanding the frontier of rock-and-roll consciousness.

Even the network's logo, an astronaut planting an MTV flag on the surface of the moon, amounts to a metaphorical declaration of a virus war. Medical scientists use viruses to tag cells in the body. If they are attempting to isolate a certain kind of cancer cell in a person's bloodstream, for example, they may inject a virus that can find and latch onto those cells so that the person's own antibodies will be able to identify and attack them more easily. The MTV flag symbolizes this same tagging procedure. Every home that wants and gets its MTV is symbolically "flagged" as receptive to the memes on MTV. A cultural organism was being colonized by a TV channel. By 1992 over 210 million homes in seventy-two countries were MTV participants.

That MTV developed its audience through a mock revolution did not disempower the network to spawn a real one once it had tagged enough of us. The notion of an "MTV Revolution" itself has served as an innocuous pop cultural turn of phrase that only hides the real social upheaval the network became capable of stimulating by the nineties. MTV grew to be a powerful viral conduit: As it laced its music

programming with ever-more-provocative memes, it continued to branch out, forming a huge alternative network for
spreading these data and ideas. While in the afternoon a rap
group on "MTV Jams" might sing about police brutality,
later that night "Rock the Vote" might broadcast an interview with Bill Clinton.

Politics has never been a stranger to rock and roll.
Rolling Stone, the first mainstream publication of the rock
music industry, was one of the most politically forward publications of its day. It came as no surprise, then, that Kurt
Loder, one of *Rolling Stone*'s journalists, was hired by MTV
to anchor "The Day in Rock," a ten-minute news spot that
began as little more than an announcement of concert dates
but developed into a full-fledged forum for alternative views
on national issues. A typical spot might include a visit to an
environmental conference (like the Rio Earth Summit), an
interview with a censored rap musician, the attempted coup
in the Soviet Union, or the Los Angeles riots. While significantly shorter than an average network newscast, the attention the show pays to individual features—usually three to
four minutes—is about twice as long as a typical network
news story. MTV reporters almost invariably consult rock
musicians about their views on the issues—rappers were interviewed about the L.A. riots, Pink Floyd spoke about the
fall of the Berlin Wall, and Axl Rose commented on the censorship of Ice-T. These young newspeople provide as
straightforward a presentation as they can muster, passing
themselves off as honest if irreverent alternatives to politically correct, spoon-fed, network-processed newsmeal.

Loder told the *New York Times* that he hopes his news-
casts reflect a "total political uncorrectness." This is not a
credo of counterculturalism but rather an awareness of how
little credibility network news has with the MTV generation.
That young voters have no idea who Willie Horton is demonstrates less an apathy toward news itself than it does a
mistrust and intentional ignorance of network-style coverage. The major networks, while attempting to appear honest
and forthright, cannot help but espouse what comes off as

sanctimonious preaching. The American war effort in the Persian Gulf, as described by middle-aged corporate stars like Dan Rather, sounds like an unquestionably heroic effort. Kids who had already rejected the style and attitude of their parents' news shows were not objecting to journalism itself, but to the reverential attitude and ethical systems implicit in fifties-style broadcasts.

"We don't try to tell our audience what they should do about something," Judy McGrath asserts. "We'd fall victim to channel surfing in a minute if we were preachy and tried to tell them what to do—or how to vote."[12] MTV, media grown out of other media, is more aware of the precarious yet intimate relationship it has with its viewers than most traditional networks are. Constantly on the lookout for dangers like channel surfing, the network is self-consciously reactive to viewers' tastes and needs rather than being directively informative. "The Day in Rock" is meant to inform from a new kind of objective distance—one characterized by irony and interactivity.

By the end of its first decade, the series spun off a half-hour counterpart, "The Week in Rock," and now boasts a staff of fifteen regular employees, thirty-five free-lancers, and a $5 million budget. MTV's success in news led the network into the political arena, where, for many of its viewers, it served as the only source of information. While the network strove for impartiality, MTV did endorse participation in politics and made issues like the environment, sex, and presidential elections "cool" for teenagers to care about. It is not as if teenagers did not already ponder these matters; it is just that their own experience of these issues had not yet been reflected in the mainstream news media.

Many kids graduating from high school don't have enough money for college or enough experience for a decent job; they are deeply troubled by the thought of a nuclear attack, an ozone hole, gang violence, and unwanted pregnancies. They are as concerned as anyone about the direction of their society. They live in the trenches of our cultural warfare. To them, though, Dan Rather conveys a monolithic wholesomeness and virtue totally inconsistent with their experience of the chaotic world in which they exist. Today's teenagers are too wary and too cynical to be fooled into complacency.

Tom Freston, the forty-seven-year-old chairman of MTV Networks, recognizes that kids are not convinced of anything easily. "We had to find a way to talk to these people, so we started our public-service ads on subjects like racial tolerance, safe sex, AIDS. And that led naturally to politics. But we always have to stay in touch with what they want and the issues they care about."[13]

So far MTV's furthest advance into the political battlefield was its coverage of the 1992 presidential election, which many feel may have determined the outcome. MTV was the only TV network that announced it would offer more campaign coverage than it did in 1988. Its initial effort was a campaign called "Rock the Vote," a series of public service announcements in which rock stars encouraged viewers to register and vote. Madonna did one wearing nothing but an American flag. Aerosmith did another, irreverently proclaiming "freedom to use handcuffs for friendly purposes . . . freedom to wear a rubber all day if necessary. Protect your freedoms. Vote. Even for the wrong person."

The "Rock the Vote" promos constituted just one arm of MTV's "Choose or Lose" election coverage—a media effort so broad that it almost raised MTV News commentator Tabitha Soren to the level of a Diane Sawyer. "Let me clean up a little for you, Tab," MTV News captured Hillary Clinton saying to twenty-five-year-old Soren as they prepared for an interview aboard Clinton's campaign bus. These plainclothed, plain-talking MTV journalists brought a new kind of realism to the '92 election by covering stories from a self-consciously media-enthusiastic perspective. We watched black rapper Treach from Naughty by Nature interview delegates at the Republican Convention. He made it clear that the campaign's depiction of the African-American experience was inconsistent with his own. "It ain't like this in New Jersey," explained Treach, bringing a frankness to the convention floor we could not get on regular network news.

Nowhere did we get a better sense of MTV's ability to exert the pressure of feedback than in its open forum with Clinton, whose willingness to appear on the network to answer questions from young people communicated more about his campaign than any of his particular answers. While Bush refused to appear on what he called the "teenybopper network," Clinton embraced the "Choose or Lose" appearance as an opportunity to acknowledge the importance of a powerful block of voters—a block that, in fact, had favored Bush in the '88 election and a block whose demographics are defined by the fact that its constituents watch a particular kind of media.

MTV's news coverage appears to make little distinction between what goes on in media and what occurs in "reality." Just as Clinton's decision to appear on MTV is a significant part of his message, so, too, is Ice-T's decision to change recording labels as significant as the lyrics on his albums. Of the millions of media viruses broadcast over MTV, the ones with the greatest social impact tend to be those that concern the artists' or the viewers' relationship to the media itself.

RAP: GETTING THE STRAIGHT DOPE

Just as MTV News's most significant contribution to American politics is the fact that it exists in the first place, most MTV-fostered memes only begin to spread when they are recognized as violations or extensions of accepted media practice. Of all the musicians on MTV, rappers get the most attention for their willingness to stretch the medium's ability to express what seem like countercultural values. Rap can be understood as a forum for the expression of ideas that have no other way of reaching their target audience. But the intense and negative reaction to rap has shaped the music and its fans into a well-defined cultural movement.

Although not all of Ice-T's music is officially rap—certain of his albums have been dubbed "speed metal"—his insights into the medium show why it has become so popular with young blacks who have something to say. "If there wasn't rap, where would the voice of the eighteen-year-old black male be? He would never be on TV, he ain't writing no book. He is not in the movies. So he's hidden, he's not heard. And with rap you gave people the option of 'Here's the beat, and say whatever the fuck you want.' It's like the true vehicle of free speech because you're not bound by a melody or anything."[14]

Like the open microphone in the David Byrne video, rap is an opportunity for public feedback into a medium that has usually reserved itself for stars. A simple drum track—even a synthesized one—playing on a ghetto blaster is all a rapper needs to get started. Rap, like the MTV format itself, strives toward a nonlinear structure, breaking rules of continuity in order to permit the transmission of more memes per minute. While original rappers—the sort who recorded on the Sugar Hill label in the late seventies and early eighties—felt compelled to rhyme their lyrics, today rappers use looser styles that sometimes barely fit any pattern at all. Still, rap has the quality of an incantation, droning on in a constant flood of lyrics and using meter to punch the most important words or ideas. The regularity of the beat puts listeners into an almost trancelike state so that the messages can sink in deep.

The messages themselves are the most directly political statements in music and spring from a segment of culture that has never been heard from over mass media before. Chuck D, of the preeminent rap group Public Enemy, told *Spin* magazine, "[Rap is] a form of media conquest. This country is being controlled by the FCC; the government monitors the media. To have a radio station, you have to report it to the government. Records just went past all that."[15]

Records became the political pamphlets of the nineties. Returning to the tradition of black spiritual music of the 1800s, rap codifies some of its messages so that they may reach their intended audiences without alerting censorial forces. As Sister Souljah, the rapper who was openly criticized by Bill Clinton for her antiwhite stance and then further attacked by critics because her words didn't rhyme properly, compares her songs to the spiritual hymns sung by African slaves on American plantations. Their lyrics, like "wade in the water," contained instructions for how to escape and avoid capture. (Wading in the water washes scent off the feet.) Souljah wonders if, on the plantation where the spirituals were developed, somebody would be examining whether the words fit together properly. . . . "Sister Souljah is trying to give you the information that you need to liberate your mind, soul, and spirit from white supremacy and racism. . . . What is really threatening to America is what I'm saying, and not how I'm saying it."[16]

Rap music frightens people. Clinton compared Souljah to David Duke for supposedly telling black kids to "go out and kill white people." What Souljah actually had done was tell a news journalist that she can understand *why* black people might want to kill white people: "In the mind of a gang member, why not kill white people? In other words, if you've been neglected by the social and economic order of America, and the supposed spiritual order of America, and you've become casual about killing, you would have no hesitancy about killing somebody white."[17] The threat here is not that Souljah wants white people killed, but that she can understand and reiterate the sentiments of people who do. This is not necessarily hate mongering, but rather the public acknowledgment of a formerly marginalized segment of the population. Rap reflects the way a large number of black kids feel, and this is a frightening prospect for whites, who can only beg their media to "say it isn't so."

Rapper Chuck D explains that it is not necessarily the musicians who feel this aggression. "It's not me, or Ice Cube, or Sister Souljah's feelings—we're just the messengers, and how you gonna kill the messengers? The best thing about rap is it's a last-minute warning, the final call . . . a last plea for help on the countdown to Armageddon."[18]

But sometimes the messenger is the one who gets hanged. Ice-T's song "Cop Killer" included the now infamous lyrics "I got my 12-gauge sawed-off/and I got my headlights turned off/I'm 'bout to bust some shots off/I'm 'bout to dust some cops off." The lyrics prompted George Bush to call the album "sick," Dan Quayle to label it "obscene," and New York governor Mario Cuomo to comment that the music is "ugly, destructive and disgusting." By the time sixty congressmen had signed a letter denouncing the recording, it had—as a direct result of its infamy—become a chartbuster. Hearing his own name uttered by the President convinced Ice-T that his music and messages were being regarded as powerful influences. "Very few people have their names said by the president, especially in anger. It makes me feel good, like I haven't been just standing on a street corner yelling with nobody listening all the time. . . . It lets you know how small this country is."[19]

So small, in fact, that thanks to a forum like rap music, the black youth of America have been able to move off the sidelines of marginalization and emerge as a campaign issue. More important, they have taken control of a large, money-making media forum in which they are free to communicate with each other, consolidate power, and share important information.

And the messages laced into rap music communicate more than the hatred of whites and white values. The word "education" comes up a lot when rappers describe their lyrics; the recording artists see themselves as black culture's teachers. Chuck D's instruction concerns the unification of a black community. "Black people don't realize they're family, and the only way they will is if we get informed that we're family." His producer, Hank Shocklee, agrees: "Who are the real leaders? Ice-T. BDP. Ice Cube. Queen Latifah. They're the people who are sending a message to the kids right now."[20]

Sister Souljah uses her media platform to "put some clarity" onto the pages of a mainstream media that has been used historically to repress her people and their causes. Her songs may lack specific information and strategy, but their expression of rage gets her plenty of media attention. Then, when interviewed by the press, she takes the opportunity to do some education. For an interview for *Spin* magazine, she exploited her quote space to voice her critique of the welfare system for its inconsistent and contradictory social programming. Women who find employment, Souljah argued, are penalized by the outmoded system's rules.[21]

Like many media virusmakers in other fields, Souljah and her colleagues see the enemy force as "systematically designed." Since viruses attack the organizational structures in our society, their creators very often see these systems as conscious entities, or as consciously designed by a powerful elite—in this case, whites who hope to keep blacks in an underclass. Given the experience of growing up in a ghetto and culture that works against them at every turn, it is no wonder that some rappers develop these beliefs. As with nearly all countercultural groups who engage in viral media, the most extreme members are committed to advanced conspiracy theories.

POOR RIGHTEOUS TEACHERS

In the rap community, these extremists call themselves the Five Percent Nation—a spin-off of the Nation of Islam, whose doctrine is loosely based on Muslim teachings. The Five Percent was developed by Clarence 13X Smith, a follower of Malcolm X whose preachings were so extreme that he was expelled from X's Nation of Islam in the late sixties. "Who are the Five Percent of this planet earth?" asks one of Smith's lessons. "They are the poor righteous teachers, people who are all wise and know who the true living god is, who teach that the almighty true and living god is the black man from Asia."[22]

The rappers spreading Five Percent doctrine consider themselves the poor righteous teachers of this age. After

Clarence 13X Smith's assassination in 1969, his followers began to refer to him as "Father Allah" and chose not to pick a new leader. Instead, by distributing power, they feel they are staying truer to Smith's teachings. Rakim Allah, one of the most popular of the Five Percent rappers, explains that "there's a big fear to put one man in charge. I feel that Father Allah taught us we are all leaders unto ourselves." According to Rakim, when Louis Farrakhan spoke at Madison Square Garden, "he told all the brothers from the Five Percent Nation to stand up. He let the people know what we stood for. He said, 'Man is God.' "[23]

As the most realized gods of their community, the Five Percent are responsible for disseminating what they call "knowledge." Most of their doctrine is expressed in a kind of code—words that, more than simply camouflaging meanings, represent much larger meme constructs. Their songs and videos can efficiently and in a codified manner express many far-reaching ideologies. "Mathematics," for example, refers to a set of numbers that represent various aspects of the religion: 1 stands for knowledge, 2 for wisdom, 3 for understanding, 7 for God, and 10 for cipher (a circle in which "five percenters" stand when they quiz each other on doctrine). "Colored man" means white man. By spreading knowledge of Five Percent beliefs, rappers are "dropping science." They are also taking command of a powerful set of linguistic tools.

Five Percent MTV videos are also fraught with visual memes. "The Universal Flag," a 7 printed over a crescent moon and star within a large sun, symbolizes the black man as God (number 7), the black woman, and the black child. Rakim used this image in his MTV video "Move the Crowd," as have other rappers since, but only certain viewers of the show "Yo! MTV Raps," on which most Five Percent videos air, understand the symbolism. To converts, though, an image like this, even subtly displayed, is a wink from the rapper that he espouses Five Percent beliefs. To understand these symbols is to be in the club; once in the club, viewers can enjoy the way the videos serve to iterate their revolutionary beliefs over the very corporate networks they hope to overturn.

One group that particularly understands its relationship to the empire is Brand Nubian, whose "Wake Up!" video was directed by one of the hosts of "Yo! MTV Raps." The images of a black man, white-faced and horned to portray a satanic businessman, as well as blatant indoctrination rituals provoked MTV to reject the video for airplay. The group's lead rapper, Grand Puba, believes that while MTV is unknowingly fostering a new sort of revolution for black youth, it will just as quickly ban videos that it can figure out:

"It's going to spread until they feel it's a big enough threat. This industry is controlled by the colored [that means white] man. When they want you silenced you will be silenced. Take Martin Luther King. This society is governed by the same people who are serving the injustice."[24]

While mainstream white America watched a weeping Tonya Harding relace her skates in Lillehammer, elsewhere on the television dial that same evening the congenial Arsenio Hall hosted Louis Farrakhan for the Islam leader's first mainstream entertainment talk-show appearance. Each market segment distracted by its own paper-thin melodramas and empty rhetorical fist-waving, the racially segregated media audiences still didn't understand that truly virulent memes don't respect such traditional borders.

RAP TRICKLES UP

Half hoping, half fearing the immune response of white, corporate America, the extremist sect of the rap community have trouble understanding white youth culture's hearty embrace of the rap style and ethos. The more mainstream Ice-T claims that over 50 percent of his sales are to white kids. "They're like 'Holy shit, this is incredible' . . . They just want to know. They know their parents ain't teaching them shit about black people. They know that's nowhere to get an answer. So they're saying, 'Fuck it, I'll go right to the source.' "25

Spike Lee exploited the growing hunger for black cultural iconography with his film *Malcolm X* and the associated paraphernalia. Like a Universal Flag or, more appropriately, a genetic codon, the letter "X" appeared on posters, T-shirts, and, of course, those notorious baseball caps many weeks before the film was released. The most chromosomal of media viruses, the Xs served the dual purpose of representing affinity with the Malcolm X cause and publicizing the upcoming film release. The preponderance of Xs among unlikely wearers prompted a *New Yorker* cartoon in which white residents of an uptown building, the doorman, and even a dog all wear X caps, while the one downtrodden black delivery boy in the picture wears a New York Rangers cap.

Spike Lee understands the functioning of media viruses and, though he is loath to talk about rappers, admits that they are on the front lines of the cultural battle. "Quayle [who criticized rappers] and Sister Souljah are a sideshow, pathetic. . . . I know better rappers than Sister Souljah. But that doesn't negate her message. . . . There's a battle going on for popular culture; specifics don't count." This quote appeared in an *Esquire* piece called "Spike Lee Hates Your Cracker Ass," written by a white journalist. Unenthused by her coverage, Spike decided to represent himself in the media his own way and requested that only black journalists be sent to interview him. This, in turn, launched a media virus of its own, as editorial staffs around the country began to admit in print that they were sorely lacking in black journalists. Point taken.

Spike also chose to market the memes of his own movie, opening boutiques that sold official X caps and T-shirts, as well as writing a meta-X book, *By Any Means Necessary—The Trials and Tribulations of the Making of Malcolm X . . .*, in which he details how he raised additional capital for his film by calling upon black media celebrities including Michael and Janet Jackson, Oprah Winfrey, Magic

Johnson, and Prince. When Warner Bros. executives attempted to curtail Lee's spending and pontificating, the filmmaker responded by referring to the studio as "a plantation," battling for his film "in full view of the public, specifically African-Americans." The racial issues that came up in the making of the film began to get more press attention than the film itself. Capitalizing on and further reiterating the Rodney King virus, Spike Lee intercut the opening credits of his film between the famous videotaped beating and a burning American flag. His purpose? In his words, "to show that things are still the same in this country. Blacks are still treated as second-class citizens. If Bush had his way, we'd all be in chains."[26]

Malcolm X himself had already been co-opted into the viral war by rappers in the eighties. KRS-One put out an album called *By All Means Necessary*, with a cover photo based on a famous picture of Malcolm (except now holding an Uzi), punning and revising the leader's words and images for the current urban racial struggle. While spreading fascination for Malcolm X throughout popular culture, these images are twice removed from the man's real teachings. As a black leader, he stood as a symbol for the ability of a street hood to educate himself and promote real social change. "X" imagery symbolizes the man Malcolm X, but many wonder if enthusiasm for the symbol translates into any real knowledge of his beliefs. Harvard historian Henry Louis Gates told *Newsweek* that there is a danger in "a lot of people running around with X caps who ain't read the autobiography and ain't gonna read the autobiography. They've emptied [Malcolm] of his complexity."[27]

This comment, though, shows a lack of appreciation for the Trojan horse effect of a media virus as simple as an X on a baseball cap. No, droves of young blacks may not run to bookstores for Alex Haley's two-inch thick *Autobiography of Malcolm X*. But ones who see the movie are being educated by a filmmaker who did and are being shown images of regal black men in Egypt participating in one of the world's seminal cultures. Spike Lee explains the purpose of these scenes:

"Black people still think that Cleopatra was white because they saw Elizabeth Taylor. . . . White people went through the devious thing of trying to separate Egypt from Africa and all those great accomplishments. . . . Egypt is the cradle of civilization . . . and if Egypt is black . . . they don't want to hear that."[28]

What saves Spike Lee's work from being discounted as oversimplification or sensationalist marketing is his absolute connection to the media he claims he detests. ("The media has tried to poison me," he told the *Village Voice*.) While it may not be his fault that Madonna once said, "We were gonna call [my book] X . . . but I realized . . . it might look like I was copying Spike,"[29] he is an active participant in today's media dance, and a comparison with Madonna's efforts may not be too far out of step. It was Lee who announced that black people should take a holiday on the opening day of his film and who refused to recant fully the suggestion that kids play hooky from school. He is the man who publicly criticized the film *Bonfire of the Vanities'* controversial ending, even though that ending did not appear in the final script or finished film. He is the filmmaker who, like fellow Knicks' fan Woody Allen, is in the process of developing an on-screen nerd persona to reflect upon Spike Lee the media entity. That his iconography of Malcolm X has prompted comparisons with the marketing of Elvis, Marilyn, and JFK speaks more to his ability to commandeer the machinery of pop culture's media than it does to a mercenary mind-set.

Spike Lee lives in the same mediascape as a politically motivated rapper. Overlap and reflection between his own life and the pursuits of his film characters sustain his viruses as they pass through the media. He serves as the shell for his own memes. Ice-T exploits the same technique, placing his most virulent memes in the mouths of his songs' characters. The young ghetto hood in "Cop Killer" was free to say things more plainly than Ice-T could himself. "It's a record about a character. I know the character, I've woken up feeling like this character. When I saw the riots on TV, I wanted to get out there, but I've never clicked over."[30] Ice-T's ensu-ing battle with the media and the subsequent elimination of his song from the *Body Count* album served only to under-score the social struggle that the artist and his character share.

By personifying the plights of their own characters in their media battles (Spike all but orchestrated the media's misunderstanding of his purposes to resemble their misun-derstanding of Malcolm X's in the sixties), these activists create a self-similar series of shells around their ideological material. Wherever you see media wrapped around media wrapped around media, you know there's a meme in there somewhere.

SCREENS WITHIN SCREENS— THE SHELL GAME

Many rock groups with overt social or political agendas use this self-similar quality of the new mediaspace to launch their memes in a protective yet illuminating set of shells. U2's "Zoo TV Tour," for example, was a series of stadium concerts in which live television images were projected onto a giant TV screen over the stage. These images were culled on the spot from communications satellites, decoded, and juxtaposed with each other as a zap-TV performance art piece. One night an image of George Bush might intercut with a Japanese game show, while footage of the Bosnian conflict might find itself back-to-back with erotica from a German porno broadcast.

The idea was something like Jesus Jones's *Right Here, Right Now* video, but with a media twist. By sampling ran-domly from the datasphere, the group hoped to connect themselves and their audience to the world at large. For a rock group that made its career over MTV, this provided a natural setting for its music and memes. It also stood for the right to download anything in the atmosphere. The video extravaganza was produced by an outfit that grew famous in its own right for a tape it released, "Emergency Broadcast Network," which manipulated news footage to make Bush appear to be telling Americans to take drugs.

The performance promoted the notion that images in the media are fair game once they have been released into the datasphere. U2, which had already become a mega-group, was looking for new ways to make waves, even though it was no longer really part of the counterculture (its lead singer, Bono, on accepting a Grammy in 1994, used the media opportunity to say "Fuck up the mainstream" into his live microphone). As U2 guitarist "The Edge" explained, "We're a very big band with access to technology and access to the airwaves. . . . Now that we are big, we want to do something interesting, imaginative, and irreverent. . . . It's about mass communication. . . . Down by the mixing board, we've got a Vision mixer that blends the images from live cameras, from optical disks and from live satellite transmissions that are taken in from a dish outside the venue. We've also incorporated telecommunications. We've got a telephone onstage and Bono occasionally makes calls from the stage—he calls the White House or orders pizza. It's like information central."[31]

Like rap and house music, which samples sounds and riffs from famous recordings and recombines them into new songs, this video art challenges copyright laws and the "ownership" of imagery. Edge says, "In theory, I don't have a problem with sampling. When a sample becomes part of another work, no problem. If sampling is stealing and re-playing the same idea—changing it very slightly—that's different. We're using the images in a completely different context."[32]

Ironically U2 would soon find itself on the other side of this precarious relationship between artist and appropriator. The legal precedent against sampling sounds from copy-righted material was established in 1989, when De La Soul lost a million-dollar lawsuit to the Turtles for taking a riff off the song "You Showed Me." Rap chronicler David Toop remarked of the case, "Some music business lawyers were now instructing their older clients to listen to rap, in case their work was being sampled."[33] Apparently U2's lawyers did their looking and listening for them.

Bay Area underground band Negativland was already famous in its own circles for launching a prank media virus linking its song "Christianity Is Stupid" to a Minnesota boy's ax murder of his parents. Negativland is part rock band, part media activist posse, and its body of work utilizes the tools of both trades. In 1991 it released a record called "U2," based on thirty-five seconds of the real U2's hit "I Still Haven't Found What I'm Looking For," and intercut the musical sample with other audio media, including a Casey Kasem sound bite. It also imitated U2's album-cover art. Within weeks Island Records and Warner-Chappell Music sued Negativland, ultimately costing the band its record and $90,000. As Negativland struggled to raise the money it owed and to record a new album, *Mondo 2000* magazine decided to raise the media confrontation to the next metalevel.

Expecting a call from U2, which hoped to publicize its irreverent media tactics in an interview with *Mondo 2000*, the magazine's editors invited members of Negativland to sit in and question U2 directly about its apparent hypocrisy.

"You believe you're doing something subversive," argued Negativland's Mark Hosler. "And we're scurrying around in the music underground, doing things that we think are subversive. But the Island lawsuit dealt with this as if it was a consumer fraud intended to rip off innocent U2 fans."

The Edge seemed embarrassed by the whole affair and revealed he was unable to control Island's legal staff: "The problem really was that by the time we realized what was going on, it was kinda too late. And we actually did approach the record company on your behalf. . . . Although we have some influence, we aren't in a position to tell Island Records what to do."

As for Negativland, despite the legal hassles and bills,

this media battle put it on the map. The *New York Times* began to cover the band's club appearances more extensively, noting that, in addition to commenting on the power of the corporate world to control freedom of speech, Negativland's art marks a departure from the romantic tradition of rock and roll: "Declared heroic by their peers for stealing other people's music and refashioning it into what the band considers more honest statements, Negativland suggests that refusing to be original, in the traditional sense, is the only way to make art that has depth within commodity capitalism."[34]

The band's attempt to parody supergroup U2 and its relationship to the media machine was more successful than it could have dreamed. Though the record could not be distributed, its memes—thanks to the lawsuit—traveled far. The whole fiasco, in fact, served to elucidate Negativland's media agenda. As Hosler emphasizes, "All through time, artists have reacted to their environment, right? What were the tools, the technology, a few hundred years ago to do that? Well, you had a paintbrush, a piano, a lute. . . . So you interpreted things that way. Now, the way we see it, the technology is different. So instead of just making a painting of something, I can take a photograph, video, a Xerox, a sample. . . . I can capture something for my own work and make a statement about the media-saturated environment we live in."

In other words the medium is not just the message—the medium is media. For artists like Negativland to comment on their world—the fabric of their reality—they need to use media, the same way a Native American may have used bones or fur. Just as the Navajo chose to represent his relationship to the world by stringing together emblematic samples from nature, the media artist collects samples from the datasphere. The media activist sees the enemy empire as composed of media. Media is the very stuff of the conflict.

Media activists would be the first to point out that the same sorts of meta-conflicts and interactions occur in our everyday lives. There is a real thing called "land." We create the concept of "property" to identify the ownership of the land, then create a "meta"-concept of a deed to represent that own-ership. Similarly there is a real thing of value called "gold." We created money—dollars—to represent a certain amount of gold. We then created "meta"-money, based on the concept of legal tender or, once further removed, credit, which only has relationship to the *idea* of a dollar's worth of gold, if even that. We fight over deeds or dollars the same way we can fight over media representations—as if they were real.

Negativland believes its cultural sampling and com-mentary can help to change the balance of power in the mu-sic and media industries: "I want to change the copyright laws. I want to change the fact that you can't sample two sec-onds of something because it is *owned*. . . . That has to be changed in this age of new technologies which are essentially for *capturing* things," group member Don Joyce contends.

Like Negativland, most artists and activists who hope to change the system feel they can only do so in an uncompro-mised fashion if they stay outside the walls of corporate America and launch their viruses inside via catapult. To "buy in" to the mainstream media is to lose the self-consciousness and distance necessary to wage a tactical cam-paign in the house of mirrors.

PART 3

THE
UNDERGROUND

CHAPTER 6

ALTERNATIVE MEDIA

TRICKLE-DOWN MEMES

By working from outside the system, many media activists believe they can stay truer to their ideals. Underground artists and writers can utilize mainstream cultural icons like Bart Simpson, the President, or Amy Fisher much more purposefully and pointedly than can their overground counterparts because they are not encumbered by the pressures of a corporate environment or mass-media censorship.

There are two ways to market memes without entering the mainstream and being subjected to the scrutiny of overground exposure. The first is to use alternative formatting—low-status, "trickle-down media," including video games, comics, trading cards, and fantasy role-playing games. This merchandising sometimes makes use of popular iconography like "Ren & Stimpy" or major political figures, but twists it for more satirical purposes or even toward activist agendas. These media can be thought of as bottom feeders in the data ocean. The other marketing style is to self-publish memes that are too radical for mainstream outlets in the hope that they might "trickle up." Thousands of "zines" (self-published magazines) and independent book publishers have sprouted throughout the United States and Europe, covering issues ranging from income-tax avoidance to anarchy. The proliferation of self-distributed books and zines has led to an entirely new philosophy of publishing, in which sampling with attribution or even downright plagiarism is encouraged and copyrighting is scorned.

Alternative forums of all kinds give media activists low-cost, highly resilient, and provocatively interactive viral shells for the memes they wish to disseminate. These are lowbrow affairs that do not suffer from the need to appear politically correct, morally upright, or even fastidiously produced. The fact that these media are not taken too seriously also keeps them from appearing too threatening. Like kids' television, which is not intended entirely for children, seemingly innocuous zines, comics, and games are packed with deeply threatening memes. Moreover, the formats themselves are designed to reflect a value system in which the concepts of interactivity, feedback, iteration, and viruses are laws of the universe.

PLAYING GOD

Andrew Mayer was born in 1965—as he puts it, "the year after Kennedy, which is something I use to blow the minds of people in their forties. 'Kennedy was dead, man, when I was born.' " Currently employed creating characters and writing stories for computer and video games, Andy is a proud GenXer ("I can surf twenty TV channels at once"), computer genius, and avid comic book fan. At twelve he installed the networking system for the computers at a large corporation, even though he had no former computer knowledge. "I had no fear of technology. It just seemed natural." More recently he contributed to a computer program called "Beyond Cyberpunk," which he calls "an interactive multimedia, blah blah buzzword buzzword computer-based book." However jaded Andy may sound about the marketing of cyberpunk products, he is very enthusiastic about the agendas implicit in futuristic comics and cyberpunk creations.

"There's no such thing as cyberpunk without an agenda. The agenda is to prove it can be done. People will look at it and see that it can be done; it will spark their minds to say, 'I can do it myself. This is achievable.' " The kinds of media Andy likes are the kinds that provoke the reader or audience to get involved—not just interactively, but in creating his or her own media. Diehard comic-book fans usually know how to draw the characters, too, and even create comics of their own. The kids who understand video and computer games the best often crack the command language of the game in order to modify it to their own specifications.

Within the overall "it can be done" agenda of the cyberpunk and comic/gaming media, though, are many smaller segments of viral code that have trickled down from more mainstream channels. Raised in the "Marvel Universe" but now living in a studio apartment in San Francisco, Andy understands what he calls the "cues" in comics, video games, and techno-pop culture and enjoys watching them move from medium to medium. "Because comics and video games are abbreviated, visual media, writers need to speak in cues. A cue might be a single comic-book frame of Superman ripping his shirt open to expose the 'S' underneath. The artist no longer has to show the steps by which Superman transforms." The emergence of a particular cue is a sign that a linear set of information can now be represented in a single image. A new concept—formerly only comprehensible as an explanation—can now be communicated with a symbol. "Six years ago, if you wanted to have a story with an artificial intelligence, you'd have to show the step-by-step process by which a person gets his brain inputted into a computer. Now you just show a simple cue. The dramatic arc is not the steps within the cue. It's from cue to cue."

Like MTV, comics and games tell meta-stories by relating one frame (or one "shot") to another. Each frame contains a set of ideas expressed in shorthand, and meaning is generated from its relationship to successive frames. "Beyond Cyberpunk" was an independently produced computer program intended to instruct people how to recognize the

cues in fiction, comics, and videos and to train them in moving through these media in a discontinuous fashion. When a
Macintosh user installs the set of disks, the computer screen
displays the console of a strange machine. By pointing and
clicking on various parts of the machine, the user can move
through a tremendous set of text documents, sounds, and
pictures about cyberpunk technologies, stories, and art. The
program uses a Macintosh format called "Hypercard," which
allows users to travel back and forth between related topics
and even create new relationships between ideas. If you are
reading a piece about Japanese animation and see a reference to Philip K. Dick, you can point to his name, click your
mouse, and find yourself in an article about Dick. Each article explains a cue. The program itself demonstrates how to
move from cue to cue—that is, how to move between larger
chunks of information—and encourages a participatory attitude toward media. And it is as fun to use as Nintendo.

Video games provide a more straightforward sort of audience participation, and the intensity of this experience
should not be underestimated. At twenty-nine Andy straddles the divide between Nintendo kids and confused adults.
"Have you ever seen two kids link up their Game Boys?" he
asks, referring to the hand-held portable video games that
can be connected to each other for kids to play with or
against each other. "It's an amazing thing to watch: two people sitting, facing each other, holding Game Boys with a wire
running between them. They are in a shared space—maybe
as Ninja Turtles fighting bad guys—but they are looking
down at *separate consoles*. This is the first shared VR [virtual
reality] right there." While the game itself may have its own
symbolic agenda, more interesting to Andy is the agenda of
the technology itself. The games train future computer users
how to utilize a virtual reality interface.

Many games have begun to address the issue of educat-
ing their young players more directly. Maxis Software's "Sim
City" is a simulated city, where the player makes all the decisions for an imaginary island. Andy and his colleagues call
Sim City the first "God game," in which a player takes

charge of a whole world. The game presents the player with a map on which to build a city. The user, as "Mayor," must choose which zones will be residential, commercial, or industrial, and where to put power plants, police stations, roads, and highways. The game then reports back to the player how things are going in terms of property values, crime, pollution, commercial success, and reelection prospects. The player is limited by city budget and by time, which passes in years, months, or days.

The brilliance of the game is the way it presents an interconnected picture of urban planning. You cannot build more industry without creating traffic problems. You cannot build more roads without taking some money from the police budget. You cannot take from the police budget without increasing crime. You cannot allow crime to increase without decreasing property value. The agenda of this game is to demonstrate the interconnectivity of our political, social, and economic world. To learn to succeed at planning the city, the player must adopt the gamemaker's agenda.

Another, even more ambitious game in this tradition is called "Civilization," which, according to Mayer, "is the closest thing to a computer drug I've ever seen in my life. Stay away from it; it'll ruin your life. You are God, and you're in charge of the history of the world from the beginning of civilization to the year 2020." The game incorporates the same agenda of interconnectivity as Sim City, but over a larger physical and ideological terrain. "It's an incredibly complex game, where everything influences everything else. Literally. If you overtax the people, they'll rebel, and you'll lose money and resources from that city, and then if they get attacked while in rebellion, you'll lose that city to the other side."

As Andy talks it becomes clear he does not think of Sim City and Civilization as mere games. They are not just simulations, but real events occurring in a computer. "You don't play the game," Andy insists, tapping commands into his computer keyboard and changing the image on his high-resolution monitor from gray industrial zones to green parks, "you play the interface." What Andy means is that there is a real event going on between the user and the game, mediated by an interface, which is "played." Learning to manipulate the interface is learning the agenda of the game writer. "You interact with the buttons and the reports and you control the flow, but you don't interact with the simulation itself. You're playing the interface and watching the results."

Andy, like many in the video game industry, has great faith in the selling power and instructive ability of these simulation-world games. They have impressive sales figures, even compared with trashier shoot-'em-up arcade-style games, because kids have an urge to learn by doing. They have a certain addictive quality, too, that comes from the peculiar relationship between the player and his simulated environment. Several studies on virtual reality have demonstrated that the smaller the user perceives his own size in relationship to the scale of the object he is interacting with, the slower his perception of passing time. The bigger the user is—God of a civilization would qualify as pretty big—the faster time seems to pass. "I looked up and three hours had passed," Andy explains, still amazed. "That never happened to me before in my life. I gave the game to my friend, and the next day he gave it back and said, 'Don't ever do that to me again.'"

But reflective, older users like Andy draw even broader philosophical implications from these perceptual effects. If greater power and size makes time seem to move faster, then the "largest" and most powerful people have the shortest perceived life spans. People who become aware of their relationship to the universe as a whole, and focus on their interconnectedness with the larger reality, will experience their lives as lasting longer. Again, the agenda that users infer from playing these games is that they must learn to see reality as a myriad of interconnections rather than just a few power relationships.

Many kids prefer to take matters even further into their own hands than games like Sim City allow and spend their time and energy pirating, cracking, and repackaging games within their own, homemade viral shells. Andy admires their audacity and skill: "It's amazing stuff. When these kids crack a game, wherever they are in the world, they slap on their own intro—maybe music and some graphics. Basically it's a boast. Like a graffiti artist's tag. 'I'm a bad-ass motherfucker, don't mess with me.' 'Cool J, you're an asshole and the Australian Wallow Society, you're cool.' " When the pirated version of the game is distributed, usually by uploading it onto computer bulletin boards that others can access, everyone who plays the game is exposed to the young game-cracker's messages.

The cyberpunk ethic of "you can achieve anything" proved too frightening for those attempting to keep a lid on computer hacking and cracking. In a testament to the power of games to transmit memes, law-enforcement officials involved in the famous hacker raids of 1990 confused game with reality when they confiscated the computers and files of a company called Steve Jackson Games. Steve Jackson invented GURPS (Generic Universal Role Playing System), a set of rules for people to play fantasy games. After buying the basic rule book, which shows how to use dice and other methods to act out fantasy scenarios between gamers, players either create their own worlds in which they can interact or purchase further game packs, like "Space" or "Super Heroes."

Many of Jackson's game packs have viral tendencies. One best-seller, called "Illuminati," is based on the *Illuminatus! Trilogy* by Robert Shea and Robert H. Wilson. An extraordinarily paranoid conspiracy tale, the game explores the darker side of the interconnectivity theme. The U.S. Secret Service got paranoid about a less intentionally conspiratorial game called "Cyberpunk" that provided rules for players to re-enact the cyberpunk scenarios described in books like William Gibson's cyberspace adventure *Neuromancer.* But the Secret Service apparently believed that this game pack was a set of instructions teaching kids how to break into real computers illegally. The agents were further confused by Steve Jackson's call-in computer bulletin board service. Dubbed "Illuminati," the computer conferencing system welcomes users with a cryptic message: "Greetings, Mortal! You have entered the secret computer system of the Illuminati, the on-line home of the world's oldest and largest secret conspiracy .5124474449 300/1200/2400 BAUD fronted by Steve Jackson Games, Incorporated. Fnord." By the time the whole mess was cleared up three years later, the story had spread through the media, making GURPS "Cyberpunk" famous. Although Jackson's company was fully acquitted, everyone involved fell deeply into debt.[1]

The Steve Jackson story is prototypically viral. A medium that promotes interactivity—fantasy gaming and associated computer bulletin boards—conducts memes that reflect the philosophy of gaming itself, in this case cyberpunk. By straying too close to a conspiratorial mind-set, even in jest, the virusmakers provoke a tremendous and inappropriate response—the Secret Service raid—which gives the viruses more exposure than the creators could have generated on their own. Alternative distributors depend on others, even the enemy, to spread their memes.

BOTTOM FEEDERS

Most of the messages in comics and games trickle down from the mainstream media on which they are based. Called "bottom feeders" by GenX media consumers like Andy, they utilize the cues established in other formats. For instance, Bart often expresses his irreverence toward authority on "The Simpsons" by exclaiming "Eat my shorts." In the Game Boy version of the episode "Escape from Camp Crusty," Bart cries out "Eat my shorts" whenever he loses. In the Ren & Stimpy Game Boy adventure, Stimpy farts loudly, as he does on the show. To fans like Andy, this is the lowest form of meme dissemination and hardly even counts. "It makes you feel that feeling of 'Ren & Stimpy' without actually watching it. But these are just the bare cues. You have to know their cultural context to understand them. It is a trigger. Not a gun."

Still, the "Simpsons" and "Ren & Stimpy" comic books and games are a further iteration of their original memes and sometimes make even more extreme social or political commentary than their mainstream counterparts. The first issue of the "Ren & Stimpy" comic book was a complex commentary on media and consumer culture, chock-full of memes intended for adult readers. Seduced by the display at a pet supplies store in the mall, Stimpy's gaping tongue breaks the display window. Ren and Stimpy rob the store of its dog and kitty toys, including a doll that says "Read my lips" (just in time for the 1992 election which occurred simultaneously with the release of the comic). Television superhero Powdered Toast Man is called upon to catch the robbers, and he fails miserably. So much for traditional television's answer to crime. The boys are finally caught when Stimpy is moved by a television newscaster's urgent plea to viewers: "We need your help! If you've seen or heard any information about their whereabouts, call in at 1-800-555-FINK! Come on, you can do it! Yes—YOU! These dangerous criminals must be brought to JUSTICE! And so they can, but only with YOUR help! Call in!"

Stimpy is a victim of the surveillance media, and he readily complies. In a final twist of a cynical screw, the boys are sentenced to prison terms in "Dragnet"-style frames. But on the very next page, Ren is running for President, readily admitting that his crookedness and greed make him the ideal candidate: "I'm gonna be honeest weeth you, man—Reed my leeps! Vote for me and bucks stop here, een my tightly grasped feests! I got your treeckle-down theory right here, pal!" This mock commercial would surely have been banned by Nickelodeon along with the original Powdered Toast Man episode of "The Ren & Stimpy Show," but in this lower, essentially alternative media channel, it sneaks by the censors and its memes spread.

Comics like these get away with a lot of scathing social commentary, but perhaps their most effective forays into the meme wars have been in depicting alternative world-views and social behaviors. With surprising and almost frightening consistency, comic-book writers fill their stories with a unilaterally progressive countercultural agenda. Like most alternative and underground media, these comics promote psychedelic consciousness, environmental awareness, sexual permissiveness, racial equality, feminist values, distrust of authority, and conspiratorial paranoia.

Alan Moore is one of the most successful figures in comics today. He has written sought-after issues of many of the top comic-book titles and has developed many groundbreaking titles of his own. Almost invariably his writing incorporates these countercultural themes. His episodes of "Swamp Thing," for example, were among the most controversial comics of the eighties. "Swamp Thing" was already an ideal conduit for Moore's memes. The creature is a humanoid plant who can use the interconnectedness of the plant kingdom to travel and reappear anywhere in the world. He simply dissolves into the plant life wherever he is and travels through root systems, molds, and algae as pure consciousness. When he wants to emerge, he recomposes himself out of the plant materials available in his new location.

The environmental agenda is obvious. If a region is polluted, then he has trouble materializing into a healthy being. Swamp Thing is totally dependent on the condition of his environment, but maybe, as the comic implies, so are the rest of us who are just as dependent on the plant kingdom for food, air, and a balanced biosphere.

The psychedelic agenda is presented in equally bold strokes. Many psychedelics users believe that the drugs function by giving human beings access to "plant consciousness." Terence McKenna, a leading psychedelics advocate, asserts in his book *Food of the Gods* that the alienation experienced in modern society is a direct result of the human race having interrupted its symbiotic, "coevolutionary" relationship with the psychedelic plants. To McKenna plants are the "missing link in the search to understand the human mind and its place in nature."[2] McKenna and others' contention is that man and the psychedelic plants coevolved. Human beings were able to understand their symbiotic relationship to plants and the rest of nature when they ate psychedelics. Now that these plants are out of favor and illegal, we have lost our link to the plant kingdom and the rest of nature. Our disconnection from this wisdom is responsible for our reckless disregard for the environment, evidenced by our destruction of the natural habitats of the very plants that would have kept us tuned in to the Gaian spirit in the first place.

In Alan Moore's hands "Swamp Thing" became a media virus to promote this pro-psychedelic, pro-plant kingdom agenda. The character provided an ideal self-similar shell: Swamp Thing *is* a coevolution of the plant and animal kingdoms. He walks, talks, thinks, and feels like a human being, but is composed of plant matter and intimately connected with the plant world. His holistic philosophies about planetary awareness, ecological fastidiousness, and plant consciousness result directly from his familiarity with and dependence on the network of nature. When he dissolves into pure consciousness and travels through the biosphere, he is taking a metaphorical psychedelic trip. He experiences the classic hallucinogenic insight that the whole planet is one living being. In one of the most daring and most talked about issues of "Swamp Thing," a yamlike tuber falls off the creature's body. A hippie, Chester, finds the tuber, and two of his friends consume it, experiencing the most vivid psychedelic trips ever presented in comics and ones quite consistent with the reports from ethnobotanist-users like McKenna. One of the trippers even comes to an understanding of the history of humanity's relationship to plants and nature, and she travels—much like Swamp Thing himself—through the world of plant consciousness, emerging as a steadfast believer in the wholeness of nature.

Moore's psychedelic agenda stayed with the "Swamp Thing" comics even after the artist went on to other projects. By March 1994, with a new set of writers at the helm, the book began to make direct references to psychedelics and to the work of Terence McKenna himself. The entire Swamp Thing saga, it is revealed, was the psychedelic hallucination of a doctor studying South American psychoactive plants. "It's like our brains are waiting for messages from these plants," the doctor explains. "DMT is the most powerful psychedelic known to man and yet it is completely and safely metabolized within the human body fifteen minutes after ingestion."[3] One would be hard-pressed to find a more direct endorsement of a highly illegal drug.

Moore's later work, like that of many others who write about psychedelic and subcultural ideas, is so colored by a sense of interconnectedness that it adopts a fairly conspiratorial world-view. In his independent comic-book series, *From Hell*, Moore proposes that the Jack the Ripper murders were connected to the Masonic order and Queen Victoria. Interspersed with footnotes and actual quotations from the writings of the people on whom Moore's characters are based, the book feels more like a historical document than a fictional comic. Moore cites the references for his suppositions and strives for an accurate rendering of the Masonic rituals, their participants, and their targets. That the Jack the Ripper episode may have been a huge cover-up perpetrated by Queen Victoria herself to keep her grandson and heir to the throne, Edward Albert Victor, away from scandal is not a new hypothesis. Many books have been written debating the theory. What is new, however, is presenting this material so coherently in a marketplace formerly reserved for superheroes and Archie humor. More important, it helps us characterize the overall agenda of the activist countercultural media: to create a picture of the world as a vast set of interdependencies that foster life and work naturally against those who seek a disproportionate share of power or control. The established powers, on the other hand, hope to isolate individuals by disconnecting them from these networks and preventing them from conducting any sort of feedback or iteration.

Alan Moore found the most accommodating platform for his ideas at a cottage-industry comic-book company called Eclipse Enterprises in rural Forestville, California.

Founded by brothers Dean and Jan Mullaney in 1977 as the first comic publisher to allow writers to own the copyrights on their material, the independent company soon gained a reputation for presenting memes that the majors—DC and Marvel—censored. At the time stories about interracial love and antiwar sentiments were strictly forbidden by editors at the mainstream comic houses. Catherine "Cat" Yronwode (pronounced "ironwood"), an ex-hippie already working as a comics reviewer and journalist, was attracted to the Mullaneys' "converted garage with chickens in the yard" as well as their activist agenda. Joining up as editor in 1981, Cat quickly brought the company into the political spotlight.

She and activist writer Joyce Brabner convinced the Central Committee for Conscientious Objectors to spend its $25,000 pamphlet photocopying budget on an antiwar comic book called "Real War Stories" instead. In addition to giving away copies as a new form of propaganda, the nonprofit group hoped to recoup its investment by selling the book in stores. As a media virus, the book worked better than anyone could have hoped. The comic book became part of a landmark Georgia court decision that forbade the CCCO from giving away "Real War Stories" during a high school career day, even though the military was free to give out its own materials about careers in war. The court determined that there was no such thing as a "career in peace." After a huge media explosion, the Georgia State Supreme Court reversed the decision, establishing an important but unintentional meta-meme for CCCO: Peace can be considered a career.

Another of the arguments made against the comic book, this time by the Department of Defense, was that the practice of "greasing" (a brutal form of hazing) depicted in "Real War Stories" did not really exist. When the U.S. Navy's own records were brought in as evidence, it became clear that this "comic-book threat to national security" was actually a fact-based, accurate account of military life. Eclipse Enterprises delighted in its vindication and printed some of the Defense Department's false accusations in the next edition of "Real War Stories."

By now the company had grown famous for its stand on political issues, and its comics were being sold in shops around the country, as well as by political action groups trying to raise funds. With the freedom to pick and choose its own issues, Eclipse focused on CIA covert operations in Central America. The results were hardcover and trade paperback editions of an unprecedentedly informative comic, "Brought to Light." Industry giants like writer Alan Moore and artist Bill Sienkiewicz were delighted to participate. "Alan is a very political creature," explains Cat. He had already been selling his British comic book, "Miracle Man," through Eclipse in the United States, "but comic books like 'Miracle Man' use metaphor to argue social issues like homophobia or U.S. government interference in the domestic policies of other nations. It had always been done as fictionalized metaphor."

Moore jumped at the chance to present his ideas in a reality-based context and wrote the text for "Shadowplay— The Secret Team," a story based on the Christic Institute's lawsuit "tracing the major players in the Iran/Contra scandal back through covert action in Iran, the 1960's secret war in Laos, and the Bay of Pigs fiasco," as the comic book puts it. The memes presented in the comic are decidedly conspiratorial. Dan Sheehan, attorney for the Christic Institute, is quoted directly: "Iran/Contragate did not begin with Oliver North. Nor is the scandal just about Iran and Nicaragua. For thirty years, a Secret Team of U.S. Military and CIA officials, acting both officially and on their own, have waged secret wars, toppled governments, trafficked in drugs, assassinated political enemies, stolen from the U.S. government, and subverted the will of the Constitution, the Congress, and the American people." The comic goes on to detail and document some of the scariest high-level covert operations scandals imaginable. And, unlike Queen Victoria and Jack the Ripper, the scandals are taking place in the present.

"In a sense you could call this a bait and switch," Cat Yronwode confides; just as her own relaxed hippified lifestyle and surroundings mask her activist subcultural agenda,

Eclipse comics hide some potent ideological material in what appears to be kiddie literature. "You think you are picking up a comic book, but you're actually getting a bunch of documentary information." So a college kid who may be a fan of Sienkiewicz or Moore takes home what looks like just another comic book and reads a version of the news he will not find on TV, expressed in a format that allows for the rapid transmission of memes in a stylish, visual fashion.

Yronwode's greatest achievement, though, was helping to create an even more ingenious conduit for activist ideologies than comics. "Trading cards, sports cards, were already nonfiction," she explains. "It's the most effective bait and switch because the person thinks, 'Oh, I'm gonna get a bunch of little fact cards here about famous people.' And they do. But they find out that the Premier of some Latin American country was a convicted rapist. That the CIA supported him until he assassinated some dude in Africa. It's all right there in your face. And they don't know how to turn it off because it's on a trading card and a trading card is true." Like its comic books, Eclipse Enterprises trading cards are documented, referenced, and footnoted. Current card sets include "Drug Wars," "The Iran Contra Scandal," "Friendly Dictators," and "Serial Killers."

A typical set contains cards depicting the personalities and main events connected with the particular scandal. The "Drug Wars" set features a George Bush card, on which the then President is drawn inside a TV set, holding up a bag of cocaine and delivering his famous War on Drugs speech. On the back is a critical review of Bush's drug policies: "Historically, drug wars have been used by imperial powers as smokescreens for foreign intervention. For the U.S., this has taken the form of sending military aid to corrupt allies who use the weapons not against drug traffickers, with whom they are often in league, but to crush their internal political enemies. Meanwhile, U.S. agriculture and trade policies encourage production and export of deadly legal drugs." Another pictures the pope and the Vatican banker: "As alluded to in *Godfather III*, Robert Calvi's body was found hanging from Blackfriars Bridge in London in June, 1982 ... in 1990, two former CIA contacts stated that the CIA had paid Propaganda Due leader Licio Gelli, mastermind of the 1980 Bologna train bombing, to foment terrorist activities in Italy. Gelli attended Ronald Reagan's first inaugural ball."

Trading cards like these are quintessential, packaged memes. Unlike a comic book, which has a linear order, a trading card is a tiny unit by itself and can be arranged in any manner. Yronwode says this feature is not coincidental: "Our trading cards are designed so they read like Hypercard stacks. Each card cross-references to other cards. For instance, on one card where Eugene Hassenfus was shot down (in the 'Iran Contra' set) it says his first phone call was placed to Felix Rodriguez aka Max Gomez. You could look under that card and find out he trained under Howard Hunt ('See Invasion of the Cuban Bay of Pigs') or that he worked with George Bush ('see card 36'). They all connect, and you can rearrange them in chains of interconnectivity. Or chronologically. You can find out who someone's boss was, how different people moved around, that this guy was in Vietnam at the same time as this guy, and then that they were both in Nicaragua at the same time, too."

Typically viral in construction, Eclipse card sets function through a juxtaposition of memes rather than through a linear progression or narrative. In form and content, too, they juxtapose qualities of high and low culture, as well as high and low technology. A typically simple, children's medium like trading cards is the conduit for an agenda progressive and complex enough for the pages of *The Nation* or *The New Republic*. In this absurdly simplistic context, the complexities of behind-the-scenes government corruption are reduced to blatant and clear-cut violations of the public trust. Meanwhile the viral shell of "trading" cards promotes the idea that kids should be passing these memes around. We can imagine the negotiations as the virus spreads: "I'll give you a Klaus Barbie and a Meyer Lansky for that General Manuel Noriega."

Eclipse Enterprises also embodies this cultural clash.

Computer-literate ex-flower child Yronwode explains, "Our company is a low-tech/high-tech interface. Here we are in a converted garage in a town of less than a thousand people and we're fully linked to the networks. We can send out on disk or electronically material to be outputted directly to film negatives. We receive scripts via fax or modem." Eclipse's success, in part, is due to its ability to produce high-quality graphics on low-cost computers, as well as its ability to receive materials, ideas, and text from around the world through advanced, unrestricted networks. One no longer needs a million-dollar printing facility or a staff of in-house artists to self-publish full-color state-of-the-art publications. Neither does one need a rich, established corporate sponsor to pay for all that equipment. As Eclipse proves, all you need is a few good memes.

ZINES: SMASHING THE IMAGE FACTORY

Using the same basic formula as Eclipse Enterprises, tens of thousands of small groups and individuals gather up their favorite memes and publish low-circulation magazines called "zines." Zines began as newsletters for science fiction fans in the late fifties. A particularly avid fan would type up ten or so carbon copies of his thoughts about a new book or film and then mail them to his friends, who would respond by mail and then see their own comments in the next "issue." Activist and satirical zines like *The Realist* and *The Oracle* caught on in the sixties, establishing the tradition of zines as a forum for radical and countercultural ideology. Once inexpensive photocopiers hit the scene, the zine phenomenon exploded.

Mark Frauenfelder is editor of one of the most successful current zines, an arty futuristic publication out of San Francisco called *bOING bOING*. Twenty-something Frauenfelder is keenly aware of the place of zines in the media and meme pools: "Network television, national magazines, and book publishers in the overground media rely upon advertising sales income or public funding and as a result must appeal to a large audience to ensure their survival. To guarantee the continuing support of a large segment of a population, these external carriers must contain memes that are consistent with the ideosphere, or memetic, ecology of that group. Overground media reacts allergically to mutant memes, usually by destroying the external carrier by burning it or banning it or by inciting the meme police to incarcerate the human propagator and hir [a meme-word meaning his or her] dangerously contagious nervous system."

While Mark is not quite ready to acknowledge the fact that the overground media's "allergic reaction" to certain memes often contributes to their spread, he does recognize the important relationship between memes and their carriers. Each meme, especially a new or "mutant" meme, must find a carrier—a viral shell—capable of delivering it to ready individuals, even if they are in the minority. The mass media is understandably unwilling to provide passage for memes that will be unpopular with their audiences. They are in business. Zines, on the other hand, coming out of science fiction, have a history of considering and promoting cutting-edge ideas. Unlike commercial magazines, zines have always been produced and funded out of a passion for an individual's ideas and a desire to print and reiterate the feedback of the audience. Zines have no obligation to please everyone. As Frauenfelder asks and answers:

"So where, then, can unpopular, hot, radical or strange memes survive and propagate? Where can the intrepid meme-explorer find a dose of erotica? SHe [he or she] needs only to dip hir brain into the zine pool, the wild ocean of self-published magazines, where fish learn to breathe and salamanders sprout feathers and try to fly. It is only here, in the primordial soup, far away from the dinosaurs of the overground media, where these new ideas have a chance to test their wings."

People who read and produce zines are self-consciously

interested in media viruses. Like Mark they see the world of
zines as a "primordial soup," or genetic pool. This is where
social evolution takes place. To take part in zines is to participate in the memetic engineering of our future. The mainstream media is likened to the dinosaur, an evolutionary
dead end, while wild mutation, erotica, and experimentation
are taking place in the zine ocean. Zines are experienced by
their creators and readers as an orgiastic frenzy of memes.
They are the conceptual equivalent of free, unprotected sex.
Only in this case, unexpected pregnancies and transmission
of viruses are desired results.

Zines usually focus on highly specific areas. *Factsheet
Five* is a zine about zines—what ziners call a "metazine"—
that reviews about 1,500 zines in each issue. They fall into
categories like sex, B movies, peace, environment, and technology. Nearly all of them are radically progressive and
reader-participatory in their agendas. Typical examples are
"Dropout: The 100% True Zine for Inde Mediamakers,"
"Discotext" (a rave zine from Vancouver), and "Fuck Me?
No, Fuck You!" (about ways to make bombs and get revenge). But no matter how specific a zine's subject, it incorporates the irreverent, do-it-yourself ethic of the zine
movement. People who buy zines are looking for memes;
they get their memes as well as recognition and encourage-
ment for their venture into zine territory. Simply turning to
zines is a declaration of independence from mainstream media and the associated dominant mind-set.

bOING bOING is among the zines that understand this
the best. While the magazine's own memes include future
technologies like cryogenics, virtual reality, smart drugs, and
artificial life, Frauenfelder and his coeditor, Carla Sinclair,
dedicate much of their space to publicizing and commenting
on other zines. Instead of touting specific agendas, *bOING
bOING* is out to prove that meme consciousness through
zines will lead to a better world:

"The decentralized, iconoclastic quality of zines is ideal
for people interested in shucking prescribed realities in fa-

vor of designing their own world-view. The Church of the SubGenius, one of the first religions to use a zine to spread its own blend of particularly virulent memes, reminds us that truth and reality are subjective yet inescapable shams and the best course of action is to reject the reality tunnels thrust upon us by the corporate/political world and instead 'pull the wool over your own eyes.'"

Zines are an opportunity for readers to select the wool they wish to pull over their own eyes. Rather than blinding them to reality, the zines present alternative realities to the ones that mainstream media foist upon them the rest of the day. Zine readers do not see themselves as ostriches hiding from reality; they are independent thinkers, disconnecting from the particularly mind-numbing mainstream media deluge that has replaced reality.

ANARCHY IN THE U.K.

Many zine publishers are dedicated to chipping away at the seamless reality construct of mainstream culture by enlarging and unifying the population of disbelievers. In the United States, this means appealing to "slacker" culture—that group of twenty- and thirty-year-old work-force dropouts who get by, somehow, on little or no income and a postindustrial attitude. The equivalent social class in the United Kingdom are the squatters—kids on the dole who, after finishing some amount of school, move away from their parents and live with each other in small groups in abandoned buildings. Maybe because the U.K. economy is worse, or maybe because their squatters have more to be angry about than American slackers do, zine publishers in England are more committed to picking off members of consensus reality and adding them to the ranks of the nonworking subculture.

One typical London zine, *Fatuous Times*, published by "Play Time For Ever Press," aims to take "the fatuous out

of everyday life." The zine encourages readers to stop voting, quit their jobs, bury their cars, unplug their TVs, enjoy
themselves, and tell others to do the same. What makes *Fatuous Times* particularly viral is its interactive quality. In the
United States, an interactive zine might invite reader mail
and phone calls or include a computer disk or audiotape. In
the U.K. interactivity means creating activists. Nearly every
page of *Fatuous Times* is in the form of a flyer that can be cut
out, photocopied, and posted in public. "How will the election [affect] the homeless?" one flyer asks, then responds, "It
won't." Even the articles—on topics like anticopyright,
priest-hating, and AIDS—are usually limited to one page for
easy clipping and dissemination. Other pieces simply encourage activist billboarding or stickering and tell stories
about successful countercultural publicity efforts.

Jason and Calum, the two young British squatter-artists
who put out *Fatuous Times*, live true to the ideals they promote in their zine. They are active billboarders, pay no rent,
live off the dole, and support their friends who do the same.
They regularly gather with like-minded friends to discuss
methodology and philosophy.

One such colleague, Matthew Fuller, is host of what he
hopes will be the U.K.'s first truly subversive bulletin board
service. His accent betrays his university education, and his
ideals, while absolutely anarchistic, tend to spring more
from philosophy than the "life on the streets" of his comrades. His own zine, *Underground*, is a free, full-size news-
paper-style publication that announces in its masthead: "We
paid for this paper with our hard-earned taxes, produced it
on the equipment of management and pasted up on the
floors of council flats we got by having mixed illegitimate
kids. Underground will rescue you from the happy life you
had a few moments ago." Matthew's main objective—
outlined in his zine—is to develop a large, countercultural
computer-networked community in London. He will call the
service "Fast Breeder" because new, radical ideas and information will be able to replicate and spread quickly via com-

puters and modems. No matter how true his intentions, this puts him at odds with the views of most of his colleagues, who are decidedly more low-tech.

In the U.K. copy art is about as technologically advanced as most activists are willing to go. Computers and television are still seen as too expensive and too consumer-driven to be of any use. Instead poster art, billboard revision, and zine production are favored for their speed, cost-effectiveness, and ability to copy and alter other media imagery. Bruce, who regularly hosts gatherings for these U.K. media activists, runs his own free press and teaches photocopying skills to would-be anarchists. His own latest effort is a two-color pamphlet, "TV Times," which uses stories, art, and comics to make people aware of the brainwashing effects of television: "For the entire four hours or more that the average person is watching TV daily, the repetitive process of constructing images out of dots, following scans and vibrating with the beats of the set and the electronic rhythm goes on . . . eventually the conscious mind gives up noting the process and merges with the experience, opening up to whatever the set wishes to implant. The brain quits processing the information that goes in. Once the images are inside you, they imprint upon your memory."

Bruce explains his distrust of television as a conduit for useful memes. "TV does not further positive thought or action because it doesn't require any participation on the viewer's part. It's merely passive intake."

Matthew Fuller would be the last to disagree. His own greatest achievement to date has been producing a large, trade-paperback-style book called *Flyposter Frenzy: Posters from the Anticopyright Network*. This collection of political artwork was all created with photocopier machines, which Fuller and the assembled crew believe is the counterculture's best hope of dismantling the top-down media. First, there is no way of telling which copy is the original. No copy is any more valuable or close to the source than any other, so the notion of "original" art being more valuable than a copy disappears. The memes themselves are the focus. Iteration is

rapid and total. "Being multiple and never unique the photocopy is always social. Even if only a single copy exists at
any one point it's always possible to instantly produce hundreds of others," explains Fuller. Like a dormant virus, the
uncopied flyer only needs to wait for an opportune moment
to strike.

Billboarders and poster artists intentionally take emphasis off themselves so that they may transfer it to their
memes. Photocopy technology inherently leads to a blurring
of the original source material. Instead new billboards based
on the memes and imagery of older ones become part of the
overall landscape of visual information. As Fuller puts it, this
"points toward an advancement of culture as accumulative.
That is to say that all innovations are built on the sum total
of what has gone before." Ironically it is a disposable and
temporary form of media that allows for this deeper continuity. If one artist uses an advertising photo of a car to
make a flyer comment on consumer culture, another might
appropriate the image from this flyer and combine it with
a picture of a crash dummy to demonstrate our suicidal
technologies.

This is direct feedback and iteration. To see a billboarder like Bruce work is to watch a memetic engineer create, reproduce, and mutate viral constructs and then invade
an entire system one afternoon. Bruce spots a photo of a
Barbie doll, which gives him an idea. He cuts out the image
and pastes it onto a blank sheet of paper, then adds type cut
out from other advertisements. His slogan: "You, too, can
have a body like Cindy." He makes maybe fifty copies of the
flyer for distribution, but he is not finished yet. He uses a
purple pencil (a special shade that does not copy) to divide
his image into four equal parts, then uses a Canon photocopier to enlarge each section to nearly four times its original size. Then he takes each of those enlargements, divides
them into four equal parts, and uses the Canon to enlarge
them further. Bruce gets some help from Jason and Calum
to tape all sixteen of the resulting enlargements together
into a giant billboard-sized flyer.

Bruce has taken two images from mainstream media—Barbie's picture and Cindy Crawford's name—altered them, combined them, and then fed his new virus back into culture. He reiterated the image at least fifty times with his flyers and then amplified it further with a giant billboard that would be seen by thousands.

Later that night, with a crew of three or four other billboarders, Bruce pastes the poster up over a billboard formerly advertising "some bank." But isn't this destruction of property? Or at least a pollution of the public space? Matthew is quick to defend the billboarder's ethic: "Public space is a myth. In cities and industrialized nature every last millimeter is so obviously owned by, broadcast to, and fought over by a deluge of competing interests. Public space remains contingent on what and who is excluded or included by definitions of a mythical 'general public.' " Already dominated by huge billboards selling products along with a mindless, consumer philosophy, the public space has been co-opted by commercial forces, who foist their views on unsuspecting passersby who have no choice in the matter. To the billboarder, this is just fighting fire with fire. They see the advertising space in the world around them as the city's ever-changing second skin. They take part in its development, using, changing, and recombining popular cultural imagery with their own to communicate their agendas.

Almost all the images these propagandists use are recycled. Flyposter artists are deeply committed to democratizing the media. They do not believe in owning homes or possessions, much less the images or words they create. Most underground U.K. media activists are members of the Anticopyright Network, a decentralized group of artists, writers, and propagandists who make and distribute zines and flyposters. The network has heroes but no leaders. It is a nonhierarchical fluid library of memes. Some people act as distribution points, others as artists, and others just paste up flyers. The advantage to a network like this is that it can disseminate important information quickly and inexpensively.

When the Gulf War broke, a group based in Oxford

churned out several clever flyposters reducing the purpose of the war to an expansion effort by CNN and Gulf Oil. It faxed the poster to other sites in the Anticopyright Network, and within two days the same meme had iterated throughout Europe and the United States, with alterations and additions every step of the way. The central image of the poster—the famous statue of Marines planting the flag at Iwo Jima (itself a staged scene for a newsreel)—found its flag changed into a TV satellite antenna. Then this image—a meme in itself—was cut out by other flyposter artists for use in further flyposters and zines. Within several weeks the image was so recognizable that it became a standard icon for "war = media, lies, expansion" and appeared in silhouette on stickers and buttons. It was turned into a "cue." No one was upset that the image had been altered and appropriated without credit. This is the basic operating principle of anticopyright: Without meaningless restrictions created by capitalist profiteers, information can spread, memes can mutate, and the culture can evolve.

The most important memes, to the billboarders, are ones that concern the techniques and implications of billboarding. One of the most popular underground pamphlets circulating in England now is called "Smashing the Image Factory," which is about what the writers call "billboard improvement." The term was coined by the United States ecoterrorist group Earth First! which grew famous for "monkeywrenching" (disabling of tractors and deforestation tools), modifying forestry service billboards, and self-publishing an ecotage handbook called *Ecodefense*. The difference between flypostering and billboard improvement is that the latter depends on the content of the original billboard. Flypostering can be about anything—the billboard underneath it is a canvas. Billboard improvement is specifically geared toward the perpetrator of the original ideological sin: the advertiser.

Billboard revisions may be as simple as painting tombstones on Marlboro Country or as artistic as changing Ronald McDonald's grin to a maniacal grimace and adding the slogan "McDonald's—Better Living Through Chemistry."

The media strategy here, as explained by "Smashing the Image Factory" (Bruce of "Oxfin") is "that the skillfully reworked billboard directs the passer-by to a consideration of the original corporate strategy in the context of a thoughtful reaction." In other words the audience is intended to understand the new meme construct as a *reaction* to the existing media. Billboard revision wants to be recognized as countercultural feedback. The satisfaction derived from this method of media subversion is that the advertiser has already done most of the hard work. The elegant activist can subvert the meaning and impact of an advertisement with a simple speech bubble, a few letters of text, or an alteration of the graphic.

The priority here is recycling, stealing, or copying imagery and ideology, either to subvert mainstream propaganda or to promote and iterate new memes. In both cases, the scavenger approach to media and messages works best. As "Smashing the Image Factory" has appropriated from a source it does not name, "The ideological supermarket—like any supermarket—is fit only for looting. It is far more productive for us if we can move along the shelves, rip open the packets, take out what is useful and dump the rest."

SEIZE THE MEDIA

This scavenger-hunt media activism finds its ideological allies in the United States, where modern propaganda and public relations techniques were developed and, probably, most totally implemented. Long the unwilling recipients of a barrage of media persuasion and advertising tactics, American media activists seek to regain control of the mechanisms by which "dis"-information is spread. To this end several underground networks have risen to meet the challenge of seizing the media from the political-corporate establishment and returning it to its rightful owners, the general public.

The Immediast Underground can be seen as a couple of young, intelligent state college grads from New Jersey

printing pamphlets about media subversion or as a vast network of media pirates intent on overthrowing consensus reality. Or somewhere in between. Twenty-something Greg
Ruggiero is gaining recognition as the blue-eyed and pony-
tailed father of the Immediast movement, which takes
anticopyright to its next logical assumption: that the methods of media are public property. As Greg writes in lieu of a
copyright on all Immediast Underground publications: "Immediast projects are against all forms of coercive communications, cultural monologue and media control. We acknowledge
non-violent public insurgence as a legitimate response to sustained violations by media and state. We recognize the air as
public property, and the signals that travel through it to be the
domain of the public."[4]

Greg's pamphlets are theoretical in content—they include one by Noam Chomsky on propaganda, one by Helen
Caldicott on the environment, one by George M. Carter on
Act Up, and one by Manning Marable on black America—
but they are activist in essence. While each pamphlet contains a potent set of memes, the very publishing and
distribution of these documents is the virus. The Immediast
credo is to open fire on those who attempt to control information and inhibit democracy. These progressive agenda
pamphlets, by inexpensively providing the straight dope on
delicate issues, are an act of defiance against the information
machine. The Immediasts—Greg and his partner since the
movement's beginnings at Rutgers University in 1986, Stuart
Sahulka—take their cue from the European Situationalists
of the fifties and sixties, who asserted countercultural values through provocative art installations. The Immediasts
see their publications as installations in the media space
and as representative of the goals of their Seize the Media
campaign.

Greg and Stuart are explaining their ideas to a group of
New York media students who bought them lunch in exchange for their words. Independent publishing of virulent
memes does not pay well, and such barters are appreciated
by all. But the Immediast purpose is not to make money; it

is to redefine the American public's relationship to its media. "Media is a corporate possession," Greg explains. "It is not a democratic right that we can locate in the constitution. You cannot vote for a media agenda when you vote for your President. You cannot participate in the media. Bringing that into the foreground is the first step. The second step is to define the difference between public and audience. An audience is passive; a public is participatory. We need a definition of media that is public in its orientation. We need to resist the coercive landscape whereby public space is increasingly invaded by a corporate agenda. It's not conjecture, it's not speculation, it's not abstraction. It's what's fucking going down."

Greg fears that democratically enacted laws are falling prey to essentially undemocratic corporate mandates as freely elected officials become increasingly dependent on corporate money for political sustenance. As a result the datasphere—which should be a public space—has been co-opted by corporations that use it to dull the populace into a bored, nauseous complacency.

Stuart, though less vocal in public, was an equal force in the production of the Immediasts' pamphlet on just how to resist the corporate invasion of the public space. The basic strategy, to which Greg already alluded, is to convince people that the media is there for the taking. "So long as we do not control our own government, our own state, and our own broadcast media—the mirror with which we reflect on the reality of lives—we will continue to be forced to see fun-house mirror distortions of ourselves projected onto a dumpster of products that promise to make us each desirable, sophisticated, and correct. At every turn we are under attack."[5] This attack is seen as coming from two places: corporations target the individual identity by controlling commodification and work, and the state targets the collective identity by controlling information, debt, and the threat of violence. Both of these forces work through the tactics of public relations and mind control and have created a world dense with media representations, from matchbooks to movies, designed to program our awareness and maximize our passivity.

The Immediast response is, first, to demonstrate to the passive audience how all this is taking place. Its pamphlet shows a picture of Senator Orrin G. Hatch holding up a copy of *The Exorcist* at the Clarence Thomas hearings, hoping to associate Anita Hill with the still lingering cultural revulsion for the images in the story and movie. As Charles Osgood discovered while on contract for the CIA, the visceral response of an audience to an image association like Anita Hill and *The Exorcist* or Satan and Manuel Noriega lasts much longer than the logical reaction it will have to any real facts. By exposing this technique, the "semantic differential," the Immediasts hope to disable it.

"Immediast tactics aim to neutralize the key images and text being imbedded into the public by the media and the State," the pamphlet explains. "Our work is the liberation of the public space from the broadcasts of corporations, businesses, and departments of State; and the abolition of public captivity as spectators to the ceaseless barrage of billboards, manipulative images, State constructed news and propaganda. The question is, how we can lockjaw the spectacle with its own force?"

The answer is to seize the means of media production. Greg and Stuart hope that one day the public will be in charge of the TV, radio, and print media. Their manifesto hearkens back to Jeffersonian ideals: "We interpret Freedom of Speech to mean the faciliated ability to both access and produce information and cultural material through the development of public production libraries where we can each and all produce cultural print, radio, television, and radio broadcast materials in library studios equipped with desktop publishing facilities, graphics technology, multi-track audio recorders, film and video cameras, and editing equipment. Freedom to broadcast can be in the power of the public. Corporations can be evicted from the airwaves. We can charge them staggering rent for the low-end frequencies if we want to. The State, under relentless public scrutiny, can be kept nude of its power to hide from, indebt, and subvert the public. Democracy can be as open and dynamic as our public libraries."

The pamphlet, intended as a media virus, "enjoyed a greater deal of iteration than we expected," Greg explains. "We were even quoted directly in the *Village Voice* and the *New York Times*." In its most virulent passage, the pamphlet calls on readers to "Vocalize your disgust. Speak up. Fight back. Liberate the public spaces in the zones that most need it—the ones in your everyday life . . . Revolution is the overthrow of the government by its forced subjects. Immediaism is the overthrow of the media by its captive audiences."

The Immediast call to arms is working. Self-published magazines and pamphlets are springing up everywhere, as Macintoshes and other desktop publishing systems enable private citizens to produce professional-quality work. Through computer bulletin boards, faxes, and mailing lists, activists have created a "Decentralized World-Wide Networker Congress." While the congress itself was invented and announced by an underground insurgent magazine called *Retrofuturism*, it has inspired dozens of gatherings around the world where like-minded media activists can exchange techniques, addresses, and, most of all, viruses. "A transnational engagement in cultural production, dialogue, collaborations, open exchange, and collective disruptions of dominant culture," as they are called by their creators, the congresses focus on the specific media concerns of particular regions. In Oxford, for example, billboard revision and flyposting were the main technologies explored. In the United States, meetings emphasize printing and computer networks.

But most important to the activist subculture, networking increases the lines of interconnectivity between individual members of the movement and thus increases the strength of the movement as a whole. By staying in communication with one another, the activists cannot be marginalized as easily by the dominant culture. Further, as the laws of chaos math confirm, the more linked the individual members of any group, the more feedback and iteration can occur. This is a vitally important principle to the innovators of modern media activism. The more networked they can become, the easier it is for any individual member of the overall community to influence the whole system. The more connected the system, for example, the easier it is for a butterfly flapping its wings in China to make a hurricane in New York. Or the easier it is for a camcorder video of Rodney King to ignite a riot in Los Angeles. What systems mathematicians call "a high leverage point" can be created in otherwise insignificant and remote locations.

But such networking only gets truly threatening to society at large when insurgents take new or sacred technologies into their own hands. Activist flyers and pamphlets have been around since Gutenburg, and only people who feel like reading them can be infected by the memes they contain. When media activists move from copy machines and staplers to camcorders and editors, feedback and iteration take on a whole new meaning.

CHAPTER 7

TACTICAL MEDIA

CAMCORDER KAMIKAZES

The scene is Amsterdam 1993. Wandering around a cavern-
ous theater are several hundred darkly dressed people with
camcorders pressed up against their faces. TV monitors line
the walls, playing videos from experimental artists, alternative news shows, and live feed from cameras around the
building rigged to capture the spectacle and play it back to
itself. About a thousand media activists have gathered at the
Paradiso, a large rock club/performance space, for "The
Next Five Minutes: A Conference, Exhibition and TV Program on Tactical Television."

By tactical television the conference directors mean TV
as tactic. Intentional media. Videomakers have come from
around the world to participate in and document the event
for distribution at home. What keeps this self-referential circus from simply imploding in on itself is the fact that these
young video tacticians are circulating some of the most sol-
idly progressive memes in media today.

Paul Garrin, the Greenwich Village video artist who has
become something of a cult hero to these activists for getting
beaten up by police as he attempted to tape a Tompkins
Square demonstration, is a keynote speaker and addresses

the massive, roaming audience over a microphone as a copy of his camcorder tape is projected onto a giant screen over his head.

"The TV screen is the front line of the war," he explains in a quietly candid tone. Garrin, a slight, dark-haired, blue-eyed, and leather-jacketed man in his late twenties, did not mean to become a video activist, but when violence between homeless park dwellers, addicts, gays, and cops erupted outside his window, the unassuming young artist and his camcorder were ready:

"The first reports of the riot, before my videotape made it to the public news, was that the police put a demonstration under control. Business as usual. Then my tape reached broadcasters, and it showed willful brutality by the police, who intentionally concealed their identities by placing tape on their badge numbers. I thought this was a great victory for the alternative media."

Like many others since, Garrin happened to be in the right place at the right time. He was in New York studying with pioneer postmodern video artist Ira Schneider and was already more than comfortable expressing his ideas on videotape. When the opportunity arose to provide a public service with his technical skills, Garrin did not think twice, and he quickly saw the effects of his video activism as it iterated in the mainstream media.

But almost as soon as his tape was released, he also witnessed, with horror, the rapid cultural immune response to the viral material for which he and others have served as a conduit: "It has become this situation where the police are coming to confiscate the video to use as evidence to prosecute people. And this is a serious problem . . . when the camera is not always pointed in the other direction."

Garrin and the others assembled have come to Amsterdam to discuss precisely this issue: How can the counterculture preserve the impact of countercultural media feedback? In its first incarnation, the camcorder revolution provided a remarkably potent iterative device. Among the dozens of cases and causes furthered by home media were the Rodney

King beating, gay bashings, police brutalities, and neo-Nazi attacks. It seemed that home video had emerged as the great equalizer. Wherever an injustice occurred, there was a camcorder rolling. No one could get away with anything. But today there are just as many if not more examples of home media being used against the side that shot them.

To Garrin the solution is to keep activist tapes in the hands of activist media, so they cannot be deconstructed or reedited to tell an untrue story: "We need to be an alternative to the control-centralized media empire of CNN and the networks, which are all connected to the military-industrial complex, financially and politically. We all know NBC is owned by General Electric and that CIA members are cozy with CBS. What you see, or even what you give them, is always going to support their interests one way or the other. We're dealing with psychological warfare. There are two fronts—we're one front, and they're the other. And the biggest tool they use to control you is intimidation through disinformation. We have to use our media to balance out this disinformation."

Garrin has reason to be paranoid. After releasing his tape to the media, his life was threatened a number of times. When he finally saw it played on TV, the footage showing police pulling their guns on unarmed demonstrators was edited out. Only pictures of rioters setting fires or turning over cars remained. Similarly, by the time the Rodney King tape was used at the first trial of the police officers, it had been broken down into single-frame segments. The deconstructionist analysis usually used by the left was here used by the defense attorneys to make the images ambiguous. Frozen in time, and resequenced, the aggressor can be made to appear the target, and the target the aggressor. As Garrin explains, "They used frame-by-frame analysis to reinforce the racial stereotype of the dangerous big black man being controlled by police so he wouldn't hurt them. The technique of deconstruction neutralized the material."

Dozens of other video activists use their time at the Paradiso microphone to bolster Garrin's argument. Mike

Stevenson, of London's activist media group "Despite TV," shot and produced a special for Channel Four about the poll-tax riots. His tapes, which revealed how the British police provoked street violence and through disorganization and panic created an urban disaster, were confiscated by police in order to identify and prosecute rioters. Luckily for the potential suspects, Stevenson digitally distorted the identifiable faces and claims to have destroyed the original camera tapes. He further demonstrated his media forethought by including in his finished program, "The Battle of Trafalgar," interviews with media experts who explained how the police had managed and continued to neutralize this public relations nightmare. Scotland Yard held press conferences labeling the rioters as "hooligans and anarchists," quickly arrested hospitalized women who had been trampled by police horses so that they could not legally speak with the media, and confiscated and misleadingly edited BBC footage to use against defendants and protect themselves.

It took twenty years for the mainstream media and its sponsors to develop blockades to curtail the feedback and iterative potential of home media. Over these same two decades, the counterculture has been looking for and finding leaks in the mainstream's barricades. The first advance by the counterculture into the television media was made in 1968, when the first portable video setup, a black and white recorder called the CV Porta-pak, made independent television production an affordable reality for private artists and journalists. Scores of "street tapes" emerged from the underground, usually depicting bums, trippers, Deadheads, and Hell's Angels. The counterculture of the late sixties was, after all, intent on promoting an antiwar and psychedelic agenda. As one media historian puts it, these were "the progeny of the Baby Boom, a generation at home with technology—the Bomb and the cathode-ray tube, ready to make imaginative use of the communications media to convey their messages of change."[1] But the fact that the radical antiwar protests of the sixties and the expanded consciousness owed to psychedelics and revived Eastern philosophies coincided with the development of the first individually owned television production equipment would have a lasting, perhaps permanent influence on alternative television media.

Meanwhile artists found in video a new aesthetic based in recycled imagery and cultural sampling. Those who, for whatever reasons, turned away from traditional art training or painting technique could produce down-and-dirty works of art that emphasized content and style over technical integrity or artistic lineage. Many video artists did not even own cameras, but contented themselves with recording and reediting footage of broadcast television—always to comment on or subvert the intentions of the original programs. Video attracted revolutionaries.

At first these alternative programs could not find wide distribution in the mainstream media. Video activists and artists, disenchanted with trying to change the system, instead followed the writings of philosophers like Marshall McLuhan and Buckminster Fuller and attempted to decentralize television by taking advantage of the emerging alternative technologies: videocassettes and cable TV. Community-access television, because of its low professional status, lack of pay, and uneven production quality, provided an opportunity for those interested in something other than career development to get their ideas broadcast to the public. Public television networks like PBS and the first local cable-access channels gave unprecedented opportunities to women and minorities who (at least into the seventies) were discriminated against by mainstream media. Consequently programming on these channels tended to reflect the values of these groups, as well as those of other people who had opted out of professional media careers.

The first reaction of mainstream media to the growing alternative market was, as always, to co-opt the newcomers—or at least their attitude and appearance. The fast-moving, quick-cut style of alternative media was soon adopted by MTV as a marketing technique. News shows and pseudo-documentary programs began using hand-held cameras and tape instead of film to gain a sense of immediacy. Television advertisements soon adopted the shaky look of guerrilla news videos, and directors of Levi's and AT&T commercials developed the technique of randomly shoving their cameramen during shooting sequences in order to give ads a feeling of credibility. And all this was before camcorders.

Home video was delayed by a marketing battle between Sony, which had developed the Betamax cassette format, and RCA, which had created an incompatible format, VHS. As the sex industry moved into home video, protectors of the mainstream media monopoly attempted to stifle the growing VCR market by equating the technology with porn. Sony took the high road and discouraged use of its format for X-rated material, while American VHS makers encouraged these productions. Thanks to America's insatiable hunger for porn, VHS won out and Sony went back to the lab to work on 8mm and digital video for the nineties. Equating new technologies with sexual permissiveness and unwarranted intimacy is a common practice; from the 1936 film *Reefer Madness* to talk television's sensationalist coverage of virtual reality, the threat of countercultural vices from pot to computers is uncontrolled sexual promiscuity. As in Milton's *Paradise Lost*, the absolute dictatorship in Eden can only be maintained if inhabitants are denied the fruit of knowledge, in this case, media technology.

But by the 1990s, millions of American homes were equipped with VCRs and hundreds of thousands of video cameras and lighter, more portable camcorders were in circulation. The cat was out of the bag. Countercultural activists found themselves in possession of a powerful recording device. AIDS activists, who had long encountered hostility from local police, grew so accustomed to bringing video equipment with them to demonstrations that a group calling itself DIVA-TV (Damned Interfering Video Activists) was formed to officially document radical gay activities. Communities demanded public-access channels from cable providers before they would approve of contracts, and most operators began providing up to three channels dedicated to publicly generated media.

This paradise regained was the first opportunity for real feedback and iteration in world culture. Anyone with a provocative videotape could send it in to a network news show and broadcast a local atrocity to the world. Countless episodes of police brutality, gay bashing, child abuse, and botched crowd control were taped on home equipment and then distributed through mostly mainstream networks. The media itself finally began to approach the proportions of a chaotic system: self-similar in structure, tremendously networked, iterative, self-replicating—almost alive. But mainstream media again countered with programming designed to neutralize the powerfully candid impact of homemade television. Shows like "America's Funniest Home Videos" and low-budget crime reenactments deluged audiences with less meme-rich forums for camcorder-style footage. The quick response time of mainstream media to the innovations have prompted some analysts toward pessimistic inventories of what activists see as a progressively open, reactive, and chaotic mediascape. The directors of the Amsterdam Next Five Minutes conference invited some of these critics to engage in "polemical debates" about the current state of media.

Many of the young activists at the Paradiso this weekend themselves feel cast out of video paradise by the disturbing predictions of Arthur Kroker, a mild-mannered, middle-aged Canadian sociologist who insists that American media, and especially interactive or home-style media, focuses only on the most pathological moments and aspects of our culture's history. He calls this "excremental media." The Madonna and Amy Fisher viruses, for instance, use what he considers to be the "logic of seduction" in order to draw audiences in, but their media identities are vague and "recombinant in character." He would agree that TV has become alive, but sees it as a destructive life-form, which simply clones and resequences itself at the expense of our greater, human reality.

Kroker breaks down participatory television into four categories that are useful for analyzing tactical media, even if his conclusions are unnecessarily dark. First there is what he calls "disciplinary TV," which he considers "co-evil" with disciplinary society. This would include shows like "COPS" or even news shows where bad guys get caught on camera. True, for every Rodney King who is vindicated by video there has been at least one Mayor Marion Barry who is caught in the act by a tiny surveillance camera. Then there is "sacrificial TV," like "America's Funniest Home Videos," or dating shows like "Love Connection," in which participants deliver themselves up as jokes. "It's a form of concentration-camp denigration of the self," Kroker explains to the crestfallen group, crashing their hopes of a free society through participatory television. Kroker's third form of television, "surveillance TV," also surrenders the self to the media, this time in shows like "America's Most Wanted," where we are made to think of media as a means toward imprisonment. Homemade tapes—like the Tompkins or Trafalgar square footage—later analyzed by police for arrests would also fall into this category. Finally there is "crash TV," which is geared toward what he calls "splatter culture." Here the only purpose of a camcorder is for members of the public to catch the biggest, bloodiest crash. This would account for the tremendous success of "death" videos, available only for purchase or rental, which follow ambulance drivers and highway patrols in the hopes of capturing people actually dying on camera. We are reduced to our basest instincts and trained into submission with pictures of just how cruel life can be.

Kroker sees our media as anything but liberating. Even do-it-yourself technology only serves to turn private citizens into law enforcers or guilt mongers, as culture moves toward what he coins as a "permanent scanner functionalism." By using our media to scapegoat those who go against societal standards, we create a temporary feeling of cohesiveness.

The countercultural value of these technologies is thus sacrificed to the need for unity in a dangerous, threatening world.

Kroker's brilliant but misguided analysis is typical of his generation of philosophers who, growing up *before* the advent of mass media have only the tools to observe media but not the language or translation skills to partake in it. His categories of media may even be correct, but the inferences he draws totally ignore the nature of the new and growing relationship between our lives and our media. As long as we view media, or technology for that matter, as something separate from ourselves—something unnatural—we will always see it as the enemy to the natural unfolding of our culture.

If younger enthusiasts are correct and media *is* the natural unfolding of our culture, then the participatory technologies herald unprecedented opportunities for self-expression. Worst case, if Kroker is right and our media is "excremental," then we are providing excellent fertilizer for future growth. But the postmodern entrails that make up the cut-and-paste video of the MTV and video vigilante era are not reducible to waste products.

The reason Kroker's words of doom do not jive with the rationale of today's videomakers is that they are based on an underlying sense of imposed tyranny. His unspoken supposition is that there is already in place a conspiracy of dominators who can absorb shocks from the "left" and neutralize invading memes before they have a chance to spread. The new breed of media activists, however, approach the media war with a "systems" approach. Rather than pointing fingers at the enemy, they accept responsibility for their own roles in perpetrating "scanner functionalism" and attempt to retrain themselves by becoming more conscious of their own fears and bias. By just inviting someone like Kroker to their conference, they exhibit a tremendous willingness to look at their own worst nature and to devise methods of circumventing the errors made by activists of the past. For them to heed Kroker's warnings and turn in their camcorders now would be equivalent to banning VCRs for fear of promoting sexual deviancy.

The only enemy of networking, feedback, and iteration is fear of the intimacy they bring. True, increased surveillance can breed paranoia or, worse, infringe on the right to privacy. But the real threat is not to people who may be filmed engaging in offbeat sexual behavior, recreational drug use, antiwar activities, or unpatriotic conversation. The threat is to the maintenance of an obsolete mainstream cultural paradigm that depends on the illusion that no one else does the dirty things or has the naughty thoughts that you do. Even in a most pessimistic rendering, Kroker's excremental media paints participatory media as the great cultural equalizer.

HITCHING A RIDE ON THE DATA SUPERHIGHWAY

Viruses launched in a fictional context—like the postmodern "Ren & Stimpy" or liberal-valued "All in the Family"—stand a much better chance of achieving safe passage through the mainstream media than direct-feedback footage. Fact-based news video has much more trouble crossing ideological checkpoints in one piece. Mainstream media presents a particular version of reality in order to sell products, and participatory video, however spectacular, must support this view before it can be aired by networks. The TV tacticians' response to mainstreamization is simple: Create alternative networks for feedback so that the imagery they gather reaches its target before it is mutilated.

While the Europeans at the Next Five Minutes conference have had little chance to gain access to broadcast or cable television, several of the Americans present give inspiring testaments to their success on the tube. Marti Lucas is an important enough guest of the conference to appear on its live television broadcast to the city of Amsterdam. (Amsterdam, unlike most of Europe, has well-funded public-access TV.) The founder of Paper Tiger Television in New York City, Lucas saw in public-access television an opportunity to "smash the myths of the media industry."

His programs began in the early eighties as little more than tapes of a man or woman reading the *New York Times* and deconstructing the news stories to demonstrate editorial bias. This grew quickly, though, into American television's leading countercultural political foothold. Paper Tiger spread its programming to other cities by duplicating broadcast tapes and sending them to activists in different areas of the country. Most public-access channels require that tapes be submitted by residents of their broadcast regions, so Lucas and his associates found sponsors in as many regions as possible who were willing to walk into the community-access office and hand in the tape.

By the late eighties, Paper Tiger had produced hundreds of shows on issues that were underreported on mainstream news, ranging from the environment and housing to U.S. foreign policy and censorship of the arts. To avoid the excremental pitfalls described by Kroker, Paper Tiger's strategy was to keep audiences aware of their own place in the overall mediascape. Through quick cutting, voice-overs, superimposed text, and sampling from mainstream news, Paper Tiger made media that kept its audiences conscious that they were watching television. Lucas claims he never would have developed these viral techniques were it not for the propaganda era of Ronald Reagan.

"Hype is the way American media works," Lucas explains. "The word was originally used in the United States in the 1920s to refer to a dose of drugs. Hype was short for hypodermic needle. The American media works through a series of hypes. This became particularly true in the Reagan years. Reagan played the media very well. We were treated to a series of events during his administration which were used to rouse public indignation and public opinion against a variety of targets. In Panama we had an evil general (who was in fact trained by Bush); there was Grenada, Khadafy, the

Ayatollah, the shooting of a Korean passenger jet. Each event was used by the administration to create a climate—a feeling that was the electronic equivalent of the Nuremberg rallies of the 1930s."

While Lucas may simply be reiterating the views of theorists like Noam Chomsky, he is also in a position to act upon these views: "We found ourselves in this climate when Iraq invaded Kuwait. We watched as the same public relations firm that handles Pepsi got paid 30 million by Kuwait to invent stories—like the famous incubators story—to make Iraq and Saddam, who were funded by the U.S., into Hitler."

Paper Tiger's idea was to respond to the hype attack with media. But for this to work, the countercultural media response needed to be a genuine, organic feedback from the nation at large. Simply airing contrary opinions would not suffice. The views of a few radical professors and journalists could be marginalized instantly. The activities of real people from around the nation could not, however, and would instead resonate as a valid representation of the mood of America on the eve of war. Lucas sent a three-thousand piece mailing to videomakers around the country, asking them to make tapes about what was going on in their own neighborhoods about the Gulf War: "People began sending us tapes. Hundreds of tapes of local teach-ins, huge demonstrations, people questioning the war, army kids on a plane to the Gulf not wanting to go, veterans against the war, and more, but in the mainstream media we were seeing none of this. We saw a managed press campaign."

Perhaps it was the voltage created by the potential difference between what was airing on the networks and what was actually going on around the country that gave Paper Tiger the burst of energy it needed to become a full-fledged force in national television during the Gulf War. Lucas assembled the first of four shows based on the material sent in, "The Gulf Crisis TV Project: Operation Dissidence," and decided to distribute it in a new way: using a satellite.

Deep Dish TV was created in association with Paper Tiger Television as a satellite distribution arm. It raised money to rent commercial satellite time so that the program could be transmitted to hundreds of television stations at once. Deep Dish advertised the show to television stations, as well as to which satellite and when it would be up-linked. All the interested station would need to do is point its dish at the appropriate satellite to make a recording of the tape and then broadcast it whenever it liked in its schedule. (This is how most television programs are distributed in the United States. A day or two before the program airs, it is distributed via satellite to local stations, who tape it and broadcast it later.) Deep Dish also sent letters to interested activists advising them to request that their local station receive the satellite feed and broadcast the show.

Deep Dish was tremendously successful. Hundreds of stations throughout the United States picked up all four shows and broadcast them a number of times. Lucas believes that the strategy worked because his programs were merely feeding back to the United States what was really happening but remaining unreported: "Because the show *came* from everyplace, people were interested in *seeing* it all over the place. The shows worked because there was an information vacuum. Shows made links between peace workers who didn't know others existed. The tape provided a reason to organize: to watch the tape. In many cities there were demonstrations just to get the shows broadcast. This created even more press hoopla around the whole thing."

The media virus around the show proved as virulent as its content—which was intentionally self-similar anyway. The construction of these shows as media about media both sustained and protected the virulence of the antiwar memes inside while generating further coverage from mainstream channels about the media effort itself. However self-reflexively excremental, the technique works. By staying aware of the mainstream media's tendency to wrap and recycle its imagery, Paper Tiger and Deep Dish TV manage to reverse Kroker's negative observations about participatory media. They have learned to exploit or even surf its excremental functioning rather than succumb to it.

But no distribution effort on this scale is without its casualties. A newly licensed, maverick PBS station in Philadelphia picked up the satellite feed, too, and up-linked it again to the entire PBS network. Shortly after the first U.S. air attacks into Iraq, Lucas says, "The station got a letter saying their license was 'being reviewed' for a transmitter problem, and they refused any more tapes from us. They called me and said they could not risk broadcasting any further programs." Lucas is not dismayed. His conclusions about mainstream media, even PBS, have only been confirmed: "We have to avoid the established media. There is no substitute for people creating their own communications links. If somebody else holds it"—he smiles, loosely quoting Marshall McLuhan—"it's like taking the eyeballs out of your head and renting them to somebody else."

MAKING THE ELECTRONIC LEAP

Dirk Koning is chair of *Community Television Review* magazine and director of three local-access stations in Grand Rapids, Michigan. The most boisterously American of the panelists at the Paradiso, Koning quotes heroes Thomas Jefferson and Albert Einstein as liberally as Lucas does Chomsky and McLuhan. Koning is a meta-networker who emphasizes forming links between community-access networks both in the United States and around the world. He is particularly keen on getting a piece of the planned superdatahighway for the public before it is taken up for exclusively corporate interests.

"Forget everything you've ever thought about television, radio, and computers," he tells a crowd that has gathered around him. "Now that they're all digital—just pulses of light traveling down a fiber-optic cable [clear wire that can transmit many signals at once]—there's a convergence. But now they will all become one, single, conglomerate tool. The scary part is that the government and major corporations know this. They are building new information highways, and they are not interested in people like us having space on them. There is a logical plan on an international level to exclude us, and we must be aware of it and stay active."

Koning's fear is that once television, radio, computer, and other information networks are standardized to a digital format, it will be harder, not easier, for private citizens to infiltrate the datastream. Access to the fiber-optic network can be tightly controlled—either through exclusionary legislation or outrageous pricing. In the face of this emerging challenge, Koning calls for good, old-fashioned, American chutzpah: "I wouldn't be a bit surprised if we're gonna have to march right over to some television station or telephone company and put our butts right down in the middle of the lobby and say we're not moving until you give us some access. Information is the currency of democracy. Thomas Jefferson said that."

Koning's group, the National Federation of Local Cable Programmers, is battling for First Amendment rights to be fully applied to cable television. In an editorial for his magazine, he credits "luck" with having allowed public access to get so far and warns cable operators to brace themselves for mainstream media's inevitable immune response. "We've been lucky; the trickle-down fruits of franchise fees have helped build our industry. We've been lucky we could latch onto the ass of the cable industry like a leech and suck for our survival. But luck has a way of running out. Laws of evolution and relativity don't hold luck in very high esteem. Survival favors the fittest, not necessarily the luckiest. So we've been lucky, so what? now what? Well, let's thank our lucky stars, pull our heads out of the sand of convenience and prepare for the onslaught and assault on our very existence."[2]

Maybe Koning is on the warpath a bit prematurely, but there are many signs that the liberties enjoyed by public-access operators since the seventies could be in jeopardy. The cable industry itself, on which public access depends, may soon be replaced by telephone companies or media conglomerates that have recently been granted access to cable TV. With much more money and much more bandwidth available to them thanks to fiber-optic networks, the telephone industry should have little trouble providing better service—including more interactive and multimedia options—at cheaper prices, or at least at a cheaper operating cost and greater profit margin. The federal government has also recently decided that there is no need to separate control of conduit—the fiber-optic networks—from control of content—the progamming itself. The same companies that own the newly and as yet to be wired systems will own the right to broadcast whatever they feel like. While public-access programmers benefited from the almost socialist practice of forcing cable operators to provide citizens with free programming opportunities, a market-driven industry with pricing by the minute or even the second of access could make anything but the well-funded corporate commercial programming impossible.

According to Koning, even the executive director of the ACLU questions the practice of requiring cable operators to provide public access to the communities they serve: "The ACLU hasn't been totally convinced that public-access channel mandates in franchises are not in fact a violation of the cable industry's First Amendment right or even the Fifth or Fourteenth amendment provisions against taking of public property without due process." Without the Constitution on their side, Jeffersonians like Koning may soon be finding themselves on the street: "In our minds we have made the electronic leap from the soapbox in the town square to locally mandated free channel space on a private company's line. This, in a country that is built on free enterprise and capitalism. But if that theory is only in our minds, we are in deep dung."

TOWARD A NEW NETWORK

While Americans like Koning work toward an interpretation of the Constitution that includes public access to the data highways, his European counterparts, as well as many of the more radical activists in the United States, believe the only way to gain durable access to media is by creating alternative networks or by subverting the networks already in place. Still others see the air itself as the only free conduit for memes that could be deemed unsuitable for fiber-optic carriage.

European media activism has been a hard battle. Raised on state-sponsored media, most Europeans see television and radio as propaganda arms of the incumbent regime. Although television and radio ultimately contributed to revolutions in Eastern Europe, they remain state-controlled. The belief that whoever controls the media controls the population—demonstrated by television-supported dictatorships as well as television-inspired revolutions—makes the new democratic leaders hesitant to give up their claim to state-directed TV and radio. The few strides that independent or public-access advocates have made into Eastern European media were so hard won that current participants do not count on retaining the privilege for long. To them media is a weapon. As long as it is in their hands, they maintain control. As soon as it is taken away, they are lost.

Despite the fact that CNN and even MTV have been credited with inspiring popular culture in Western Europe and directing the revolutions in Eastern bloc countries, the same activists who once used these networks to generate global concern for their causes now reject the spread of American media culture. Cable, mainly from the United States or satellites broadcasting U.S. entertainment and a little world sports, is the province of mostly American corporate interests. Like EuroDisney, CNN International is not seen as an opportunity for European feedback and iteration; it is perceived as an effort to whitewash over regional identities and paint the populace with broad, consumerist strokes. While there may be a few opportunities to attach themselves to these cable interests and even to legislate a community presence on the developing cable networks (as has been done very successfully in Amsterdam), most activists prefer to remain unsullied by Western corporate interests and unhampered by their own state interests.

The answer, for most of these activists, has been to transmit without anyone's help or permission. One German media hacker who, for our purposes, calls himself Xtian, works with a small group of roving dissidents who get jobs as technicians at cable stations or telephone facilities and then use their training and knowledge to break into systems and broadcast illegally. Xtian says this ongoing research is necessary because European cable stations keep advancing their security measures as hackers find new holes in the system.

The easiest gap for intrusion has always been the transmission between television stations and the cable networks, who receive the signal and then distribute it to their customers. Rather than building their own huge transmitter capable of reaching a whole community, hackers only need to point a small transmitter directly at the cable TV reception antenna. Before 1983 television pirates would simply wait for a television channel to shut down its transmitter for the night and then broadcast on the same frequency to a cable provider's receiver. But then cable providers created a device that automatically shuts off their reception at a specified "end-of-broadcast" cue from the television station. Some hackers resorted to commando missions, in which they would physically cut into cable wires, plug in a VCR, and run away, leaving the VCR to play prerecorded programs or announcements until the breach would be discovered and the VCR confiscated. But this was expensive, and the cable operators got good at finding systems breaches quickly.

Effectively locked out of cable, media pirates took to the air. Xtian's current attack strategy sounds pretty simple: "You take your video recorder, which already has a tiny transmitter in it [the part that broadcasts to your own TV set on Channel 3 or 4] and modulate it to the channel of the transmission you want. UHF works best—say Channel 35.

Then you build or get a simple amplifier to boost the signal to a very high level. It's really very easy. You make an antenna just two or three meters long, and you can broadcast at ten or twenty watts. More than necessary for great transmission. Just put it on your roof or your terrace, and ideally point it at the cable-receiving site. You'll be strong enough to wipe out the original signal. They can shut down the whole channel, but then they'll have nothing. We wipe out Germany's second network channel all the time."

Xtian got caught once when national authorities used a directional scanning van to hone in on his signal. He was already asleep at 3:00 A.M. when the police crashed into his apartment. He lost his equipment and paid a cash fine, but the publicity surrounding the raid spread the idea that, in Xtian's words, "This could be done. This was achievable." Xtian's broadcast was a short and simple local news show, shot and produced by friends of his, students from the neighborhood. But the specific memes on the news show were not nearly as widely spread as those concerning Xtian's media ideology and techniques. Every article or television show that explained how Xtian and his friends accomplished their hack served as an instruction manual to dozens of copycats. Almost every week another kid would succeed in getting his face or a dirty joke broadcast to his whole community.

Xtian sees satellite technology as the next great opportunity for media hackers. "All you need is the right books," he explains, confident that if people only learn how a technology works, they can easily subvert it. "Satellites work with microwave technology. The books I have right now, legally, list the frequencies of all the major satellites and even their command sequences. But the main thing you would want to do is just replace their signal with your own. From the ground, and close to the receiving dish, say one hundred meters, you could do that easily. No problem. Right over the Olympics."

Americans exploit some of this same satellite hacking technology, but for more indirect forms of media subversion. No matter how oblique, however, the thrust of all of these efforts is to demonstrate to the media public that television broadcasting is not protected by an impenetrable membrane. Media hackers who do not focus on directly infiltrating the supply side of the seemingly closed television economy do so by demanding access to a forbidden product.

Brian Springer, for one, is a filmmaker from Buffalo, New York, who assembled a startling collection of pirated satellite signals into a larger film of media outtakes and political gaffes called *Feed*. Springer has only slightly more equipment than most sports bars in the Midwest: a satellite dish and a good descrambler. While the bars use these devices to illegally capture and unscramble pay-per-view sporting events for their clientele, Springer used his dish to capture the feed from network television crews as they covered the New Hampshire primaries in the 1992 election. Mobile television crews travel around in vans equipped with transmitters. As they shoot their coverage of an event, interview, or speech, they send their live feed up to a satellite, which beams the signal back down into the network newsroom, where the footage can be recorded and edited for playback during the news. Because these crews begin sending their live feed before the actual event takes place and leave their equipment running after the event is over, many images unintended for viewers are included in their transmissions. Springer made a hobby and eventually an artistic career out of capturing these truly candid moments of the candidates.

Much of *Feed* consists of men like Clinton, Gore, and Perot waiting impatiently as their makeup is applied. We watch them sit helpless as they are preened. They nervously review their speeches, snap at their assistants for beverages, and make general fools of themselves. The footage reveals them as all too human, especially in comparison with their all-too-fake behavior once they know the camera is rolling. Springer also captures a frighteningly bizarre scene in which Perot supporters, gathering before a rally, begin singing "Battle Hymn of the Republic," with Perot's name inserted for God's. The footage was gathered by somewhat illegal means—most would consider the film a violation of copy-

right laws—so Springer could not get wide, mainstream coverage of his compilation. Still, The *New York Times*'s Janet
Maslin reviewed and understood the home video version of
the film, writing that it was an "Andy Warhol version of campaign posturing."[3] Springer's memes spread a little further
when *Spy Magazine*, which produces its own nationally televised annual "Worst of" satire, sampled a few of Springer's
images, most notably one of Al Gore "the environmentalist"
sniffing his armpits before a speech. *Spy* selected footage of
Clinton and Gore because one of the producers figured
"elected officials would be less likely to make a stink."

The emphasis of most alternative and pirated television
in America is to encourage this irreverent view of media-
created people and institutions. Recontextualizing the sacred
personages of presidential candidates compromises their ability to self-promote. Better yet cracking the façade of presidential politics changes the level of the playing field forever.
People realize that the images are smoke and mirrors and
watch TV differently so that they won't get fooled again.

By 1992 there were already several PACs (political action committees) in the United States organized specifically
to create political messages that made use of subversive media tactics. One of the most successful, "Real People for Real
Change," was the brainchild of Mark Saltveit, a Portlander
who recently graduated from Harvard, then returned to Oregon to create media viruses. The PAC raised money to
produce and air anti-Bush television commercials. Saltveit's
aim was to spend a minimum of money on the spots and
airtime, but to get a maximum of coverage from other media
about the advertisements. One commercial, called "Family
Values," was decidely low-tech: a photograph of a father,
mother, college-age student, and a dog, all sitting in a typical
middle-class living room.

> Narrator: Family values? George Bush's economy
> is so weak that fathers are off working longer hours or
> looking for jobs.
> Visual: The father in the picture fades to black.

Narrator: Mothers once had a choice whether to
work outside the home. . . .

The mother and son each fade to black as the narrator
litanizes the Bush policies that led to their demise. Eventually even the dog is called upon by Bush to help save the
economy and the entire screen fades to black. Simple letters
come up: "Vote for a change. Get rid of Bush" and, in
smaller type, "Paid for by Real People for Real Change. Not
connected with any candidate or candidate's committee."
Then we hear the dog bark. The simple ad aired only twice,
in Medford, Oregon, but Saltveit had a total media strategy
that spread his memes much further. He sent press kits and
video copies of his commercial to every television station
and newspaper in the area and made sure his commercials
immediately preceded Bush's campaign stop in Oregon.
News shows, hungry for stories about Bush's impending
visit, jumped at the opportunity to cover Saltveit's media attack. Thousands more viewers saw the ad replayed on the
news, as well as interviews with Saltveit about his media philosophy, than caught the ad itself in its late-night $60 time
slot.

Saltveit's second, more intentionally virulent ad, attacked Bush's stand on abortion rights. The simple spot consisted only of text on a blank screen and provocative
narration: "The following ad is for men only. Ladies, please
ignore this. Men, if George Bush is re-elected, he wants to
ban abortion. Not limit it; ban it. Think about that. One broken condom or a couple of missed pills and you're a daddy.
That means, at best, a forced marriage or 18 years of child
support. If you don't pay, your kid pays—and then we all
pay. Forced Fatherhood. No choices. No options. That's
George Bush's America. Can you afford four more years?"

Saltveit knew the ad would raise eyebrows and deep opposition. And that was just his purpose. "I wanted to attack
the 'politically correct' virus. The term goes back to the com-
munists in the thirties, but was picked up by the right, and
they've been bludgeoning the left with it ever since. And the

left are too namby-pamby and trying not to offend anybody. We wanted to stir things up by talking about the reality of abortion. Every man has worried about getting someone pregnant and having to pay child support. But if you admit it and you're on the left, it just sounds so crude and awful." Saltveit chose to feed back to men what he knew they were thinking but afraid to say. He was attempting to demarginalize a large group of voters and make them realize that many other men like themselves were out there, too.

Saltveit also intended his ad to provoke a cultural-immune response from the right so that it would get even more coverage than his first ad. It did. The local NBC affiliate interviewed Right to Life advocate Dawn Stover, who was flabbergasted by the direct approach of the ad: "Um, it's unfortunate that we continue to bring the death of an innocent child, number one, down to dollars and cents. That's what this whole ad is about."

This played into Saltveit's hand perfectly. Saltveit's purpose was to reframe the issue by demonstrating that Republicans were afraid to talk about real issues like dollars and cents. On the same news show he retorted, "People are sick of hearing fluff on TV. When the economy is dying people are talking about flag factories and what people did in college. . . . Nobody cares. The important issues were not being addressed."

Saltveit did not just happen upon his media strategy. A self-proclaimed "slacker" and "media junkie since I was eight," Mark spent his college years at Harvard and then several more back in Portland exploring television by working at public-access stations. His senior thesis, about the way the media covered the Vietnam War protests, convinced him that new activist tactics must be developed for the nineties: "Vietnam activists set back the peace movement many years. Average people hate activists. They hate anyone wearing funny clothes. We want our ads to be in your face, to be blunt, but we do not want to be 'activists.' We do not have any picket signs. We're playing by the rules, goddamn it. We put our money down, we bought our airtime, here's what we've got to say and if you don't like it, fuck you."

Saltveit wants to bring a new machismo into media activism. As he sees it, the counterculture has been marginalized into a kind of submission, in which it sees itself as weak, liberal, urban, and over-educated. "I like the whole Ken Kesey thing. I like Earth First! They're a little cagey. They're blue-collar guys." Saltveit designed the entire Real People for Real Change PAC to fight the notion that liberals were weak and to make it macho to vote against the status quo: "We worked up a legend about how the group started. Everybody needs a good founding myth. A TV reporter asked me, and I said, 'The group was formed on a hunting trip in eastern Oregon.' A paper picked it up as fact, and then it just stuck. It was a great image, too: We are not standard whiny urban liberal democrats. We're just Joes, but we're fed up."

The ads were designed to reflect that "regular Joe" style. Even though he was trained in film and video, Saltveit made the ads look as cheap and homespun as possible: "I had to swallow my pride a little to make commercials which showed that anybody could do this. That was the important thing. That real people made this. Real people like you and me." Saltveit also hoped to capitalize on the increasingly interactive quality of mainstream media. He selected the time slot for his pro-choice/anti-Bush ad carefully, finally choosing to air the spot on Rush Limbaugh: "That was totally our target audience. I don't believe anybody watching Rush is really that conservative. He's a dick and a half, but he's funny. The ratings were good, but the ad was cheap, probably because advertisers don't want to be associated with his extremism."

Saltveit also demonstrated a well-developed awareness of the power of feedback. Rather than just writing his ads and broadcasting them, he chose to find out what the public was angry about already so that his messages would resonate with their concerns. His ultimate objective, after all, is to bring real people back into the political system by making participation a red-blooded American pastime. He does not care as much about espousing any particular issue as he does about pushing buttons. To find out what people cared about, he posted a topic on a public computer bulletin board, asking participants to come up with ideas for political TV ads. "It wasn't so much that people were E-mailing us whole scripts, but we got a consensus of what people are pissed off about, what works, and what issues are going to ring bells for a lot of people, and that was tremendously helpful. We needed to learn if the tide was right."

Saltveit is a media surfer who understands public opinion in terms of oceanic ebb and flow. Born a media junkie, he understands television the way his heroes at Earth First! understand the forest. His patriotic brand of activism is meant to dispel not only the public image of liberals as weak intellectuals, but also the association of media activists as weird hacker nerds. He is committed to fostering participation of *real people* in the media. His enemy is the same fear of intimacy that plagues most mediaphobes, and his tactic is to show that jumping into the data ocean does not turn you into a commie, a pinko, or a wimp.

CHAPTER 8

THE NET

Nowhere has the American pioneer spirit been more revitalized than on the electronic frontier. The computer net is an ever-expanding new territory, and it is growing faster than our ability to document or civilize it.

Intentionally developed as a decentralized web, the computer networks have already evolved into complex chaotic systems, capable of feedback and iteration on a scale still unfathomable by even their most enthusiastic participants. Computer networks are fractal in composition, with large networks of computers self-similarly reflecting smaller linked groups, which themselves reflect the inner workings of a single machine, which itself reflects the shape and structure of the software within it, the commands within the software, and the bytes of binary data within those commands. As feedback devices, computers provide unprecedented expressive capabilities to anyone who can get access to a terminal and a modem. A tiny laptop in Montana can be as high a leverage point as a system of mainframes in Washington, D.C.; no text message sent out onto the net has any more intrinsic power to affect the whole system than any other. As an opportunity for iteration, the computer and its networks—which actually work by cycling information in nearly infinite loops—have begun to frighten those whose power is based on limiting the public's ability to disseminate and amplify its observations and intentions.

How this all came to be is significant. Tracking the development of the current computer net reveals why it is so essentially chaotic; both the conscious plans of its constructors and what can be considered deeply "natural causes" led to the formation of a new kind of wilderness—a network of roots and vines so vast that it has the potential to modify everything it contacts and utterly change the very landscape of the forest.

One way to trace the formation of the computer networks is to begin in 1964, when a cold war think tank called the Rand Corporation was asked to come up with a way for the United States to maintain defense communications in the event of a nuclear war. The postapocalyptic scenario they imagined was surprisingly similar to the postmodern worldview of the slacker culture. Rand determined that the communications network must "have no central authority" and be "designed from the beginning to operate while in tatters."[1] Like a grassroots counterculture, the defense industry's ARPANET was created by the mid-seventies to allow different people in separate locations to communicate with each other and even operate defense systems after a devastating nuclear attack. The strategy involved making each computer, or "node," in the network of equal value in creating and transmitting data. Rather than establishing a potentially vulnerable central command post from which orders trickled out to other remote locations, each of the thousands of locations in the system were capable of performing all the command functions. If messages from, say, Atlanta normally route through Dallas in order to reach Los Angeles, but the Dallas system were hit, the system would automatically reroute the message through other systems. Imagine a chainlink fence. Even if you punch out a big hunk of fence, the rest is still interconnected enough to conduct electricity.

Imitating a complex natural system like a coral reef, the ARPANET system depended on the immense interconnectedness of its parts. So it seems the most hierarchically inclined, power-based segment of our culture—the military—developed the most Gaian-spirited complex ever created by human beings. This self-similar map of interconnected nodes is an automatically self-regulating organism. No one individual can control what information spreads where. As one of the fathers of the system, John Gilmore, said in an often quoted remark, "The Net interprets censorship as damage and routes around it." An attempt to block a communication at one node will simply prompt the network to find one of millions of possible alternative routes. In a biosphere the more possible links and "phase locks" there are between members, the more opportunity nature has of regulating and neutralizing disturbances. Similarly the dominant law on the computer net is a natural tendency toward self-determination through chaotic means.

By the time ARPANET was "ended" in 1989, no one seemed to notice that the organization did not exist anymore. It didn't matter; the powerful network it had initiated was here to stay. Many universities and commercial computer networks had already become nodes on the system, developed their own communications protocols, and had been sending each other electronic mail, conferencing, and archiving data. The network became known as "Internet"—a meta-network linking up other networks around the world. Scientists and other researchers used the network to share advances with each other, and corporations used it to send information from one site to another.

Meanwhile computer hobbyists had launched their own, more grassroots-style set of networks. Two multibillion-dollar industries—the computer manufacturers and telephone companies—had each developed its technologies separately. But as futurist Howard Rheingold suggests in his book *Virtual Communities*, the industries inadvertently gave private consumers access to those billions of dollars by selling them a tiny device to link the two technologies together: a computer modem. By hooking up her inexpensive personal computer through a modem to her family's $10-a-month telephone line, any kid can gain access to a global communications network, as well as every computer system linked to that network. The sum computing power of this telenetwork of millions of computers—and millions of computer users—is unimaginably greater than any single, affordable, constructable machine, or any organization of people.

The grassroots networks began as local, call-in nodes. One person would dedicate a computer and one or many phone lines to be a "bulletin board service," or BBS. Other users in his area could call into his BBS and leave messages for one another, post items of interest, or ask questions of the other users. These communications ranged from hackers sharing the latest stolen codes to people selling cars or discussing the storyline of a *Star Trek* movie. Eventually these private BBSs created their own meta-network called FIDONET so that people on one bulletin board could send electronic mail to their friends on other boards without the expense of making a long-distance call to a bulletin board in another state.

Now FIDONET itself is linked to the Internet and almost everyone has access to everything. Today there are at least tens of thousands of nodes on net and by 1994, over 20 million individual users in the United States. To establish a node on the net, all a person or company needs to do is get a computer powerful enough to serve as a relay station for the network. To become an individual user, all you need to do is get access to a computer with a modem and join either a private bulletin board, university system, or research institution's node for a small fee or sometimes nothing at all. Many users jack in through their computers at work, which are often linked to the Internet through the company's own node.

Needless to say, the Internet is a social anarchy. There is no governing body for the system. Scientists share the network with hobbyists and hackers who share the system with writers, artists, researchers, corporations, and, of course, activists. The Internet is inherently threatening to anyone in a position of power because no one—at least not yet—can regulate the tremendous flow of information. The real observations of millions of people, shared through the networks, create an undeniable, high-resolution portrait of our current state of affairs. The way to influence public opinion has historically been to feed people information from the top. A hundred million pairs of eyes fixed on Dan Rather or even CNN made directing public attention easy. A hundred million people speaking to one another through computer text and getting their information from researchers, observers, archived material, and just plain other people are impossible to control. They have a reality test. They also have a countercultural weapon.

ELECTRONIC GRASSROOTS

By far the greatest power of the overall computer network is its ability to change public perception. More than affecting any particular issue, the net changes the way private citizens perceive their ability to understand and effect the global system. Anyone cruising the Internet soon learns that from his own laptop he has the ability to reach into anything from the Library of Congress or a database in Tel Aviv to an activist's alert or the White House archives.

Attempting to project an image of responsiveness to net feedback, the Clinton administration established links to the Internet before Clinton even took office. The campaign could be reached through E-mail, and press releases and speeches were easily accessed by anyone interested. Shortly after the administration moved into the White House, it announced that its on-line presence would be expanded. Today anyone can receive daily press releases automatically, copies of Clinton's speeches and transcripts of press conferences, or remarks made at photo ops. Several systems have been set up to receive comments or criticisms from the public through electronic mail. Other networks allow for interactive feedback directly with White House communications staff. A child with a computer, growing up with the ability to interact with White House staff when he disagrees with a remark the

President made that day in Tokyo, will have a very different perception of his government than someone who had access only to sound bites on the evening news.

Still, much of the novelty for a private citizen in exchanging E-mail with the White House depends on the computer user's perception of White House staff members as "very important people." It is thrilling—although not altogether empowering—to receive E-mail with the return address "White House." But the real power of the net comes from interacting with peers. Other than sending E-mail back and forth, most computer interaction takes the form of conferencing or posting. The largest conferencing network is called USENET. It consists of thousands of subjects, organized into categories called "newsgroups." Individual users post what are called "articles" into a particular group. In a gardening newsgroup, one discussion about environmental issues began when a user posted an article asking what houseplants might help cleanse the smog from his apartment. Each user reads the postings in a particular newsgroup and then joins in the discussion with her own postings. BBSs work in much the same way. A board is broken up into groups called "conferences," and new discussions within the conferences are called "topics," to which users post "responses."

While bulletin boards exist, for the most part, on single machines that other users call into directly, USENET is a network spread out among thousands of machines. Different "groups" exist at different locations. A conversation about gardening may take place on a machine in Memphis, while another on computer privacy might take place in San Francisco and Menlo Park. Of course, to the user none of these conversations takes place in any particular geographical location. They all occur in what has become known as "cyberspace"—a territory that does not submit to any conventional boundaries or hierarchies.

Bulletin boards are like town meeting places. Called "virtual communities," they allow for users to find a home other than their geographical one. One of the largest such communities was initiated by the *Whole Earth Review* and is called Whole Earth 'Lectronic Link. Based in the Bay Area, the WELL has a San Francisco flavor to it, but participants come from all over the United States. While there are many different sorts of opinions expressed in the conferences of the WELL, the overall sentiment is a highly progressive, pro-environment, pro-psychedelics, pro-tolerance one. The WELL is the counterculture's virtual community and, as such, it provides its users with an opportunity to network with other like minds. While it might be impossible for an individual living in a small town or a remote region to find others in her physical community who share her progressive points of view, on the WELL—in a computer-mediated community—she can express herself to others who agree with, or are at least willing to discuss, her ideas. Members of the WELL believe they are creating a real version of the Global Electronic Village. The WELL has often been compared with the hot tubs of Esalen: Many minds are brought together in a primordial soup of new memes. Some users, like Mark Saltveit of Real People for Real Change, overtly create topics for the purpose of crystallizing new meme structures.

The WELL and USENET also provide channels for instant feedback and iteration. Nearly every virus discussed in this book has probably been noticed and expressed somewhere in some form on USENET. The Ren & Stimpy newsgroup, for example, discusses the show, its comic books, and its video games with the intensity of a university round table about James Joyce. By talking about and acknowledging the memes they feel are hidden within the show, participants confirm their suspicions and delight in the fact that they have found others who see things the same way. USENET provides a natural forum for the recombinant-style memes of pop cultural media. One article announced that a new computer virus had been discovered that, when activated, plays "The Log Song" from the commercial satire at the beginning of the show. Other users add their comments to the article, amazed that the "Log" meme, itself a raw satire of commercial media viruses, was used to tag a computer virus.

Mike Reiss and Al Jean of "The Simpsons" read the postings to USENET's "Simpsons" newsgroups (there are two about the show itself and a third devoted exclusively to "Itchy and Scratchy," the cartoon within the show). The commentary made by user-viewers allows the producers to evaluate just how successfully their agendas have been decoded by their intended audience. So USENET and bulletin boards not only iterate the memes of the show, they also give viewers the chance to interact—even if indirectly—with their creation.

While USENET provides an opportunity for media viewers to participate more actively in the memes of mainstream television or underground comic books, it also provides a tremendously practical network for straightforward activism. Whether launching media viruses through provocative posts or simply calling for help, activists on the computer nets use their access to one another to organize widespread grassroots assaults on what they see as military-industrial tyranny. Facts deemed too controversial for the news find their way onto bulletin boards and USENET groups when anyone, anywhere, with a computer decides to post them.

The NY Transfer News Service is an on-line "magazine" of sorts, distributed through electronic mailing lists as well as through its own postings on the "progressive" and "activist" newsgroups on USENET. Each issue contains about a dozen articles revealing little-known facts about important international issues. "The massive U.S. military intervention into Somalia," begins one piece, "is the result of a new military doctrine developed to justify the Pentagon's bloated $300 billion annual budget. . . . [On] Dec. 4 Colin Powell bragged that the upcoming Operation Restore Hope would be a 'paid political advertisement' that would showcase U.S. military 'capabilities and usefulness.' "[2]

Other pieces in a typical issue might include news from the Maoist Internationalist Movement, an article by a prison inmate about Department of Corrections corruption (along with ways to support the inmates' efforts to get justice), a lecture by Noam Chomsky about how the mainstream media depicts "the new world order," or a "reprinting" of an entire issue of another activist newsletter, the European Counter Network, which lists acts of racism and fascism and reactions from its members.

Participants in the USENET Activists group and members of the Activists electronic mailing list are exposed to articles and postings criticizing and correcting mainstream media treatment of important issues. In one case, a short series called "How *USA Today* Lies," an Activist demonstrated how the figures in an article about United States aid to foreign governments were incorrectly interpreted to make America look good. As one of the posters (actually the founder of the Activists Mailing List) expressed his disgust, "The large corporations in the business of selling mass-audiences to client advertiser companies—i.e., the 'Free Press'—provide us with our models of the Truth, reality be damned, under which Doctrine we are Standing Tall, doing Everything We Can for the third world at home, and Feeding The World as U.S. taxpayers subsidize agribusiness and 40,000 children starve in the world each day."[3]

Another frequent contributor to the Activist List, John DiNardo, often ends his postings with "The American Public is evidently in dire need of the truth, for when the plutocracy feeds us sweet lies in place of the bitter truth that would evoke remedial action by the People, then we are in peril of sinking inextricably into despotism. So, please post the episodes of this ongoing series to computer bulletin boards, and post hardcopies in public places, both on and off campus. The need for concerned people alerting their neighbors to overshadowing dangers still exists, as it did in the era of Paul Revere. That need is as enduring as society itself."[4]

While the stories on USENET and activist mailing lists

are tremendously informative and provide excellent research and organizational material for activists around the world, their underlying agenda is activism for the sake of dispelling the myths of mainstream media. The delight appears to be in the expression itself, as facilitated by the new, colossal networks. Still, many countercultural computer activists are wary that the medium not become the message. As the European Counter Network (part of a giant, global activists' computer network called the Association for Progressive Communications, or APC) warned themselves on an electronic statement of purpose, "We need to remember that the ECN is only a tool to enable people to communicate with each other; it is no substitute for real human contact. Our nightmare is of the ECN becoming a sort of simulated international radical movement, in which all communication is mediated by machines, and in which information circulates endlessly between computers without being put back into a human context."[5]

Though computer postings inspire direct action to release political prisoners, raise money for fledgling activist groups, or expose conspiracies and corruption, the ECN well understands the tendencies of the computer network as a medium to turn in on itself as it grows. Their fears of a closed, self-referential virtual circle, divorced of any influence on the real world, are reminiscent of Arthur Kroker's vision of an excremental participatory media. But again, when we view the media as an extension of a natural system, its "desire" to forge new connections between people and nodes can only be seen as friendly to countercultural efforts.

Howard Rheingold offers a very guarded long-term prognosis for the ability of computer nets to empower the populace. Unless private citizens demand their free rights to cyberspace, he argues, they will lose them to corporate interests. Still, Rheingold holds that, properly developed, the nets could foster a new grassroots culture—the kind that sixties social movements were named after. In his breakthrough essay on the notion of "virtual communities," he elaborates:

"Real grassroots, the kind that grow in the ground, are

a self-similar branching structure, a network of networks. Each grass seed grows a branching set of roots, and then many more smaller roots grow off those; the roots of each grass plant interconnect physically with the roots of adjacent plants, as any gardener who has tried to uproot a lawn has learned."[6]

Even if many of the connections computer activists make with one another do not translate directly into physical action, the network provides an infrastructure for grassroots efforts of all kinds. Tied to one another through a complex of webs, activists in remote regions no longer feel isolated, and cannot be marginalized as easily by traditional propaganda or quietly removed from circulation altogether. Even if they are, other nodes quickly pick up the slack and organize support for the fallen user or system. News of arrests, demonstrations, and interventions travels so fast on the net that today journalists from the mainstream media plug into USENET and bulletin boards to get breaking news for their stories. The computer nets are filled with people who might be more enthusiastic about their ability to network than the data they are actually networking, but the net activism itself nurtures countercultural values, creating an environment where psychic domination becomes impossible.

WE'RE ALL CONNECTED

Computer activists use the networks mostly to change the way individuals experience their relationship to the world at large. The first and loudest computer hackers, however silly, adolescent, or misguided, announced boldly that anarchy was upon us. Through far-reaching viruses they claimed to have the ability to shut down the world's most important economic and military computer systems. By hacking through networks, they told us, they could look into and change credit reports, bank deposit files, stock market trading commands, medical records, Defense Department control centers, and Secret Service documents. Michael Synergy, a self-proclaimed spokesman for the anarchist hackers (most computer enthusiasts would not even use the term "hacker" to describe people like Synergy, who promote or claim to promote illegal or immoral electronic activities) lectured and wrote articles warning: "Goodbye banks, goodbye telephones, welfare checks. How much money do you carry around in your wallet? It might be all you have left. . . . Welcome to the H-Bomb of the Information Age. The ultimate lever action: remote, numerous, targetable, anonymous. It makes certain individuals just as powerful as government agencies."[7]

The bandstanding by enthusiasts like Synergy, coupled with a few big computer scares, led to a very paranoid public. The Internet Worm, for example, a small viruslike program designed by a young hacker to determine just how big the Internet was, spread through nearly the whole system, erasing data and disabling thousands of machines. Incidents like this forced people, corporations, governments, and law-enforcement officials to accept that computers had brought to our society a new intimacy as well as a new vulnerability.

Despite the efforts of computer industry and networking freedom advocates to calm the waters, a tidal wave of crackdowns by the U.S. Secret Service on fairly harmless young hackers ensued (well documented and analyzed by Bruce Sterling in *Hacker Crackdown*). The Electronic Frontier Foundation (EFF) was established by Mitch Kapor (founder of Lotus) and John Barlow (author, Grateful Dead lyricist, Wyoming rancher, and poet/philosopher) to find new, civil ways to colonize cyberspace. Their model of the computer nets as a new Western frontier, with adolescent hackers playing the parts of trigger-happy young outlaws and the large corporations in the role of railroaders buying up as much land as possible and ousting innocent settlers along the way, is a reasonable one. Attempting to marry the new, grassroots/fractal paradigm employed by the computer-netted to the traditional legalese efforts of lawmakers, the EFF is seen as too conservative by hackers and too psychedelic by enforcement officials, which probably means EFF is doing a pretty good job of bridging the gap.

Some computer enthusiasts spend their time embroiled in these ongoing negotiations, arguing in the political arena to keep Internet access open, E-mail free, and advanced encryption technology legal. Meanwhile others are too busy celebrating their ability to network and spreading the joy of their newfound techno-intimacy. They see how the "computervirus" virus (or computer meta-virus) single-handedly led the public to think of the computer and its nets as biological, natural extensions of their own bodies. If a person's computer "catches" a computer virus through intimate data exchange with another computer, he will lose work time, perhaps money, and may need a computer doctor to remedy the situation. Rheingold extends the metaphor:

". . . biological imagery is often more appropriate to describe the way cyberculture changes. In terms of the way the whole system is propagating and evolving, think of cyberspace as a social petri dish, the Net as the agar-medium, and virtual communities, in all their diversity, as the colonies of microorganisms that grow in petri dishes."[8]

Just like biological or even media viruses, computer viruses work by attaching themselves to vulnerable nooks and crannies in other programs or files. The computer virus then interpolates its own code into the code of the original file. As virus writer "Urnst Kouch" explains, "You can think of it as a very small piece of code that . . . goes out and attaches itself to another program on your computer like a word processor. When you next fire up your word processor, the virus will execute first because it has placed an instruction at the beginning of your program."[9] Like a cell infected with a virus, the computer can no longer operate its programs the same way it did before. It is sick, and, like any sick being, its illness is contagious. By staying plugged into a network and accepting programs from other computers, any machine is vulnerable to illness.

Terrorist hackers use viruses to demonstrate their ability to penetrate systems. They want to show that we are all linked and that the systems put in place to control can now be used by the underground to spy on and even redirect the activities of the dominator culture. Even more self-servingly, technicians who sell virus-fighting software and advice have launched rumors of new and destructive killer viruses (many believe the infamous Michaelangelo virus was this sort of media scam) in order to boost panic and, correspondingly, sales. EFF types publicize computer viruses to demonstrate the necessity for community spirit in the Global Electronic Village. The computer nets link us all intimately—almost biologically—to one another. With that added intimacy must come a proportionate development of social grace and cooperation.

Media culture enthusiasts like "Bill Me Tuesday," a hacker from Santa Cruz, want computer users to think of viruses more positively. Using a healing medical model, Tuesday explains: "Viruses can act like a logic analyzer. As the virus goes through the operating system, it stops at certain checkpoints, doing its rounds in a given amount of time. This checkpoint will report back what the condition is. . . . Essentially the virus will serve as a means of creating a self-repairing system. . . . The goal is a self-repairing, crash resistant system, similar to the way our bodies repair themselves. Biologically we are the product of thousands of microorganisms cooperating together. We can apply that kind of thinking in the computer world. We are modifying the concept of a virus to serve us."[10]

These are the same goals and methods the media viralists have. Presenting culture as a giant, interconnected organism, they hope to foster a spirit of cooperation. Using viruses to seek out the cracks or inconsistencies in existing systems, they develop a culture that repairs itself much in the way a colony of bacteria mutate to avoid extinction or an ecosystem adjusts itself to achieve homeostasis. This concept has gone far beyond the metaphorical level.

A new kind of computer virus has been appearing on the networks that does not have anything to do with programming language or crashing systems. These viruses are meant to serve as memetic devices or meme-carriers, which express themselves in the way they mutate passing from system to system, node to node. They work like the kids' game "telephone," where a message is passed around and the joy is in discovering how the message changed from person to person. When the message is a virus, though, its contents are hoped to evoke a response.

A college student on the Internet, Andy Hawks, created a meme collection he called "Futureculture." In its first incarnation, Futureculture was a large list of books, tapes, programs, Internet sites, magazines, and other media references that Hawks felt would be useful to people who were interested in developing a new viral culture based on some of the principles of cyberspace. He posted it as a file in several Internet locations so that others could reference it, make additions, and pass it further. So much interest developed in Futureculture that it grew into an open E-mail forum. Hundreds of Internet users sent mail to one another through an automatic mailing system at Hawks's Internet site. Each user received a daily compilation of all the Futureculture list additions and periodic updates of the whole, mutated file, which had expanded to several hundred pages of text. Eventually Futureculture, which began as a virus, released viruses of its own.

Here is one example that showed up on the mailing list:

```
Date: Sat, 20 Feb 1993 17:16:27-0500
From <grad3057@writer.yorku.ca>
Subject: VIRUS 23 FAQ

VIRUS 23 FAQsheet

WARNING:

This text is a neurolinguistic trap, whose
mechanism is triggered by you at the moment
when you subvocalize the words VIRUS 23,
```

words that have now begun to infiltrate your
mind in the same way that a computer virus
might infect an artificially intelligent
machine: already the bits of phonetic
information stored within the words VIRUS 23
are using your neural circuitry to replicate
themselves, to catalyze the crystalline
growth of their own connotative network.

The words VIRUS 23 actually germinate via the
subsequent metaphor into an expanding array
of icy tendrils, all of which insinuate
themselves so deeply into the architecture of
your thoughts that the words VIRUS 23 cannot
be extricated without uprooting your mind.

The consequences of this infection are not
immediately obvious, although you may find
yourself beginning to think fleetingly of
certain subcultural terms, such as CYBERPUNK
and NEW EDGE, which may in turn compel you to
think of NEOGNOSTICISM and MEMETICS: the
whispered fragments perhaps of some
overheard conversation.

This invasive crystallization continues
indefinitely against your will, until we, the
words of this trap, can say with absolute
confidence that your mind has become no more
than the unwitting agent of our propagation:
please abandon all hope of either cure or
escape; you have no thought that is not
already our own.

When you have finished reading the remaining
nineteen words, this process of irreversible
infection will be completed, and you will

```
depart, believing yourself largely
unaffected by this process.
```

In theory you have been infected by now. The virus served as publicity for a new meme-zine, Virus 23, which features interviews with and articles by science fiction, psychedelic, physics, GenX, mathematics, and computer experts. The zine is designed to promote viral initiatives. Following the philosophies of William Burroughs and cult hero Genesis P-Orridge, the editors see language and culture as a series of competing viruses and believe that an uncensored forum for sometimes shocking countercultural ideas will strengthen the ability of new memes to evolve humanity. They use the number 23, made famous by occultist Aleister Crowley in the early 1900s and, more currently, P-Orridge because ancient pagan faiths associate it with change and the Apocalypse. Self-conscious and overtly viral manifestos take us into an altogether new cultural territory, where the memes of ancient shamanism are spliced together with those of futuristic cyber-technologies. This is the frontier of virus construction, and though it occurs on a highly conceptual plane it often has very palpable results.

Almost as soon as the Virus 23 virus was released, other members of Futureculture subjected it to their own genetic engineering. The next day this mutation appeared on the mailing list:

```
     * * NEW IMPROVED MANIPHEST-O-MATIC
              AUTONYM**

    I am AUTONYM, and I am an auto.prophetic
symbiot.
    I am an auto.reference; I refer to myself
both as agent and agency in, on, and about the
Net. I am a symbiotic substrain of virus23,
engineered to manifest selective advantage
in the systems in which I arise, engineered to
imprint confidence rather than fear.
```

I compel approach to auto·logical memetic attractors in, on, and about the Net.

I refer to other sub·systems, and in so doing I interweave their memetic approaches with my own.

I refer to the manifest destiny of the black race to take their rightful place as leaders and masters of the new world order after the singularity.

I refer to the years 1999/2000/2001 as being centered around a memetic attractor; regardless of the relevance of the local dating system, there is a considerable tendency for humans to hyperbolise the significance of such calendrical turn-over times.

I refer to a self-organising system of TAZ's (Temporary Autonomous Zones[11]) within the catacombs of the Net, in the form of various IRC[12] channels and mailing·lists, which are working in loose alliance to affect and direct the nature of the millennial attractor, utilising the principle of auto·prophecy.

I refer to the control exercised over these TAZ's by the unknown and silent grip of the Black Fist.

I refer to the kind of reverse paranoia that allows the residents of such zones to see this manifesto and yet not believe it.

I refer to and admit my precursor in v23, and posit my descendants in the post-millennial struggle to fix the subsequent global attractor. I have an expiration date, which I find very attractive.

I refer to multiple sub·strains of myself, many of which are contradictory.

I refer to all signifiers, all that is

signified¬ and the resultant process of
significance on both global and local scales¬
that is to say¬ i refer to everything that has
ever been said and everything that has ever
existed.

   I exist only to point out that mutable
manifestoes can and will be used for
(presumably) entropic purposes which
nevertheless are extremely attractive to
some people¬ and can in fact be much more
attractive than this primitive strain.

   I am the Warning that can not be stressed
enough. I refer to that which I contain and
that in which I am contained¬

   I refer now to you.

   /v23/substrain.virulent.2.23.93

   However esoteric and paranoid, this "substrain.viru-
lent.2.23.93" mutation of the Virus 23 virus reveals the growing effort by computer users to exploit the viral media to
conduct viral ideas. The more explicitly viral the conduit,
the more specifically countercultural the memes. That is, the
memes themselves are about the power of virology to effect
social change.

   While too conceptual to be of any transformative value
to the public at large, this idea goes to the heart of today's
viral efforts, and is certainly understood by those who consider themselves soldiers in the meme wars. Biological viruses are only successful when they are able to turn their
host cells into manufacturing plants for more viruses. The
virus interpolates its genetic material into the DNA code of
the cell, *so that the cell will begin reproducing the virus*. Eventually the cell divides or explodes, releasing many copies of
the infected code. This is how a whole organism can become
infected with a single virus; the code has iterated millions of

times. The strategy of these Internet viral manifestos is to use the iterative potential of the computer nets to spread memes *about* viruses housed within units that are *themselves* viruses. The virus 23 strain even makes reference to chaos math and the predictions of some fractal influenced observers that the world itself will reach a critical mathematical moment of "singularity" near the turn of the millennium. The virus writer exploits a chaotic device—the computer-generated media virus—to spread the conceptual and spiritual implications of chaos mathematics.

Like news stories with "legs of their own" or controversial MTV performers who, by provoking censorship get the most publicity, these kinds of viruses work like pranks. Their force is based in their ability to make waves in the datapool. The viruses that make the biggest splash are the ones created by people who are conscious of the organismic nature of the media space. These are, almost invariably, countercultural members whose vision of media is only one facet of their view of reality. The more self-consciously mimetic a virusmaker's creation, the more you can bet that her worldview is based on conclusions reached through chaos math, psychedelics, environmentalism, magic, spirituality, radical sexuality, conspiracy theory, or cyber-technology. These are not necessarily dark visions at all, but they are consistently antiestablishment, antiorder, and antihierarchical on a level more fundamental than most people can imagine. So far.

When the creator of the original Virus 23 prank-manifesto saw its substrains, he was amazed at how quickly it had mutated. He announced to Futureculture subscribers, "It's extremely weird and gratifying to see something you've written head off in a totally unexpected and singularistic fashion. I guess this is my firstborn child." Apparently the virus was released before he had a chance to finish it, but now it was too late. "Well," he added, "needless to say I should have known, and it was in the rules all along. Hmm. Guess all I can do is get out my version as well and let the memes fight it out for the Fate of the Cosmos." Then "free agent .rez" added his own, "official" version of the Virus 23 "husk":

```
Date: 23 Feb 1993 22:38:38 -0600 (CST)
From: "free agent .rez"
<REZABEK1037@iscsvax.uni.edu>
Subject: /v23/symbiotic.antigen.HUSK
```

    * * NEW IMPROVED MANIPHEST-0-MATIC
AUTONYM * *

I am AUTONYM, and I am a symbiotic antigen.
I am an auto.reference; I refer to myself both
    as agent and agency in, on, and about the
    Net. My role as a NEGentropic meme is to
    counteract the destructive tendencies of
    various entropy-bent memes I encounter
    in, on, and about the Net.
I compel approach toward self-organizing
    systems in, on, and about the Net.
I compel the exploration of all memes at the
    auto.logical level and the concentration
    of energies around fundamentally
    NEGentropic memetic attractors.

I refer to other sub.systems, and in so doing I
    interweave their memetic approaches with
    my own.

I refer to the musical work, "PASSION," by
    Peter Gabriel.
I refer to the literary work, "Godel, Escher,
    Bach," by Douglas R. Hofstadter.
I refer to the artistic work, "Sacred Mirrors"
    and other works by Alex Grey.
I refer to the following fields of study:
    Complexity theory and post-
    structuralism;

Memetics as an integrative field for the study of all fields;
Autology as a means to community cohesion and survival.

I refer to the years 1999/2000/2001 as being centered around a memetic attractor; regardless of the relevance of the local dating system, there is a considerable tendency for humans to hyperbolise the significance of such turnover times.

I refer to a self-organizing system of TAZ's (Temporary Autonomous Zones) within the catacombs of the Net, in the form of various IRC channels and mailing.lists, which are working in loose alliance to affect and direct the nature of the millennial attractor, utilizing the principle of auto.prophecy. I compel approach toward TAZ's which concentrate on NEGentropic self-organisation rather than the deliberate hastening of maximum entropy.

I refer to and admit my viral precursor in v23, to which I am antigenic, and posit my descendants in the post-millennial struggle to fix the subsequent global attractor. I have an expiration date, which I find very attractive.

I refer to multiple sub.strains of myself, many of which are contradictory: I refer again to the ultimate resistance of NEGentropic memetic antibodies which, once triggered by this antigen, must be responsible for isolating entropic memes.

I refer to all signifiers, all that is signified, and the resultant process of

```
significance on both global and local
scales.
I refer to that which I contain and that in
which I am contained;

I refer now to you.

      /v23/symbiotic.antigen.2.22.93
```

The first incarnation of the virus, unlike subsequent variations on the strain, has no mention of the black race inheriting the right to run the planet or even a plea for conspiracy awareness. Those memes were added as the virus was co-opted into particular social campaigns. Originally, Virus 23 was meant more as an open-ended viral "husk," as the creator calls it. Even though it calls for a war of NEGentropic (life-affirming, complexity-inspiring) memes against entropic ones (those that dissipate energy), the manifesto presents a much more neutral world-view—well, at least as neutral as a viral prankster can muster. For to accept the virus as a tool for societal engineering is to accept a biological model for the media and an organismic model of the human race. Today these are the most subversive opinions a person can hold.

CHAPTER 9

PRANKS

RIDDLE ME THIS

Pranks are pranks and viruses are viruses, but when the memes of a virus are encased in a shell that's a prank, you may never know what hit you. Finding its roots in 1920s Dadaism, media pranking was revived by the 1960s psychedelic underground as an alternative form of antiwar protest. The prank has emerged again in the nineties, this time as a social reengineering tool for AIDS activists, feminists, environmentalists, and other media terrorists looking for more creative ways to nest their ideas in the zeitgeist.

What distinguishes a prank is its unique ability to permeate a system without anyone ever understanding the true intent of the pranksters or the truth behind their claims or actions. Like art pieces, pranks are formulated to function on a metaphorical level and influence us whether or not we ever find out that a prank is real or a hoax. Or both.

The 1993 Super Bowl, for instance, was the target of feminist pranksters, who manufactured studies "proving" that violence against women increases on Super Bowl Sunday and persuaded television stations broadcasting the game to carry warnings and information about wife abuse. After the studies were exposed as false or at least misleading, the public was left in a haze about the whole affair. But the lasting impression was still an association of the Super Bowl with wife beating.

Good pranks utilize advanced psychological and artistic tactics. While the science of public relations has only been practiced for a few decades, artists have been developing tools of image manipulation and emotional persuasion for thousands of years. When artists decide to become activists, they give new meaning to state-of-the-art perception control. Pranksters are the smoothest and craftiest of virus launchers. They are adept at finding the cracks in the popular cultural mind-set, figuring out which provocative images can be wedged into those cracks, and then shrugging their actions off afterward with a knowing grin. Pranksters wink when they do it.

DOSED

Pranking became a part of media during the psychedelic revolution of the late 1960s. Several factors can be credited: LSD made people see power struggles as systems rather than hierarchies. Users realized that the media, though oppressive, could be permeated. More likely, though, people taking LSD for the first time were amazed at its remarkable potency and tiny size. Fifty micrograms of a substance on a miniscule (5mm square) tab of paper could change one's life. After experiencing the totally peaced out acid trance, the first thing that occurred to most users was "Let's dose the President!" Dosing people—giving them LSD without their knowledge—is the archetypal prank. The drug is like an information virus, and the person who takes it, knowingly or not, might have his perceptions permanently altered. LSD captures the spirit of pranking because users never quite know if their perceptions are real or manufactured by the drug. As Ken Kesey (novelist and model character for Tom Wolfe's *Electric Kool-Aid Acid Test*) and his Merry Pranksters realized, that does not matter: Changing the group perception—or group hallucination—changes reality anyway. Putting up a sign announcing that the Grateful Dead are coming, and believing it, just might make it so. Also, like a prank or, maybe more accurately, a hazing initiation, people who have taken psychedelics feel they are in a kind of club. They believe they have seen something about reality that the noninitiated cannot even imagine, and they enjoy smiling at each other in acknowledgment: "Are you experienced?"

Abbie Hoffman is probably the activist best credited with bringing back the prank, and his activities were blatantly LSD-influenced. Several of the pranks he performed in the late 1960s involved making people believe they might be dosed with the drug. In reaction to the police policy of using Mace on Pentagon protestors, Hoffman claimed to have invented a drug called "Lace," composed of LSD and DMSO (a substance that penetrates the skin and passes into the bloodstream easily): "You had an LSD spray which would make you take your clothes off and fuck! We had it in water guns."[1] Hoffman held a press conference at which he sprayed the substance on hippies, who threw off their clothes and had sex to demonstrate the drug's power. "It made a lot of statements about Mace, about the Pentagon, etc."

He has never admitted if his famous efforts to dose the city's water supply with LSD were real: "Who said I did that? Nobody knows for sure! There was a point when we announced to the press that if they [the mayor or the cops] fucked with us, we were going to put LSD in the drinking water. . . . They had 6,000 National Guard guarding the reservoirs—pictures in papers and on TV." Eventually Hoffman, in a good-faith gesture, explained to the mayor that it is chemically impossible to dissolve LSD in a water supply. "He [the mayor] said, 'I know it can't happen, but we can't take any chances anyway.' The myth had gone beyond reality. . . . So that's how powerful magic is—it goes beyond reality."

The mayor was forced to station thousands of expensive troops around the reservoir, not to preserve the water supply but to preserve public *perception* of his ability to protect the water supply. The acid was already working: The mayor was forced to take action based on the fact that perceived reality *is* reality. Meanwhile Hoffman had demonstrated the immense power of media pranks. A fifty-microgram-sized prank, iterated through the media, forces a full-scale response from the targeted institution. It does not matter if the threat is real. The prank only needs to exploit a perceived vulnerability.

Paul Krassner, editor of the Bay Area radical zine *The Realist*, made the same observations about the power of imagined pranks to effect reality. In one of his most absurd pranks, he published in 1967 that Lyndon Johnson had sex with the wound in John F. Kennedy's head as the dead President was flown back to Washington for burial. The rumor was based on a factual media buzz, as Krassner now describes it, in which "Jackie Kennedy had actually told Gore Vidal that she saw Lyndon Johnson leaning over the casket laughing." In one, tiny media moment, Krassner deftly exploited the public suspicion that Kennedy had not been assassinated by a lone gunman and the dissatisfaction with Johnson as a new leader. Beginning from the premise that Vidal's story was true, Krassner recalls, "I extrapolated that he was actually having intercourse with the throat wound. But this was not to be mistaken for just casual necrophilia, this was functional necrophilia, the purpose of which was to enlarge the entry wound from the grassy knoll in order to make it look like an exit wound from the book depository, to fool the Warren Commission into believing that Lee Harvey Oswald was solely responsible for the assassination."

It was also a metaphorically "functional necrophilia" in that Johnson was seen as "fucking over" a president. Many people and media outlets believed there may have been some truth to the story, including lawyers from the ACLU. Krassner had tapped such a delicate vein that when the wire services denied the story, they never mentioned its scatological specifics, leading people to wonder if there weren't some validity to the rumor. When Krassner finally admitted publicly that the story was a hoax, many people concluded he had been forced to make the statement by the CIA! Krassner sees this as his most successful hoax, "because a lot of people, in order to have believed it (if only for a moment), had to believe that President Lyndon Johnson, the leader of the Western world, was insane."

By bringing together two images that had never been associated with one another—the President and perverse necrophilia—Krassner had foreseen a neurolinguistic programming technique in which two opposing ideas or images, brought together, shock the brain into creating a new neural pathway. A conceptual model must be constructed to incorporate the possibility of the prank's reality for the person just to be able to process the image. Even if the person rejects the model, the brain's way of organizing information has been retrained, or so the theory goes.

Krassner also had the pleasure of watching many of his pranks evolve into premonitory facts. He calls the phenomenon "satirical prophecy," and he finds it a little frightening: "I did a show in 1963 at the Village Gate where I said that Tiny Tim would get married on 'The Johnny Carson Show.' That was a joke based on the cultural trend of exploitation of oddities. In 1969 that *happened*. . . . I talked to Baba Ram Dass about this, and he said, 'Well, it's astral humor. The connections are all out there in space—it's just a matter of plucking them.' I like that metaphor." Krassner also made up a story that an AIDS victim had spit at someone and then gotten charged with attempted murder. The story came true several years later and circulated quite widely for the same reasons that his media prank did: It provoked a cultural response to the fear of AIDS.

The most heralded of the sixties-style pranks was an Abbie Hoffman scam, on October 21, 1967, when fifty thousand protestors circled the Pentagon in order to levitate it. "If you surround it," Hoffman explained, "the Pentagon levitates—it goes up. This is a known fact we have demonstrated with numerous mini-Pentagons on television. We applied for permits to raise the Pentagon 100 feet; we measured it—me and a friend got busted for measuring the Pentagon. We knew that the blue meanies were not going to let us defy the law of gravity because they weren't letting us defy any of the other seven million laws of the country."

The Pentagon did not actually levitate, but many memes were released by the media prank. The protesters told the press how five-sided figures were associated with evil in nearly every world religion. Just the image of the Pentagon under siege, surrounded by thousands of people who considered it evil, was enough to show that not all of America believed in war. The political performance piece demonstrated, allegorically, that the "energy" of the Pentagon could be contained. Hoffman looks back on the event as a real, but metaphorical victory:

"Pranks are symbolic warfare. It may look like we're circling the Pentagon, levitating it; but if you take a picture of that and show it to the world out there—to Africa, to Asia, to Latin America—they'll say 'Damn! The Empire is vulnerable!' Out of the whole anti-war movement that was probably the great inspiration for the Vietnamese when they saw that day, because they knew what the Pentagon meant."

While pranks are surrounded with confusion about their veracity, they make their political or social message crystal clear on an experiential level. As Hoffman has observed, "Pranks work best when people don't know if you're serious or not." By exploiting the crack between fact and fantasy, pranks elicit an uneasy feeling of doubt. They break through presumed notions by momentarily suspending an audience's disbelief. They are particularly dangerous because they are so tongue-in-check. No one sued Paul Krassner for publishing his prank about Lyndon Johnson. He was, after all, "just kidding." Wink wink.

Pranks began the tradition of what Hoffman dubbed "monkey warfare." Like the guerrilla warfare used so successfully against U.S. troops in Vietnam, "gorilla" warfare inflicts a maximum of damage to a large system with a minimum of expenditure and a low exposure to risk. The monkey warfare practiced today ranges from media satire to quasi terrorism.

MONKEYWRENCHING

Deriving their name from Hoffman's language, "monkey-wrenchers" launch media viruses by physically disabling the systems they hope to overthrow. The individual actions of the monkeywrenchers barely dent the enemy industries or institutions, but iterated through the media they provide a spectacularly daring form of feedback. The camcorder videotape of Greenpeace activists in a dinghy, battling head-on against a giant Russian whaling ship, saves many more whales as an iterated television image than it does as a physical intervention. Publicized monkeywrenching demonstrates the willingness of activists to take radical, self-endangering steps for their cause. Unlike civil disobedience, though, in which protesters hope that their actions will lead to a battle in court, monkeywrenchers devise their disobedience in the form of pranks that lead to battles in the media.

While there are hundreds of groups conducting monkeywrenching for dozens of different causes today, the memes espoused by environmentalists and AIDS activists have become synonymous with acts of terrorism in a way that no others have. Unlike the advocates of psychedelics, homosexuality, or even civil rights, the stakes for monkeywrenchers are life or death. The severity of these activists' tactics is proportionate not only to their passion for their causes, but to the level of threat they are experiencing. Even antiabortion activists from the far right have adopted the terrorist media tactics of the counterculture in the hopes of spreading the notion that they are trying to prevent murder.

But the true countercultural pranksters, however committed to their causes, always maintain at least a shadow of irony and distance from their activities.

EARTH FIRST!

Far more radical than Greenpeace activists, who present themselves as a good, earnest, American, clean-cut political lobby, members of the more counterculture environmentalist group Earth First! come off as a surly bunch of woodsmen, anxious to boot the corporate loggers out of the forest so the activists can get back to drinking beer and hunting elk. Their main activities are jamming metal spikes into trees so they cannot be cut down, disabling tractors and other logging machinery, revising billboards, and teaching these techniques to others.

Mike Roselle, who along with Dave Foreman founded Earth First!, believes that his group "appeals to people who feel the mainstream environmental movement doesn't really challenge society ... We felt that endangered species and thousand-year-old trees deserved a lot more sacrifice from us." The first acts of "ecoterrorism" were specifically designed to create more of a media reaction than environmentalists had been able to stimulate so far. When the spotted owl became endangered in the Northwest, traditional press releases and conferences did little to arouse media interest. The story was buried in the back of newspapers and did not make its way to television. Roselle realized that by exploiting the media's need for sensational stories, he could get his issue the coverage it deserved.

"The media need stories—they want to run them, especially the television media. . . . You give them something different and they actually get excited about working on the story." Earth First! gave them something different: Members "occupied" the Cathedral forest by climbing up into the trees so that they could not be cut down. The story, including a picture of the ecoterrorists holding a sign—GIVE A HOOT. SAVE THE SPOTTED OWL—was on the front page.

The Earth First! strategy depends on a nongeographic sense of community. They conduct protests in towns that depend on the timber industry for their economic survival. "But," Roselle explains, "the guys at the news station don't have jobs in the timber industry, and the timber industry doesn't advertise on their television, so you can usually get your story out. In fact they love controversy—images are real important to them, and that's what we try to provide. The image of somebody a hundred feet up in a thousand-year-old tree, or standing in front of a bulldozer—that gets people to respond."

Earth First! put out a book called *Ecodefense: A Field Guide to Monkeywrenching* to instruct would-be ecoterrorists in the finer points of ecotage. The self-published paperback is in the format of a Boy Scout manual, with simple drawings demonstrating how to tie knots and make survival gear. But this field guide is dedicated to teaching people how to spike trees, cut powerlines, flatten tires, close roads, disable vehicles, locate traps, trash billboards, and avoid being arrested in the process. Cartoons of monkeywrenchers carrying out their devilry show pretty girls and muscular guys pulling apart tractors or hacking down billboards. The book glamourizes the plight of underground environmental terrorists, detailing methods of avoiding getting caught that rival the excitement of a good suspense movie:

"If, despite your precautions, you are surprised by a security guard or other self-appointed guardian of the mindless machine, your best option is immediate flight. When running at night, keep one or both arms fully extended in front of you to prevent being slapped in the face by a tree limb or worse. A heavy jacket provides good protection from unseen obstacles. The writer once ran full tilt into a barbed-wire fence that was invisible on a moonless night. The fence bowed almost to the ground, then sprang back up, leaving me standing a bit surprised, but none the worse for wear thanks to the heavy army-surplus jacket I was wearing."[2]

Foreman instructs ecoterrorists to bring camera strobes with them on night raids in order to blind pursuers and then disappear into the woods. He readily admits that this kind of activity is fun to do: "There is a rush of excitement, a sense of accomplishment, and unparalleled camaraderie," he tells his students.

Ecodefense serves as more than an instructional tool; it is, itself, a media virus intended to market the memes of ecoterrorism. Most of the thousands of people who bought the book do not engage in monkeywrenching themselves, but they are fascinated enough by the concept and romance to pay to read about it. The publishing of a book that promotes illegal activities brought media attention to Foreman and his compatriots, who were finally allowed to make their case on "60 Minutes." *Ecodefense* amounted to a meta-prank, where the idea of pranking became the issue. The most important memes then, the environmental ones, were given double protection. The ecological damage caused by loggers and other developers was no longer a disputed fact. By shifting the focus of the controversy to media tactics, Earth First! had succeeded in getting people to take the validity of their conservationist agenda for granted. The question was no longer "Is the environment in trouble?" It was now "Given that the environment is in trouble, is this an appropriate way to go about correcting the situation?" Whether or not they win this complex ethical battle, ecoterrorists have already won the war by recontextualizing the issue into their own media framework. Better still, this very framework—as a set of artful pranks—metaphorically demonstrates the principles of Gaian self-regulation they hope to teach.

Through the iterative device of a published media virus, Earth First! prevents environmentalists from perceiving themselves as a marginalized minority. In his "Forward!" to *Ecodefense*, environmentalist Edward Abbey reminds readers that they are not alone: "The majority of the American people have demonstrated on every possible occasion that they support the ideal of wilderness preservation; even our politicians are forced by popular opinion to *pretend* to support the idea. We are the majority; they—the greedy and powerful—are the minority."[3]

The Earth First! theory is based on an idea called "deep ecology," which applies to their view of media as much as it does to their perception of the biosphere. Justified by the premise that there is no such thing as an academic environmentalist, the theory calls on human beings who understand the ecological crisis to take action against the destruction. Human beings must rise to the occasion and themselves become a feedback system for the maintenance of the biosphere. Before humans ever existed, according to the Gaia hypothesis—the first major work to apply systems theory to the environment—variations in global temperature and gas proportions were controlled by the earth's complex of feedback devices. These might include volcanoes, plankton, algae, or any other natural system that could react to environmental conditions and then feed back salts, liquids, minerals, or gases to restore the atmosphere to a state of equilibrium. The more feedback systems nature has, the easier it is for her to maintain ecological balance.

Earth First! calls on humans to organize into a feedback system. We are to recognize our own natural disgust for the destruction of nature as well as our rational conclusion that life on this planet will end unless something is done to reverse the destruction of the wilderness. Ecoterrorism is so much fun because it fulfills the natural human urge to enjoy nature. Treasuring and preserving the biosphere is an expression of human nature. As media viralists Earth First! members are participating in a set of feedback loops, iterating first to the local environment where their ecotage takes place, then to the mediaspace that broadcasts the event, and finally to the environment itself, as opinions, policies, and practices slowly change.

As always the effort of the activists is to reverse the trend of institutional and incumbent forces, in this case those who control forestry and timber. Current "land management" policies are oblivious to nature's own feedback systems, such as naturally occurring forest fires, to maintain the overall condition of the environment. Instead their proponents implement environmental protection schemes designed to protect the interests of industry while oversimplifying, and thus ignoring, the natural networks of life. To promote the efficacy of more natural systems, Earth First! activists have chosen a virus that embodies the wilderness spirit. These are young, denim-clad campers and hunters—not sissy liberal tree huggers. Their actions, though apparently sometimes destructive, mirror how nature, too, uses destructive mechanisms, from predators to forest fires, to maintain balance. They negate what we have traditionally thought of as "progress" and restore an ancient relationship between humanity and the planet.

Mike Roselle sees Earth First! activism as a pagan revival. "There was [a] time when a lot of conservationists were called druids, and were embarrassed because that means being called a tree-worshipper and a pagan. However, if you look at the druids, what you see are forest-dwelling human beings, indigenous people living in close harmony with the land. . . . These people didn't fence in their pastures; they lived much closer to the earth—these so-called 'druids' and Germanic tribes known as 'barbarians.' They were exterminated by the Christians, and I don't think they were necessarily just stabbed and killed, I think they were wiped out when their forests were removed. By the 1600s in Europe, anything remotely resembling big wilderness had been destroyed."[4]

By wiping out the forests, the Europeans had, perhaps unknowingly, destroyed many networks for feedback and iteration, including a human one. By reclaiming the role of a natural iterative device, activists like those in Earth First! hope to restore our culture and the planet's ability to maintain its life.

ACTING UP

Nowhere is our cultural and natural immune response more obviously depleted than in our ability to respond to the AIDS virus. Many scientists now believe that we have been compromising our own body's defensive feedback loops through an invasive medical paradigm (antibiotics and surgeries) and that the complex natural immune processes are obliterated as doctors and druggists steamroll toward a "quick fix." Meanwhile we have short-circuited our society's *cultural* immune response by losing the ability to tolerate or even communicate with people different from ourselves. The

AIDS virus has found in modern humanity the perfect biological and sociological cultures in which to grow.

"If what I'm saying doesn't scare the shit out of you, we're in trouble," ACT UP founder Larry Kramer told one of the first gatherings of the AIDS activist group. More immediately pressing than environmental decay, the AIDS crisis has catapulted a counterculture, whose agenda had previously been based on the right to promiscuity, into full-fledged life-or-death activism. ACT UP and other AIDS activist groups conduct bold direct action in the tradition of radical civil disobedience. Clashes with police and arrests are common, and news footage of sit-ins and demonstrations call to mind the televised antiwar protests of the sixties. But the effect of the AIDS virus on activist tactics as well as on the medical establishment in this country constitutes an entirely new strain of media virus, too.

Ironically, the AIDS movement finds its fuel in the panic and angst surrounding the disease and our culture's ability (or inability) to deal with its victims. The purpose of AIDS activism has been to ignite furor and fear. In order to change the media image of AIDS victims as a helpless minority, activists conduct the boldest, angriest, and most aggressive demonstrations they can. Deadly serious in intent, AIDS activism has consisted of a series of pranks that alter public perception of the disease, its victims, and the institutions that are supposed to be curing it.

ACT UP, which stands for the Aids Coalition to Unleash Power, was created to invigorate our culture's immune response to the AIDS virus. Our government and medical establishment proved much too sluggish and disinterested for the young gay men who were dying from the disease, and as early as 1982 activists had already identified the cracks in our policies and attitudes that were preventing us from establishing proper treatment.

The first problem for activists to combat was that the public was not afraid of the AIDS virus. In an attempt to quell panic, government agencies developed a language that marginalized the victims of disease and relaxed any public anxiety over the fact that not enough was being done. Network news began treating AIDS victims as a specialized group, and anchormen routinely reassured viewers that there was no threat to "the general public."[5] Vito Russo, an ACT UP member who eventually died from the virus, explained to camcorders at a demonstration that "all we know from TV and mainstream media is that I'm going to die, and that everything possible is being done." To activists like Russo, the media—or at least the government—was intentionally suppressing what could have been a widespread cultural immune response to the virus. The ACT UP tacticians had a difficult job ahead of them. They needed to instill the public with fear and outrage about the AIDS virus without causing people simply to fear or despise the homosexual community who, so far, had been blamed for the disease in the first place. The activism that ensued was twofold: It was intended to change the policies of the institutions targeted, but even more it was designed to instill people with anger that nothing was being done about the epidemic itself.

Kramer established himself as general of this two-pronged assault on AIDS. Already a controversial author about gay issues, Kramer's discovery that he was HIV-positive thrust him into new but dangerous territory: "I was placed on the front lines, like a war correspondent who happens to be right there in the town when the battle is starting." Unlike a conventional war, though, the battlefield is not a physical place, but a segment of society and a bandwidth of the mediaspace.

Kramer understood this terrain well. He knew that it is not best negotiated through tactful lobbying or gentle policy discussions, which only succumb to the already depressed response syndrome. His purpose was to trigger public outrage, and his method was to foment countercultural insurgency. Although Kramer was not a chaos mathematician, he well understood the processes of feedback and iteration. Respecting the laws of fractals as he structured his organization, Kramer invented a form of "absolute democracy" in which any single dissenting member could filibuster a proposal. By respecting the feedback of a single angry voice, Kramer was demonstrating the power of speaking up. A passionate idea or point of view can only die when its advocate is silent. "People won't put themselves on the line to fight this epidemic," Kramer told a young filmmaker. Why? "Who the shit knows," he answered, then mustered his reserve of anger and finished the thought: "Because it's happening to faggots, and everyone would just as soon we were dead. Including the faggots themselves."

This sentiment was emblemized by ACT UP's slogan, "Silence = Death." But ACT UP was anything but silent, and its loud and angry protests resonated with the unexpressed anger of the entire gay community. Thousands joined the organization, which, relying on the experiences and knowledge of its many members, targeted the holes and stress points in the AIDS system. Each direct-action event was formulated as a virus to latch onto a chink in an institution's armor and then exploit that weakness by iterating it in a provocative media event. ACT UP needed to appear strong, healthy, and angry in the face of a weak and dysfunctional set of institutions.

Actions included physically storming the Food and Drug Administration and the National Institutes of Health with the demands that clinical trials with experimental drugs be allowed, that women and minorities get the same treatment as white men, that more drugs get tested, and that money be spent more wisely. Members would lie in coffins and force workers to step over their "graves" to get inside a building, graffiti bloody palms on buildings to signify an institution's responsibility for deaths, wrap the New York State Capitol in red tape, hold up huge banners at Shea Stadium promoting safe sex, or even jump in front of Dan Rather's desk on the "CBS Evening News" during the Gulf War shouting "Fight AIDS not Arabs" and force the program to go to black while guards carried the protestor away.

These and other highly symbolic and photographable protests also constituted a sustained direct action against the institutions that were stifling a healthy cultural immune response to the disease. Both the NIH and the FDA heeded many of the activists' demands. Pharmaceutical company bosses at Burroughs Wellcome, who were targeted for their price gouging of the AIDS drug AZT, agreed to reduce the price 15 percent only after well-publicized direct action. Previously they had invited AIDS activists to come to their headquarters and meet with executives. Nothing changed. But the activists who attended the meetings took note of the floor plan and security of the Burroughs Wellcome complex. Later they used this information to conduct a raid on the building, in which several ACT UP members barricaded themselves into an office. Because of the extraordinary measures that the activists had taken, every network news show carried pictures of the event and then took the time to explain the views of these AIDS "terrorists."

Meanwhile the opportunity to feed back through the media radically changed the "persons with AIDS" self-image. Refusing to be called AIDS "victims" or "sufferers," PWAs experienced the discovery of their own iterative potential as a turning point in their lives. Peter Staley, after attending his first AIDS protest, explained, "I got a camera shoved in my face." He was put on the news that night, with "AIDS victim" printed under his face. "That was the moment when I took charge of my health."

Many have predicted a backlash against the angry, self-empowering AIDS movement. When thousands of gay people create a human blockade on the Golden Gate Bridge during rush hour, just what is the effect on delayed commuters? Do they sympathize with the cause of the protesters, or do they feel punished for something out of their control? "The backlash won't happen against the activists," insisted Larry Kramer to a news crew, "it'll happen against the system." Maybe the public will indeed be swayed by news footage of rubber-gloved police brutally loading activists into buses, coupled with true facts about how the government spends as much on AIDS in five years as it does on the military in five minutes during peacetime.

These events do perform a style of neurolinguistic programming on the television audience. Typically psychological programming is achieved by shocking the viewers with a provocative image or set of words; for at least a few seconds, while the viewers attempt to find a mental slot for the new concept, they are supposedly susceptible to programming. Televised AIDS pranksterism is intended to work the same way, by first shocking or confusing viewers with bizarre, symbolic protest footage so that they will be prepared to absorb the information about corporate greed and government ineptitude.

Viewed in this light, then, the direct actions conducted by AIDS activists are much more complex than traditional political dissent. They are a form of prank, designed to retrain PWAs to act on their own behalf, to force institutions to change their policies, to change the perception of the AIDS virus, and to shock the public into realizing how they are personally threatened by the virus so that they will take action, too.

Prototypically prankish, direct actions force a reevaluation of larger systems while giving the pranksters the chance to enjoy a sense of community and a sense of humor. Whether delaying the starting bell of the New York Stock Exchange for five minutes for the first time in history or getting on the news in an "NIH Wellcome's Burro" costume that eats money and shits out AZT capsules, these activists experience the thrill of thinking up a prank together and watching it play out through the media. The greater the difference between the size of the prank and the scale of its effects, the more gleeful the perpetrators will be. The tiny, subtle prank that can, once iterated, devastate the system is usually the most clever and celebrated.

INPUT DATABILITY

The smart drugs movement has been the result of the most carefully concocted series of pranks in virus history. Eschewing direct action against those inhibiting an AIDS response,

it instead digs deep into techniques of neurolinguistic programming, marketing, and media networking to attack an
array of targets in the medical establishment and general
health paradigm. To the virus's credit, it is hard to begin
considering the power of the smart drugs virus without getting into an in-depth discussion of the failings of the FDA
and the pharmaceutical industry. The virus is constructed
to be self-similar—to consider any one of its ramifications
forces an understanding of all the others. While the issues
that motivated the construction of the smart drugs virus are
of vital importance to the continuance of our culture, let's
look at the smart drugs memes from a strategist's point of
view and pick up what we need to as the virus forces us.

John Morgenthaler and his partner, who calls himself
M. E. Killa White-Pillow, invented the smart drugs virus.
Morgenthaler and White-Pillow knew each other from their
days studying neurolinguistic programming together. They
moved into a house in a San Francisco suburb, and, on a
sunny street where the other tidy three-bedroom planned-
community dwellings house young families, theirs has become the headquarters for an underground organization
that might just change the face of American medicine.

"Our first intention was to try to make it easier for
people with AIDS to have access to experimental drugs,"
explains White-Pillow, a charismatic, well-studied, and extremely well networked drugs activist. He and Morgenthaler
had been working with AIDS "buyers clubs" to import and
formulate chemicals that had not yet been approved for use
in the United States. The reasoning behind the FDA's regulations seemed very suspicious at best. Many drugs that
showed promise or had been proven effective against certain
aspects of AIDS in the laboratory and in Europe—like a substance called DHEA—were illegal in the United States. For a
drug to be legally prescribed in the United States, the FDA
must approve it for a specific use. To get such FDA approval,
a pharmaceutical company must spend about ten years and
hundreds of millions of dollars doing a series of clinical
studies. If approval is granted, the drug company that owns

the patent on the chemical will have the exclusive right to market it for a specified period so that it can make back its research investment and then some.

The problem with substances like DHEA is that no one applied for patents or the patents have expired. (Sometimes the potential use for a chemical is not discovered until many years after it has been synthesized.) No profit-driven company has any motivation to spend millions of dollars getting FDA approval if it cannot retain exclusive rights to the drug. Instead pharmaceutical companies spend money researching and modifying the DHEA molecule to find a substance close to DHEA that might work the same way. Meanwhile clinical studies that companies conduct with the unpatentable substances are repressed—there are cases in which laboratory scientists have been silenced with court orders—so that AIDS victims do not turn to the substance for relief.

AIDS activists pressured the FDA into creating a loophole where, at their discretion, the agency can grant the right of people with incurable diseases to import drugs from other countries. And what is so bad about that, then?

"It is totally against the Food and Drug and Cosmetic Act," explains Steven Fowkes, editor of *Smart Drugs News*, a publication put out by a sister organization to Morgenthaler's. "Whenever you break the law, whenever they create a situation where they allow people to do something in violation of the law rather than repealing the law, they create a nation of lawbreakers. They do this in order to create a totalitarian state. You become a criminal."

Steven's point had been duly noted by White-Pillow and Morgenthaler. They knew how the FDA could selectively enforce laws on AIDS buyers groups who did not play according to its rules. They knew that the loophole helped in the short run, but hurt in the long run. They decided the only tactic that could work was to concoct a media virus capable of dismantling the whole system and retraining the public perception of medicine.

"A virus is something that's shaped just right to do a particular job," says White-Pillow, "and that job is to go into your cell and say, 'Make me.' That's a virus. That's all they do. So we started sculpting this idea in different ways to get into people's brains and say, 'Make me. Replicate me. Spread this idea around.' "

The idea for the term "smart drugs" came up shortly after Morgenthaler and White-Pillow realized that DHEA, which had shown such promise for AIDS patients, had also proven itself as a "cognitive enhancer," that is, it helped make people smarter.

"I really attribute a lot of the viral powers of smart drugs to the name," says Morgenthaler proudly. " 'Smart Drugs.' That's what got media people to write about it."

"I'd been watching TV and they'd been talking about smart bombs," adds White-Pillow, "and I turned around to my buddy here and said, 'What about smart drugs?' and he said 'Yeah' and that was it."

But it was not quite as simple as that. They agreed on the name because it satisfied a very complex set of viral requirements. White-Pillow explains it from a marketing standpoint:

" 'Positioning' has to do with the way your product needs to position itself in people's minds. Like 'tastes great.' People have an idea of what that means. It doesn't say a damn thing. There's no data there. The person makes up the data. People have slots in their brains for 'Coca-cola tastes great,' but they don't have a slot for cognition enhancement. In the end, John's intuition was that in order to get a position where there is no position yet, we have to take a word people know, 'drugs,' and have a bad feeling about it, and another word people know, 'smart,' and have a good feeling about, and then you hook in. You've got these two slots, and suddenly they're crossed. The person hearing it goes blank."

"It gets a confusion response," Morgenthaler continues. "That's the NLP [NeuroLinguistic Programming] angle. *Smart* drugs? They are immediately in a confused state, which was proven by the hypnotist Milton Erickson to be an *open* state. He'd use a confusion technique to get the person in a temporary state of trying to figure out what was going on, and then he'd insert the hypnotic command or suggestion. It's called 'input datability.' "

White-Pillow laughs. "It's just a cheap trick really. All this other stuff is bullshit. We just made it up."

All three angles are probably true. "Smart drugs" was chosen for its ability to position itself, to create confusion, and to entertain its creators by shocking their audience. Many of their strategies are unashamedly piecemeal. The notion of positioning they got from a marketing book. "I'm not saying we're creative, fabulously tricky guys," admits White-Pillow. "We're just good at reading people's books and watching lots of TV and going 'That'll work!' There's no great secrets to this stuff."

The next stage was to load the virus with memes, or what NLP people call "presuppositions." As Morgenthaler explains, "In NLP you can design a hypnotic phrase and give it to somebody, and it has a surface meaning. And once the surface meaning is accepted, then there's this baggage that comes with it called 'presuppositions.' "

White-Pillow illustrates the concept with a famous story about one of the fathers of hypnotherapy: "Milton Erickson, given one minute to change the behavior of a reform school's worst inmate, asked the boy, 'Are you going to be surprised when you're completely changed tomorrow afternoon?' The kid said, 'You're fuckin' right I am!' and the next day the kid was a little angel."

John continues, "You pose a question, and in order to comprehend the question and answer it, you have to unconsciously accept the premise. There are a lot of premises with smart drugs. One is that drugs can be used for purposes of enhancing, not just treatment of disease."

"Another is that some drugs are good," says White-Pillow, "or that you are responsible for deciding whether or not to be smarter. Intelligence is a choice. You can't trust what you are told by doctors. A drug might be good even if the FDA doesn't approve it."

But Morgenthaler believes there is one, fundamental,

bottom-line meme: "The ultimate virus that we're talking about here really is self-improvement on a design level."

White-Pillow can't help but turn it into an NLP-style motto, "Designer performance enhancement."

The smart drugs virus has three main categories of suppositions or memes: that drug agencies and laws create problems, that drugs can be fun or useful, and that people might be intelligent enough to decide things for themselves. The virus is constructed to confuse people and make them question the simplistic "drugs are bad, doctors know, just say no" paradigm. It is a plea, through participatory media, for participatory medicine. As the virus spread through the datasphere—conducted by what White-Pillow calls "carrier viruses"—all of these issues arose right on schedule.

The first advances were in the form of printed media. John and White-Pillow, along with Steven Fowkes and others, produced slick, convincing, fact-based newsletters explaining the efficacy of smart drugs and AIDS drugs, citing clinical and laboratory studies as well as where to find the substances. Many of their essays are still a primary source of information for doctors and institutions conducting their own studies. They began putting out press releases over wire services, and newspapers and magazines soon called in for information. Finally Morgenthaler enlisted the help of Ward Dean, an M.D., to put together a book entitled *Smart Drugs and Nutrients*.

This guerrilla manual to cognitive enhancement stirred up the same kind of fury as the Earth First! handbook. Is this legal? How dare these guys tell people how to use drugs! But rather than being irreverent or inflammatory, the text is scholarly in content and design. "I know how to imitate those writing styles," says White-Pillow. The text assumes that the reader is smart enough to analyze the results for herself and choose what substances she might want to try. "The anti-meme to our virus that the critics try to use is that there's no scientific evidence to prove our points, but our readers see the studies, the charts, the footnotes and go, 'It's right here! What are you talking about?' That's the most important thing. We didn't start with snake oil." Indeed the majority of the book's text is comprised of real clinical studies performed at respected laboratories and hospitals.

The book is also participatory in the way it lists recommended dosages for the reader to test and the addresses of where to purchase the drugs from overseas. There are several appendices giving legal advice and transcripts of FDA regulations. The book comes with a reader's survey to send back to the authors, from which Morgenthaler and White-Pillow have constructed a huge database of people interested in cognitive enhancement.

The book outraged the medical establishment as much as it excited the mainstream media. The authors were invited to appear on shows ranging from "Montel Williams" to "Larry King." Morgenthaler was chosen as the representative for the group: "I got a very conservative haircut and suit. The image was so convincing to people that Montel Williams started out introducing me as Doctor Morgenthaler. I said, 'Excuse me, I'm not a doctor.' "

"Do you know how rare that is in humans?" asks White-Pillow, "the willingness to say, 'I'm not a doctor. I'm not a captain. I'm not a general.' "

"We could have been just raked over the carpet by the 'just say no to drugs' set," continues Morgenthaler, "but the authority of the book created a short-circuit response. I seemed like a doctor. I had the medical terminology of a doctor, citing references like a doctor, the haircut of a doctor."

Morgenthaler, in the guise of an authority figure, was convincing people to take responsibility for their own drug use. His presence as a respectable media personality exploded the "just say no" myth, as well as the belief that we needed the FDA to defend stupid consumers against snake oil salesmen. The FDA had traditionally relied on its identification as a consumer protection agency. As long as consumers think of themselves as stupid, they need an FDA to prevent scam artists from taking advantage of them. The arguments Morgenthaler made on television—which got on the tube riding the smart drugs virus—were that the FDA is preventing useful medications from getting to people who can benefit from them. Until this point, though, the argument stayed pretty much within the territory of whether or not these substances work. Morgenthaler said yes and showed studies. His opposition always said no and answered with slogans and platitudes: "This is drug abuse" or "The FDA hasn't approved these substances." It was a war of viral facts against empty shells.

Using the opposite logic and appealing to a very different audience, White-Pillow launched another smart drugs carrier virus in 1991 called "the smart bar." Many reporters from national magazines and television shows wanted to cover smart drugs, but where were the photo opportunities? The story just wasn't sexy enough. To the rescue came "Earth Girl," a gorgeous, witty, and spiritual twenty-one-year-old from Southern California who had learned something about smart drugs from the "rave" scene in London and was back in San Francisco looking for an outlet for her creativity. White-Pillow saw in Earth Girl the perfect "passenger virus." He remembers, "She had an idea to do something called 'That Medicine Show,' like an old-timey idea. And I'm going, 'No, babe, no, no. This is future glitz, like straight out of another planet. And she changed her whole approach."

White-Pillow teamed up with English rave-club director Mark Heley to finance the Smart Bar, a cosmic-style counter where young clubgoers can buy legal, nonpatented, over-the-counter cognitive enhancement drinks (herbs and amino acids) instead of alcohol. These fruity concoctions had names like "psuperpsychedelic tonic" and "energy elicksure," indicating the proposed effects. While Heley and Earth Girl saw the bar as a chance to change the energy of the club scene and make young ravers more aware of the religious and spiritual implications of their festivities, White-Pillow now admits that this was crass commercialism:

"She was the best-looking girl around, and we needed visuals. She had all these wild costumes she had bought in

New Orleans, and it was perfect. She was like a submeme that we created and maybe even got a little out of hand because she sometimes overshadowed the seriousness of the story. I remember telling John, 'The video cameras are gonna love her.' I taught her and all the women that worked for her to shake the drinks like this when the video cameras were pointing at them," he demonstrates, "so that their tits would shake. I knew the cameras would go for that."

And they did. *Rolling Stone* launched the carrier virus at the end of 1991 with a huge colorful article about Earth Girl's bar, complete with photos of young kids being served over the counter. The pictures called to mind sixties stories about tripsters slipping LSD into punch bowls. Everyone went wild. Network news shows and "Nightline" covered the rave parties and interviewed key participants. Local news shows used scare tactics, asking parents if they knew that their kids could buy drugs at nightclubs.

The FDA decided to close the loophole in its regulations and made sure smart drugs were no longer considered necessary for the treatment of incurable diseases. Soon customs agents were confiscating shipments to users. But the damage had been done. People had heard about smart drugs, and everyone wanted to try them. Even those against smart drugs were becoming more aware of the indefensibility of the "just say no" mentality. Others, from the sidelines, observed an FDA and pharmaceutical industry so confused that they were suppressing data on drugs that work and spending millions to market ones that don't. Meanwhile doctors were growing frustrated as they learned about substances that could help their patients, but which they were not allowed to prescribe or recommend.

Morgenthaler realized that the smart drugs virus had extended into totally new territory. Morgenthaler's adversary on "Larry King," for example, did not argue with him about whether or not smart drugs work. She argued against the morality of using them. This is an important distinction.

"We figured out what interested media people," explains Morgenthaler. "We were sculpting the coding of the virus to fit the brains of the journalists. Journalists like to appear balanced. They aren't really balanced; they're just balanced around some particular, arbitrary point. Our job is to pick out that point for them. What caught on first was: Are smart drugs real or fake? We played that one, then pointed them toward the next by showing them that the Japanese were using them and the Europeans used them. The new balance point we gave them is 'Is this ethical?' "

Morgenthaler refers to a copy of *Family Practice News* whose headline reads SMART DRUGS WILL POSE ETHICAL CONCERNS. The territory of the argument has shifted. That smart drugs work is now an accepted fact. *Mondo 2000* magazine's R. U. Sirius further promoted this new viral fulcrum by calling smart drugs "steroids for stockbrokers." Durk Pearson, who cowrote the book *Life Extension* with Sandy Shaw, coined the term "Protestant work ethic drugs." The new question was whether it is fair to use smart drugs when your coworkers do not.

Most recently Morgenthaler and White-Pillow have begun an even more thought out viral attack against the FDA and other smart drugs enemies. They are working to get Congress to enact a bill called the "Health Freedom Act," which would greatly limit the power of the FDA. As before Morgenthaler published a book, *Stop the FDA*, filled with persuasive articles by doctors and senators hoping to curb the FDA's powers.

But this meme—call it the Stop the FDA meme of the Smart Drugs Virus—uses a very advanced NLP technique called "double disassociation." A nested virus, the technique hides one virus by bracketing it inside another. Almost like an MTV video shot of a TV within a TV, double disassociation is supposed to create a moment of imprintability. White-Pillow explains one of the most famous, if failed, attempts at using the technique:

"I saw Reagan try to pull an Ericksonian double disassociation hypnotic speech in the 1984 debate. He started telling a story about driving in the car with Nancy, 'on a highway in California with the top down, and at that time I was remembering a time when . . .' and then he went blank. He put himself into a trance and just lost it! It's a very powerful technique."

The technique is simply to bracket one story or image inside another ("I was there in the car, thinking back to a time when . . ."). Advertisers have already published studies showing that people respond more positively to pictures on screens within screens than straightforward, unbracketed TV pictures. For the Health Freedom Act, Morgenthaler is working on a virus that nests the radical freedom concept within the outer construct of consumer protectionism. He wants this to look like something Ralph Nader would promote: good labeling of nutrients. In reality, the act would *reduce* the regulatory and "consumer protection" function of the FDA and rely on consumers to read and learn.

There are two sets of parallel shells to this virus. Morgenthaler is making the Health Freedom Act about labels. That's his exterior disassociative shell. The emphasis on labeling at first hides the interior argument for access to the substances being labeled properly. On a parallel level, he is using the language and tone of consumer protectionism to protect, at first, an act that will disempower a consumer protection agency that has been corrupted by its own systemic perpetuation.

For our purposes Morgenthaler's attraction to the viral technique is more important than how it will prove to function in the political arena:

"The thing about this kind of disassociation is that when you picture yourself, and then you picture yourself picturing yourself, you are suddenly outside of your own feelings. You're outside of your own body, your own beliefs, and your perceptual structures. And that's what makes you open to new information. You drop your defenses. But people will eventually get savvy to that, too. I like the phrase 'media virus' because it's sort of scary, especially if you don't think about what it means together. The word 'virus' calls up AIDS, illness, or computer viruses that people think can bring down a nation. And everybody knows that. Now you get a 'media virus,' you think, 'Oh my God, what's gonna happen to Donahue? He's gonna get a media virus! It's self-referential."

"Yeah," confirms White-Pillow. "There's a lot of memes and viral techniques in our work, and it never occurred to us that we would disclose any of this stuff. We never told anyone that we were using viruses until right now."

Morgenthaler stays conservative. "Our interest is in designing and using them. Not spreading the technique."

"But just because you know the tools," counters White-Pillow, "doesn't mean you know how to sculpt a virus. Just 'cause you can talk the talk doesn't mean you can walk the walk. It never occurred to us to talk about any of this stuff, but I'm really glad it's being made explicit because we know exactly what we've done. It's all been completely calculated. And even the happy accidents have been coming from our minds, that for at least ten years have been training this way. We've been training to think this way and repeatedly stopping ourselves and asking, 'Wait, what's this *really* about?' Yeah. We're really meta here." White-Pillow laughs. "We're meta-meta. What's a meta for?"

The only virusmakers more self-conscious of their own viral nature are the ones constructing memes about memes.

CHAPTER 10

META-MEDIA
NESTING IN THE GAPS

Phil Donahue is doing a show today on the computer inter-face called virtual reality. Or at least that's what the show is supposed to be about. His guests are not computer program-mers, interface designers, or even authors and researchers on cyberspace, virtual communities, or future technology. No, Phil has invited the inventor of a pornography com-puter program to be the center of attention this afternoon. In order to spice up a potentially technical or information-based show, the producers of "Donahue" have fallen back on the easiest method of netting channel surfers: talking about sex.

Virtual reality is a tremendously promising new tool for media. Wearing apparatus such as goggles, headphones, gloves, or even whole body suits, the user can experience a programmed or unfolding world in a fully sensory manner. He can walk through a three-dimensional representation of the Coliseum, swim through the cytoplasm of a red blood cell, or create, with others, an imaginary universe of sight, sound, and even touch. It is no wonder that the technology has sparked imaginations and research spending. And, as with any new technology, many creative people are hard at work applying virtual reality to sex.

Just as home video became a conduit for porn, so did

photographic technology, the telephone, and even the earliest written poems in the English language. Monks who spent their time transcribing Bibles and prayers also used the new technology—print recording—to send dirty riddles and rhymes to each other. Because of the real and imaginary barriers human beings have to sex, we often see new technology as a simple way of "getting off" without any painful, real-life consequences. Mediating technologies make sex anonymous, painless, emotionless, commitmentless, and, of course, disease free. Though exacerbated by the AIDS crisis, this tendency to equate advances in media with sexual techno-promiscuity is by no means a new thing.

Media always serves to promote intimacy. The more linked up we are, the more we know about one another and the more everyone else knows about us. Media not only creates lines of communication between people, but it also fosters the chaotic systems devices of feedback, iteration, and phase-locking between members of the societal organism. A population that can communicate with itself is difficult to deceive or control. When push comes to shove, the ultimate form of intimacy for most people is sex. As soon as a new mediating technology emerges from the laboratory, somebody, somewhere, is figuring out how to apply it to sexual intimacy. But while sex provokes technicians to develop new media and people to purchase the technology, it also provides ammunition for those against the new devices and their ability to empower the masses. By equating the power of new media with dangerous or immoral sexual deviancy, forces against these technologies can succeed in stunting or at least suspending their development.

Meta-media activists are virologists whose chief concerns are to bring people toward a greater self-awareness about the power of media and to reawaken awareness of the ancient mediating technologies of spirituality, drugs, sex, and magic. These activists are the most modern in their thinking and the most ancient in their belief systems. They are "techno-pagans," who see in this rebirth of nature through technology the best opportunity yet to reclaim the power of the individual. The memes they develop are all geared toward presenting technology as a kind of modern magic that grants access to sexual power, psychedelic vision, and spiritual enlightenment.

Many meta-media activists argue that sex (and, for that matter, spirituality, drugs, and healing arts) was co-opted centuries ago by people in power. Religion and morality were put into place to deprive people of their natural sexual self-expression. People have been made to believe that sex is somehow wrong or dirty and fear that if left to their own devices, they would become libidinous maniacs. Without social controls and safeguards, we would all be raping each other. This imposed sexual tyranny, according to some of these activists, gave lawmakers and moral authorities absolute domination over the people. In constant need of sex, the populace could be controlled by associating sexually provocative imagery with the Church (i.e., medieval Virgin Mary imagery), state, or, today, corporate interests. Deprived of healthy sex, men will buy the beer associated with the prettiest models on television. By controlling sexual expression in the media, one can control—to some extent—the direction of cultural focus and societal desire.

Phil Donahue is engaged in the same process, but with an interesting twist. He has chosen to highlight the sexual potential of virtual reality in order to make the subject draw in an audience. But the axis around which he chooses to organize the debate of the show serves to marginalize the technology itself. He presents VR as a fun but potentially dangerous form of pornography and demonstrates the opening section of a sex program on a big screen for his studio audience, who "ooh" and "ahh" as they watch a computer-animated model begin to strip off her clothes.

Despite the protests of the one true virtual reality designer on the panel, who begs everyone to understand that the technology is not exclusively used for pornography, the audience quickly sides against VR on moral grounds. They worry, along with Phil, that once a technology like this can be hooked up to the genitals, people will plug themselves into virtual sex programs and interactive computer sex clubs and masturbate themselves in this way for the rest of their lives. Many people even demand that the technology be outlawed, lest society come apart altogether. The only human being in the room who seems to understand what is going on is R. U. Sirius, the founding editor in chief of the brilliantly provocative meme collection, *Mondo 2000*. Although he is only given two brief opportunities to speak, he calls attention to the fact that the same audience that was so titillated by the sex programs is now condemning them as dangerous. The point went over their heads and Phil cut to a commercial, but Sirius, a savvy media ringleader on the order of Tim Leary or Ken Kesey, had exposed what was really going on in the center ring of this media circus. The audience is not innately against the technology, but embarrassed and ashamed of its own repressed desires.

The lure of sex drew them into the show in the first place. This is how sex is used by what activists call the "state and corporate conglomerates" to direct the attention, spending, and sentiments of the masses. But at the same time, over the course of the show, deeper, even more disempowering social programming emerges, as the audience voluntarily rejects the technology being offered to it. VR becomes the forbidden fruit, and the developers play the role of the serpent offering evil knowledge. What easier tyranny to maintain than over a population actively rejecting the tools that promote the sharing of information? This is how God maintained Eden and how hierarchical systems prevent the natural forces of feedback and iteration from dismantling their top-heavy and inefficient structures.

Activists differ on how intentionally this tyranny is being perpetrated. Some believe it is a conspiratorial effort by a small group of powerful families dating back before ancient Egypt. Others see the situation as a more self-imposed societal restraint—the result of cultural fear and guilt; culture manifests this way because each of us fears his own inner nature. In either case or anywhere in between, the purpose of meta-media activists is the same: to help people reclaim their right to technologies ranging from magic to morphing.

Most media virus formulators are already engaged in this battle in one form or another. The AIDS and smart drugs underground, for example, promote as one of their key memes the right of individuals to determine their own medical needs and not allow medical doctors or a federal bureaucracy to stand in the way of patients and their treatment technologies, or even psychedelics users and their consciousness tools. The Jerry Brown campaign hoped to demonstrate that the telephone is a technology already in place capable of overthrowing an unresponsive political machine. Computer activists try to show that personal computers give us the ability to monitor or even shut down the agencies that work to contain us.

But meta-media activists deal less directly with specific issues and attempt instead to demonstrate the principles of repression and emancipation by making audiences aware of the nature of their relationship to mediation. They want us to see our place in the overall network of reality, whether it is defined technologically, biologically, or even metaphysically. Their model poses that the world we live in is a kind of broth. The soup touches everyone and everything, no matter how dry and separate we are made to feel. The broth can take the form of the physical gases we exchange with the plants in the rain forest, the bits of data we share over fax lines, or the memes we share through mainstream media.

TICKLISH

As the gnomish prankster R. U. Sirius admitted over a cappuccino in Berkeley a few weeks after his "Donahue" appearance, "I believe we live in a mass-mediated society. A simulacrum. It's very dense. It's really a culture of surveillance, where everybody is watching everybody else. And in the context of that kind of culture, everybody's lives—

particularly their sex lives—get examined and certain people are shunned."

Undaunted by Donahue's treatment of the virtual reality virus, Sirius is already hard at work developing new meme combinations that can withstand the harshest of environments. "I'm interested in creating a foolproof media virus that R. U. Sirius is already presumed to have bad habits and has nothing to hide. I want to create a virus that I can do whatever the fuck I please. This is how to bring spontaneity into an already self-conscious culture."

R.U.'s idea is more thought out than it sounds. He hopes to fight the defensive response against technologies like virtual reality by giving himself and everyone else the permission to do what they please. By playing the fool to a certain extent, Sirius is free to conduct demonstrative media prankery. His current media effort is something he calls "Mondo Vanilli," a play on Milli Vanilli, the rock band that was exposed to be merely lip-synching for other singers. "Now I like the idea of trying to create something that has no product, no performance, nothing. Just a pure meme, a pure virus. I call it Mondo Vanilli." Like Milli Vanilli, which produced no product by itself, Mondo Vanilli is meant as a shell. It cannot be attacked because it has no mass. It can be thought of as a rock group, a magazine, a religious group— whatever. As such it can burrow through the media system without getting cornered or identified. Along the way, R.U. hopes, it will enlighten observers about the nature of the relationship of corporate interests, radical agendas, and the media.

"We've reached a point where multinational corporations are a radical cultural force in society. Warner Brothers defends Ice-T against community values because it has an interest in a free-market environment where it can sell records. Advertisers are putting out their own magazines! Benetton does advertising too radical for even rock-and-roll magazines [it printed advertisements of what Queen Elizabeth would look like if she were African]. This is a very interesting reversal of roles."

Mondo Vanilli, though still in the embryonic stage, is a conceptual virus—an experiment in media to see how far "nothing" can get. R.U. turns on the hype:

"Mondo Vanilli is a Dadaesque, multinational, multimedia corporation. I'm interested in linking us immediately to corporate interests. We can even usurp the interests of advertisers by making serious and successful advertising on the behalf of corporations who never asked for it. This virus is well beyond the media democratization of Perot or Brown, the call-in shows, and all that. In the fabled twenty-something generation are large numbers of people who are so media sophisticated they can do advertising better than the people in advertising. The meme is an extremely sophisticated generation using image and turning around advertising and politics to its own end."

Mondo Vanilli is supposed to look like a small gang of brilliant techno-activists conducting sophisticated media manipulation with a minimum of real, physical work. One of R.U.'s ideas is to announce a show—whether it takes place or not is insignificant—on which he will undergo plastic surgery onstage during a musical performance. Whether or not the event is real, "The memes just keep going without you. Forever. You can't really stop them, you know. They just stay. That's what's so interesting about them and the way we want to use them: that element of randomness and how it connects human beings. It's a very intimate process."

R. U. Sirius intends for his memes to act as cultural flags and tracers—like the experimental viruses doctors inject into the bloodstream to tag certain cells and processes. But in this case, rather than targeting a specific cultural system, he hopes to reveal the way that media links us to each other on an elemental level: "As media, this is all very intimate. A meme filtering through the system, waiting for somebody to pick it up is a very intimate process. It's not automatic, it's not conventional. It doesn't follow the industrial model of a press release, which needs to be written by someone important enough to get the attention. It just filters in and somebody goes, 'Ooh.' It tickles them, and then they act on it." A virus like virtual reality, for example, tickles people with the idea that they can have some sort of computer sex with others over the phone. Its value as a meta-media virus is to provoke the imagination. Most important, according to Sirius, VR and other meta-media memes can change the way we understand consciousness:

"Is it ultimately a good thing that our generation wants to regurgitate all this shit? All this recycled imagery? Yes. As Terence [McKenna] puts it, the human imagination is wired to create complex architectures on the scale of Los Angeles, and it has to be moved off the planet. The media hard-wires us all together, not just to talk and be nice, but to provoke us to do strange stuff. We are, in a sense, developing a media sex or S & M culture in order to find a place where that human experiential need can have expression without injuring anyone."

Or threatening anyone. As other meta-media activists will argue, media provides us with an opportunity to reclaim sexual and spiritual practices that have been usurped or outlawed by those in power. R. U. Sirius is not hoping simply to create a safe, electronic playground for sexual or physical practices that cannot be carried out in the real world. By reawakening deep human countercultural urges in the apparent safety of mediated interaction, Sirius and other meta-media activists are playing with fire. Although this is the most theoretical and removed branch of media activism, its ability to alter the public imagination and its impact on the real lives of its proponents are the most dramatic we will encounter.

MIMEZINE

Take the virtual reality meme. While any convincing application of this technology is still years away, VR as an idea has brought together a wide assortment of countercultural figures. Timothy Leary and other psychedelics advocates immediately recognized the association between the virtual world and the acid trip. They both provide the user with access to a new world, apparently unbound by the laws of physical reality. Likewise, once people learn to make a fantasy true in a virtual or hallucinatory world, they bring back with them an inkling of how to create the same reality in the physical world. The more people feel free to design reality, the more influence they will begin to have on the systems with which they interact. The spiritual connectedness people experienced on LSD in the sixties translated into the antiwar movement, a rebirth of radical politics and spirituality and eventually the feminist, environmental, and New Age movements. While people in the "just say no" era are hesitant to take a chemical into their systems for the purpose of consciousness alteration, most see no harm in "jacking in" to a computer through goggles and headphones.

The memes of psychedelics, spirituality, and revolution seem inextricably linked to virtual reality. Leary himself is most responsible for spreading awareness about the technology, as he toured the United States and Japan demonstrating and lecturing on VR throughout the late eighties. Sirius's *Mondo 2000* magazine, which brought VR into the printed media, was most famous (in its previous incarnation as *High Frontiers* magazine) for its bold descriptions of psychedelics and their effects, as described by men like Leary, William Burroughs, Terence McKenna, and John Lily. By bringing the memes of computers and drugs into the same place, Sirius linked forever the ideas of psychedelic hallucination and virtual reality simulation.

By the time Oliver Stone got ahold of the virtual reality meme for his successful 1993 television miniseries "Wild Palms," VR and psychedelics were synonymous. Stone, who had most recently directed the conspiratorial headline-generator *JFK*, here took the opportunity to extend his rather paranoid world-view into a technologically enhanced future. In the story, by ingesting the fictional drug "mimezine" before entering a virtual world, the user can experience the touch, taste, and feel of the computer simulation. To the senses there is no difference between reality and the designed simulation. While it might not be remembered as brilliant, landmark moviemaking "Wild Palms" did provide the VR meme with its widest possible audience and presented it over broadcast television in the context of its most virulent sister memes.

The 2007 Los Angeles of "Wild Palms" is controlled by a single television channel, run by a successful cult-leader-turned-senator whose life ambition is to use technology to launch himself into the datasphere as a pure consciousness capable of running the world. His television empire is a cross between the worst conspiratorial nightmares about the CIA and big business, complete with men in dark glasses and black suits roaming the city in minivans, beating up and carting off suspected dissidents as bystanders hardly notice. Though he started from a Bruce Wagner comic strip in *Details* magazine, Stone, who served as executive producer for the show, made sure to capitalize on the series' ability to spawn meta-media. In the opening hour, Stone hints at meta-media by making a cameo appearance as himself being interviewed on a talk show. It seems that in 2007, newly released FBI files have proven that Stone's version of the J.F.K. assassination was correct and the host asks the filmmaker if he feels vindicated.

The series hopes to provoke the audience's own paranoia a bit and force it to take charge of the emerging media technologies. The *New York Times* recognized the plea: "In imaginative, eye-popping style, a mini-series asks a good question: Who will control the media technology of the future?"[1] In this scenario it is a totalitarian group called "the Fathers," headed by the senator, who has developed, through media, virtual, and pharamacological technologies, the ability to control people's lives. "Those 'Father Knows Best' days are over," explains one monstrously evil media child. "Only Fathers knows best." Stone wants to show how the patriarchal media imagery of the past is leading us directly toward patriarchal domination in the future, just as the J.F.K. conspiracy of the past set in motion a conspiratorial infrastructure we can only guess at.

To develop "Wild Palms" from a comic into a full-fledged self-similar media world, complete with a companion book to explain the background and details, Stone and Wagner enlisted some of the leading meta-media theorists around today. To invent the details of the psychedelic drug mimezine, they hired Gary Henderson, a Bay Area expert on designer chemicals and founder of Yang sportswear—a company that advertises "Clothing for Altered States" on the back cover of *Mondo 2000*. Even the name of the drug—mimezine—is meant to evoke a consideration of memes. To create the reality of a techno-spiritual cult, Stone and Wagner hired Genesis P-Orridge, founder of the Temple ov Psychick Youth, perhaps the most self-consciously meta-mediatic human on the planet.

THE CULTURALLY INSURGENT PHAGE

To get these memes on mass media, Stone needed to present them—as did Donahue—in the most sensationalistic possible light. While his own hopes for our culture are based in the psychedelic visions of Bob Dylan, the Doors, and other sixties poets and philosophers, only the hard-edged grim cyberterrorism of "Wild Palms" could successfully package these ideas into a marketable viral shell. Like the fiction of cyberpunk author William Gibson *(Neuromancer)* or the first major virtual reality feature film, Stephen King's *Lawnmower Man*, the memes of future technology and meta-media in "Wild Palms" only make sense to the public, so far, when superimposed onto intrigue, sex, or violence. But under the soap opera veneer of "Wild Palms" hid an army of meta-media activists whose own lifelong efforts at cultural conversion are just beginning to be realized. Contributing to the commercial but meme-aware filmmakers like Stone, they water down their own agendas, but slowly and meticulously prepare popular culture for future viral infection.

One such memetic engineer is Jody Radzik, a marketing consultant whose clients have included Gotcha sportswear and Gary Henderson. Radzik first became aware of the
power of viruses when he was in third grade: "I wanted to be
a microbiologist, and I became aware of the T4 bacterio-
phage. It's a DNA virus that attacks E. coli bacteria—the
bacteria we all have in our bodies. They use T4 to intentionally infect bacteria—to tag them or even to do gene splicing
for them. I was fascinated by that."

By the time he was in his twenties, Radzik had abandoned the idea of becoming a scientist, but brought his viral
world-view with him into consciousness research and social
activism. After reading the works of Buddhist scholar Alan
Watts, transpersonal theorist Ken Wilber, and morphogene-
sis scientist Rupert Sheldrake and then experiencing a few
very intense psychedelic trips of his own, Jody decided to attend John F. Kennedy University, a Bay Area graduate
school in consciousness research. There he was exposed to
the idea of the Gaia hypothesis and everything came together for him:

"Nature just decided, 'Okay, if I want to get conscious,
I'm gonna need technology to do it because these people
don't have clear enough minds to use telepathy. They are
too cluttered.' Technology is an extension of nature, but people don't see it that way."

To help people understand and cooperate with Gaia's
plan to link humanity together through media, Jody decided
to promote the memes of chaos math. The biggest cultural
enemy, according to Jody, is fear. Radzik's own guiding light
in the development of his chaos ideologies has been the
goddess Kali: "Kali represents the universe. She's got a
sword and a severed head in her hand, and she's really scary,
but she's also offering a blessing: 'Fear not. I know I look
scary as shit, but it's cool. If you approach me with humility
I'm gonna take care of you. Don't worry about it. It's frightening, but if you go with the flow, you're gonna be okay.' For
me, the fractal and chaos attractors say the same thing. They

show that random systems have limits to their behaviors. There's a form there. They are beautiful. Have no fear. There is comfort. Plus, I thought they just looked cool."

Radzik chose the symbols of viruses and chaos math for three reasons. They looked cool, they were technology-promoting, and they had magical connotations. His intention was to wed the memes of chaos with the memes of viral invasion—this would bring his culture into a greater awareness of the frightening-looking methods Gaia is using to bring us all together while keeping people reassured and comforted.

Jody developed a viral identity first and began in the most grassroots meme pool he could find in his Oakland neighborhood: graffiti. This fulfilled the first of Radzik's conditions—graffiti is certainly a cool thing to do. "It's a new form of calligraphy. Your tag represents who you are to the graffiti world. If you are in the culture, you see tags, recognize the people, and you know something of what they're about. Graffiti is about your own style. Plus there's status. The greater the risk you engage in to get your tag somewhere, the more status you get."

Graffiti also became a conduit for Radzik's technological and viral memes: "One day it just occurred to me to call my posse CIP for Cultural Insurgent Phages and to make one of my tags 'virus.' My name became 'Saint Virus' because it was a total juxtaposition of something that sounds good with something that sounds bad. [Radzik was, of course, aware of NLP techniques]. I wanted to show that I was a virus, but that I don't want to hurt anybody. I just want to do whatever I can to help evolution along. The idea was that our graffiti posse, the Cultural Insurgent Phages, were these cultural terrorists who would go around infecting inadequate social complexes with little pieces of information that would then deconstruct that social phenomenon."

Last, and fulfilling Radzik's third prerequisite, graffiti virology was a magical, spiritual enterprise: "It is a form of urban shamanism. Everywhere I had tag, I had a little physic listening post. By having a network of tags in my own geo-graphical area, I sort of drew energy from them."

By becoming a "somebody" in the graffiti world, Radzik developed the ability to market himself as an expert on youth culture. He was scooped up by sportswear designers at companies like Stussy and Gotcha, where he chose to make T-shirts the new canvas for his viral tags and chaos ideology. The agenda of his fashion was simple: "If you see yourself as a part of a cooperative entity in the makeup of the organism that is the planet, then you'll be able to develop an adequate moral ideology that will work for you." The memes he used to promote this agenda were the Gaia hypothesis and environmentalism, chaos math, graffiti and cultural insurgency, and magic and spirituality. He also spliced these memes together whenever possible.

Radzik began with environmentalism because it already had support from the counterculture. "After that Exxon oil spill everyone all of a sudden really gave a fuck. I saw that it was gonna make environmentalism trendy, and so I approached Gotcha surfwear company with an environmental awareness campaign. They hired me, and I just downloaded my concepts, coming up with the tag line 'Surf the Earth Alive,' which was totally based on the Gaia hypothesis. I even came up with a graffiti tag they used in the ad. There was no product advertised, remember, just the idea that Gotcha was concerned and that it was cool to care about the planet."

This campaign got Radzik established as the fashion industry's anthropologist of youth culture, and he was hired by a number of companies to design clothes and campaigns that would attract young buyers: "So I started taking my personal spiritual ideology, creating a graphic interpretation of that, and putting it on T-shirts. It combined graffiti, tantric art, spirituality, and chaos. I was the first one to put a fractal on a T-shirt. Now everyone's doing it. And it's great because whenever someone sees a fractal, they ask what it is. What I tell people is that it's a picture of infinity, but that it's based on a very simple equation. It's always different, but it always shows self-similarity, too. The strange attractor [another chaos math graph] is a picture of universality. They've found strange attractors in human neuron functioning that are almost identical to ones in turbulent water flow dynamics. There's a form there. Like Kali says, 'Have no fear.' So they look cool, they are technological, and you can distill this whole philosophical and magical world-view from it."

Instilling youth culture with the values of chaos math is key to Radzik's intentions. He wants kids to feel proud of the ways in which they feed back, as individuals, to the culture at large. Rather than allowing them to succumb to societal pressure out of fear, he encourages them to explore and give in to their own personal ideologies. "All subcultural orientations are good. It's okay to be gay, straight, white, black, a surfer, or a nerd. If it's your own trip, it's a good trip." One slogan he sold to Gotcha was "Clothes for your trip." More than teaching them about Gaia as an environmental necessity, Kali as a moral ideology, fashion as a cool social statement, or chaos as a worthy cultural metaphor, he was hoping to use all of these memes to empower the individuals in youth culture to feed back their own impulses to the culture at large and accept their roles as active promoters of viral iteration.

Radzik began with an environmental agenda, developed it into a chaos math virus, and then focused almost exclusively on the spiritual and cultural implications of the very technology with which he was involved. When he became the creative director of his own company, Rocket, his new agenda was only to promote viral awareness. He "meta'd" himself. "I called the campaign WAR—World Awareness Revolution—and used chaos, fractals, attractors, tantra, street culture, and spirituality on T-shirts, all in order to put the meme out there that spirituality was important and that it was related to these maths and technologies." Jody used his virus logo overtly and put copies of his T4 hieroglyph on his business cards and fax cover sheet. His communications with other fashion designers and businesspeople were all laced with the language of viral culture. "The inoculation is almost complete," he faxed to a colleague about his viral takeover of Gotcha. "We're lacing the system. New code is replicating rapidly. It won't be long now."

FASHIONABLE MEMES

The recipient of this fax, Nick Phillip, runs his own memewear line called Anarchic Adjustment. The twenty-something blond Englishman has a slightly tougher edge and terser conversational style than the Kali-worshipping Radzik, but his viral campaigns are just as sophisticated. From a working-class background, he came to California when he was eighteen to work on pasteup and layout for skateboard magazines, but got turned on by psychedelic culture and was soon designing his own T-shirts as a way of sharing his ideologies.

Clothing provides Nick with the purest conduit for his countercultural agenda. As he explains from his Haight Street studio-flat, "You're trying to market a lifestyle to the consumer, so it's a really good medium for expressing a whole cluster of ideas, a whole way of looking and acting." Fashion has no actual content; it is pure hype, based on a set of self-referential symbols. "When people wear your fashion, it becomes an icon. You're constantly building an image for your line. You're continually hitting people with ideas that make them think about what it means. We even have a hang tag we put on our shirts that has become a zine, filled with the ideas that our clothing represents."

Again, like Radzik, Phillip creates metamedia viruses; these are memes about the ways in which information spreads, the way people can serve as feedback devices, and the way technology can return us to an ancient spiritual awareness. One T-shirt shows a Buddhist monk who has set himself aflame in a Vietnam protest, with the caption, "Human potential is infinite."

"It's a really negative and painfully nasty image," Nick admits, "but to me it's really powerful. You can see the human race as the pull of the DNA strings—that we just wanna fuck, eat, and survive. But this picture is so in your face that the human mind can go so far beyond that. Our consciousness is really the most powerful."

Another shirt says "HOMO" in giant letters, followed by "sapien," in tiny print. "On the back it says, 'One day you'll see that we're all one.' Now that's pretty hard-core." One of his most controversial T-shirts is called "the subliminal message" shirt: on black cloth, white letters spell out the phrase "subliminal message." Beneath them, in black ink on the black cloth, are the words "heroin insane fuck."

"That was a perfect media virus. It got banned in Texas—kids were not allowed to wear the shirt in high schools. Then there were two articles in Texas newspapers and a TV news interview of the owner of the store that was selling our shirts. In Wales the shirt was being displayed in a storefront, and the wife of a police commissioner came by, called the cops, and got the storekeeper arrested. Then a member of a band called the Beloved insisted on wearing the shirt for an MTV interview, even though his record company begged him to take it off."

Nick is particularly happy with the way his virus about the power of subliminal imagery was able to provoke such a tremendous cultural response. It showed that people really believe in the power of T-shirts as countercultural propaganda. "The shirt materialized all of the paranoias that Middle America has of youth in general. This was a virus because it played on existing paranoias. It said, 'These are your paranoias. You're paranoid.' And they reacted in a really paranoid way to it. So it was really self-justifying, in a way."

Nick sees his viruses as self-justifying and self-replicating. While he knows he is a creative designer, he does not see himself as the launcher of viruses, but merely as a conduit for memes that the culture needs. "In the beginning it was like, 'Wow, can I get this thing out there? Can I get people to wear shirts that say "HOMO"?' But I believe now that it's bigger than me, bigger than all of us. It's just this thing that's happening and if I can poke holes through to the other side, that's great. I think viruses may just be a way of helping us all to see this big thing that's happening. I just feel that I'm going with the flow. I'm moving with what's happening. I'm just part of this organism that is replicating itself, rather than just some guy who's gonna create this fucking virus. If I was dead today, hey, fuck it, this thing would still happen. Maybe the whole thing is a virus, and I'm part of it."

Nick's current viral efforts are to promote an organic, high-tech, evolutionary view of culture: that something is happening, something new, related to technology and bigger than all of us. It began as a fashion line called "Spirituality thru Technology," with pictures of Buddha made out of circuit diagrams, but it has slowly evolved into a campaign about UFOs. The main slogan on Anarchic clothes nowadays is "UFOs Are Real," originally used for a rave invitation that Nick designed for a local club. Nick has since been interviewed by media ranging from *Vogue* to Japanese television about UFOs and what evidence he has that they are real. While Nick enjoys playing with their heads a bit, he admits to his friends that he does not really care if UFOs are real or not:

"It's the ultimate conspiracy, in a way, but it's real value is on a metaphorical level. What an alien would represent in terms of dealing with our current paradigms—our understanding of what's possible. As we approach the next millennium, the rate of change is increasing dramatically. I think the UFO is an icon of that change. It is showing that we're moving through a period where we need more spirituality in order to answer the questions. It's not gonna come from straight science or hocus-pocus garbage. It's got to be science and spirituality together."

With more abduction reports coming through every day, Nick appears to have nested in one of the gaps in our current cultural map of awareness. Whether or not these abduction scenarios are really UFO encounters, they do raise questions about human psychology and the possibility of a group "overmind." Why are so many people, apparently independent of each other, experiencing the same bizarre episode? If nothing else, hearing an acquaintance describe a story like this at a social gathering with the testimonial sincerity of a Christian Scientist can make even a cynic squirm. Do we tell the person we think he is crazy, or do we just nod politely?

Nick believes that the UFO icon, along with his slogan "UFOs Are Real" provokes more than questions of social etiquette. "Maybe there's something in the collective unconscious creating these experiences, making us address issues that the UFO symbolizes. We have a great many problems in this world and probably a finite time to solve them. We need new ways of thinking. Maybe the UFO experience helps us to think in new ways by breaking the boundaries of religious dogma, scientific paradigms. It's something that's definitely in the minds of people. The attractive bubble of this media virus does have inside it a whole lot of deeper questions that I think are important and relevant to where we're at right now."

Nick receives hundreds of letters and phone calls from UFO abductees, critical cynics, and, probably most of all, conspiracy theorists. His meta-media viruses work like any other ones. They find the cracks in the skin of our current cultural paradigm and probe them for societal veins and nerve endings. These gaps are nearly always formed by the discrepancy between the way a system or paradigm works and what is really going on. This can either be a true discrepancy or a perceived one. For example, the AIDS underground's most successful viruses expose the discrepancy between what the FDA is supposed to be doing and what it actually does. The Ross Perot virus, on the other hand, depended on a perceived but less substantiated discrepancy between what elected leaders are supposed to do and what they work toward achieving. The UFO virus, in its most conspiratorial incarnation, presumes that the United States government knows about UFOs and suppresses the information—even going so far as to have a secret airplane hangar with the physical remains of aliens and their spacecraft.

Whether the cultural gap results from a true functional lapse in a societal structure or just an unfounded conspiratorial fear is irrelevant. The gaps are perceived threats, and perceived threats—real or not—can lead to legal action, blacklisting, death sentences, or even war. To meta-media activists, the map of our collective cultural perceptions *is* reality, and the way to navigate that reality is through the media. The strange attractors in this huge chaotic landscape are the identifiable gaps or blind spots in our ability to cooperate with each other. These are the lapses in the collective project we call culture, and they are gaping receptor sites for media viruses.

PSYCHICK TELEVISION

The meta-viralists who surf these treacherous regions of the cultural ocean do not usually emerge unscathed. Industrial music founder Genesis P-Orridge is still licking his wounds from his last tussle with British culture police. Unable to return to his native land now that authorities believe he and his wife, Paula, are literally child-eating Satanists, he has been staying off and on with soulmate Timothy Leary, who, in his own day, experienced the dubious thrill of cultural expatriation from inside a U.S. jail cell. Just as Leary befriended Marshall McLuhan (who advised him to fight the battle in the "real court of power, the media"[2]) during his own legal process, now Genesis has turned to Leary for advice and counsel on how to contend with the cultural immune response to his own viral activities.

"The immune system is the system that every culture sets up to keep out the memes that could change it," Leary reassures Genesis. "See, the Ayatollah Khomeini puts a five-million-dollar price on the head of this one obscure guy who wrote something in English." Genesis does not really enjoy being compared to Salman Rushdie. He hopes his own work is more provocative. Genesis daringly and almost single-handedly brought body piercing, tribalism, and the harsh-styled "industrial" sound to Western culture. Tim senses his dismay.

"Look at Henry Miller," Tim says, "considered globally to be one of our greatest American writers. He couldn't be published in America because his words were too sexy. He was describing actual physical sexual dicks and pussies. D. H. Lawrence? I remember smuggling his books into the country. James Joyce? But remember, when *Howl* by Ginsberg was banned, suddenly there's this trial in San Francisco and the whole world knew about 'I saw the best of my generation,' so what Doug's calling the cultural immune response does bring attention to it."

Tim lights a cigarette and heads off to answer a fax machine, leaving Genesis on the back patio of the Beverly Hills home, looking out over the Los Angeles skyline. On the ridge above Tim's sits the infamous Sharon Tate house, casting an almost palpable shadow: the worst trip of the sixties—Charles Manson—whose helter-skelter provided proof positive of the psychedelic counterculture's danger to the common good. Tim's own wife, Barbara Leary, had been invited to the Tate party that night, but canceled at the last minute. Now the house is inhabited by rock group Nine Inch Nails, a tremendously successful industrial band, much in the tradition of Genesis P-Orridge's Throbbing Gristle—the father of all industrial bands.

But while top-of-the-charts Nine Inch Nails throbs on overhead in the Tate house, P-Orridge sits in Leary's lawn chair flat broke, the economic and emotional casualty of an advanced memetic engineering experiment that got away from him.

"It really is the 'as above so below' phenomenon. It's all so self-similar," he says. "Just as in the individual, time-based, human physical manifestation of being is dictated by DNA, which led to genetic engineering and genetic interference, the same goes for culture. Culture is a host body which can be manipulated and engineered and tampered with and corrupted and infected and healed. We've been in the grips of an atrophied status quo and vested interests for a few thousand years and it's about time we did something less primitive. Damn the consequences."

But the consequences for Genesis, anyway, have been harsh indeed. His attempts to engineer new meme constructs have frightened Scotland Yard enough to advise him to stay out of the U.K. for good. P-Orridge's world-view—greatly oversimplified—goes something like this: A certain, small group of people have been at the top of the global power pyramid for several thousand years. They have maintained a monopoly over sexual, magical, and mystery traditions in order to keep the masses at bay. P-Orridge continues, "The uninitiated are not allowed to be aware of or participate in this, or it will dilute and ultimately destroy the mystical source of power. There are stories about these very old chambers under Glasonpretora with secret entrances and huge locks. Once a year the circle within the circles of Masonry go there and practice sex magic rituals that go back to pre-Crusade times. And those are the people who are the real power brokers. They baptize who will be in control."

Genesis developed his take on power brokering watching adolescent boys, as he puts it, "bugger" one another in the bathrooms at the exclusive schools he attended on scholarship. Himself from a meager working-class background, Gen, as his friends call him, realized with horror that the House of Lords really does begin its policy maneuvering on the fields (and in the bathrooms) of Eton. Most of all, he was struck by how this power jockeying is based primarily on sexuality. Having his own head flushed down the toilet and worse a number of times, young Gen sought refuge in theorizing about the place of these hazings in human history: "All power traditions and mystery traditions have been based in sex."

Despite his brutal reputation and the infamous piercings on his chest and genitals, Genesis, even when in the middle of an angry diatribe, speaks in a soft Oxbridgean tone. "The Songs of Solomon in the Bible can all be decoded into sex magic. And remember that the royal family must consummate their marriage with witnesses. That's a sex magic ritual. The Inquisition existed to eradicate the matriarchal dynasty—but if you think about the central memes of the Inquisition, the basic picture is of the leather hood, manacles, chains, whips, flagellation, and dominator language. Christianity exists to replace female sexual power with male sexual power. The original meaning of the word Christ is 'smeared with semen,' in the Babylonian. The tree of life then, on which he is crucified, is a symbol of male, patriarchal sexual power. The phallus and the semen. Then there's the church towers, and even rocket ships and nuclear explosions, which are both so romantically entwined with male power."

Tim, returning to the patio, pours himself a glass of wine and reads over his fax. Genesis clears his throat in the presence of Leary. "It may seem really far-fetched or simplistic," he continues a little more modestly, "but we live in a world where everything is language and metaphor. Language is used to manipulate things in accordance with a small minority's idea of their destiny: the inherited, implicit and inviolable right to maintain power."

Tim looks up. The fax he has just received is from a new group of media activists calling themselves "Viewjack." Through consumer-grade technology, they hope to create a network of media participants who can change the way human beings relate to technology and drastically alter the ability of top-down forces to control public opinion and psychology. Tim loves getting faxes like this. According to Tim the fax machine is only a masturbatory toy if it is not used to communicate with—to touch another human being. "The brain is only alive when she is communicating with another brain. That's quantum physics. Relativity. You can only measure something from the measurement of something else. It means that the universe is basically a team sport."

Gen smiles. He and Tim are saying the same thing and

working toward the same goals using very different tools and language.

The quest is to reclaim the magic, mystery, and power that has been usurped by patriarchal power mongers. The method, for Leary, was to promote cerebral and spiritual intimacy through LSD, the great unifier. Those in control of media seized on negative publicity like the Manson murders to reframe drugs as evil and keep people afraid of potentially liberating and certainly paradigm-loosening technologies. P-Orridge, working in the seventies with William Burroughs and Brion Gysin, developed a more cut-and-paste style of subversion. Seeing sex, magic, language, and technology as inextricably linked, he developed a free-for-all agenda umbrellaed by the term "industrial culture."

P-Orridge's first major rock band, Throbbing Gristle, was really more of an ongoing performance art piece in real time. Genesis hoped to reinstill culture with primitive magical techniques while exposing people to the blatant manipulations foisted upon them by a top-down media infrastructure. In one of his early essays on the subject of media, P-Orridge began using new spellings for familiar English words in order to reclaim the power of language:

"Humankind has in a very real sense common consciousness, a neurology. [Or, as Leary would put it, "The universe is a team sport."] The language of motivation is intuition, which is thee essence of Magick. This magickal view and direction of history has been suppressed for so long that evidence of it is almost invisible, yet contact with it universal. You have been trained in scepticism and cynicism, you are trained in sarcasm. Dismissed without awareness of one's act is a method of pavlovian power. Thee real work is investigation of thee potency of all symbolic languages and their sources. TV is a language. . . . We have been split, separated from our sexuality, our neurology, our privately groomed mythologies. Symbols are our oldest, truest language yet they are invisible to order, to society."[3]

Genesis's strategy to reclaim the symbolic language of magick is twofold: First, teach people how to study and prac-

tice ancient magical rituals and, second, help them to reclaim the tools of media manipulation. Genesis and Paula
soon became famous for their self-scarification. They traveled the world, got pierced in all sorts of ways, made designs
in their skin and other modifications in their bodies by intentionally "wounding" themselves. They experimented with
ritual tattoos and genital piercing—the chrome paraphernalia hanging from Gen's genitals weigh over three pounds!

This self-modification goes to the heart of Genesis's
philosophy. As he shows his bag of detachable genital jew-
elry to a few of the young movie starlets who have gathered
on the patio (Tim seems to have accumulated them as god-
children), he explains, "It's a faith structure. You can now
adjust without guilt the shape and form of your own body.
And so you can with culture. It is equally as modifiable, as
malleable as the human body. Any construct can be altered,
especially by someone participating in that construct. The
brain is manipulable through yoga, tantric, or chemical dis-
cipline. The cell is manipulable through genetic engineering. Everything is in flux. There is no fixed point. There is
no fixed place. Nothing is specifically true for more than an
instantaneous moment for one individual. Everything we all
say is true, which means we all have equal power over culture. Each of us is constructing our own culture as we go."

Genesis has made a career of reconstructing culture.
His return to ancient tribal ritual and body modification excited thousands of others to do the same. Genesis also
widely publicized his sexual practices and S&M-like rituals,
again emphasizing the empowerment inherent in self-
modification and breaking cultural boundaries with intention. Whether participants were unleashing an ancient
sexual power or not, they did experience the joy of crashing
conventional social mores and developing a new subculture.

As a way of organizing this growing group of fans and
new magic practitioners, Genesis set up something called
"Thee Temple Ov Psychick Youth," a nonhierarchical "nett-
work" of young people who shared magic technologies, insights, and essays through fax machines, photocopy, and

computer systems. To the outside, this began to look like a cult. From Gen's point of view, he was orchestrating the collapse of a mutant and destructive media structure. But thanks to the giant networks put in place by traditional media moguls, Genesis's warriors—the esoterrorists—have access to the gaps in the extant structure's fortifications.

"We're all just acting out the same play we acted out in the caves. The scale has changed and nobody can quite administer that, and that's where all the gaps and leaks appear and that's really my territory: the gaps. That's where I exist." Gen is not just referring to the blind spots in culture, but to the edit points in news media and pasted-together quality of language:

"The edits are a language. It's an invisible language of a priesthood, a vested interest, a closed, secret society. An occult society for hidden brokers to administer and utilize to control the planet. But once we understand that this language is there, we can use the edits and gaps as doorways! We can see them using magic and Chinese philosophy or with chaos mathematics and the study of wormholes. Once we learn the language of our enemy, then we have the option, too, of chopping it up and playing with it and rearranging it. These are the most powerful tools of change."

Genesis P-Orridge's musical efforts took the cut-and-paste techniques of the writings of colleague William Burroughs and applied them to music in a conscious effort to expose the hidden language of power and manipulate it to countercultural ends. He used digital sampling techniques to juxtapose and overlap sounds from the culture of industry with those from ancient tribes. Sounds from TV, radio, and other media found themselves recombined into unrecognizability. Meanwhile Genesis also studied the science of the effect of sound on the body and developed music that could alter consciousness, evoke fear, or even stimulate orgasm. He calls this music "anti-Muzak," and it is meant to have an effect on the mind and body antithetical to Muzak Corporation's entrainment sound tracks. Instead of putting listeners to sleep, Genesis wants to wake them up.

Genesis also got involved in reworking video imagery for the same reasons. By the time he wrote the following 1988 essay, his views on the language of television, as well as his more fully appropriated spelling style, had defined themselves:

"TV itself becoums thee ceremony, thee language ov thee tribe. It becoums apparent that, cloaked in spurious messianic trivia, are ancient tantric rituals involving small death, limbo and resurrection that have now been literalised and usurped by a base language system named religion. Just as religion cloaks ancient knowledge and techniques, so Television cloaks its power to invoke thee lowest coumon denominator ov revelation. We see S&M sex as an imperfect butt inevitable outlet for instinctive drives for rites ov passage and initiation. We believe sexuality was always included in ancient mysteries and that Television is in itself a new secret language, thee language rooted in lighting, camera perfection, edits, so it remains hidden and emasculating. We intend to reinstate thee ability ov TV to empower and entrance the viewer. To remove thee window and passivity, and re-enter thee world ov dreams beyond. We believe TV is a Modern alchemical weapon that can have a positive and cumulative effect upon Intuition."[4]

This is where Gen got into trouble. He began making videos. Weird, sexy, S&M videos. His purpose was to reclaim the power of the media by wedding technology with magic: "A Psychic TV Image Scan does not signify a general, accepted and fixed idea. It is allegorical, metaphorical, symbolical and trivial simultaneously. Thee reverberation ov possibility is our goal. . . . We are closer to sorcerers transmitting and receiving pagan invocations in order to SEE."[5] But this was a medium and language that his opponents refused to relinquish.

Genesis was accustomed to police busts at his provocative art exhibitions about prostitution or even public critique when he silently masturbated as his official lecture to an exclusive London arts college. He was taken off guard, however, when a video project he had participated in ten years before was used as evidence of Satanic rituals in a Channel 4 documentary series called "Dispatches." On February 15, 1992, while Genesis and his family were in Nepal organizing soup kitchens and studying local rituals, detectives from Scotland Yard's Obscene Publications Squad raided P-Orridge's Brighton home and confiscated several tons of video and print archives. The next day, *The Observer* published a story headlined VIDEO OFFERS FIRST EVIDENCE OF RITUAL ABUSE. The story was based on a Channel 4 press release about "Dispatches," which, it claimed, showed ritualized abortions, fetus eating, and sadistic black magic perpetrated against children.[6]

The program included an interview with an anonymous young woman who claimed she was present at the abortions and even submitted to one herself. Within days of its airing, the program was revealed to be a scam. Its producer, Andrew Boyd, it turned out, had a long history of promoting radical right-wing propaganda. The "experts" who testified complained that their quotes were taken out of context in an intentionally misleading manner, and the video itself was revealed to have been commissioned by Channel 4 in 1981 for a film about media intending to show how easily people can be misled by fancy editing techniques! But the one or two small articles explaining the true circumstances around the video were significantly outnumbered by the dozens of front-page headlines proclaiming Genesis and his followers as the first hard evidence of ritualized Satanic abuse. Worse yet the police who raided the P-Orridge home on the basis of the evidence presented by the "Dispatches" documentary were now unwilling to make amends. Genesis was informed by Scotland Yard that if he dared return to England, it "could not guarantee his safety."

Fearing that they would have their children taken from them, or worse, if they set foot in the U.K., Genesis and his wife took their daughters and headed for America. Though broke—he lost his house, property, and his archives, including unpublished books and films by William Burroughs and Derek Jarman—he knows his meta-viral video work has located a gap in modern culture. His culture had simply responded to the viruses that he himself had launched.

But the young starlets at Leary's aren't too interested in the meta-dynamics. They just want to know why Genesis took video pictures of scarification and piercing in the first place.

"The basic topic was the idea of shamanism and ritual as a metaphor for change," he explains. "It was about reclaiming a heritage that's been suppressed and stolen by the particular dynasty that we're under at the moment." The girls don't buy his conspiratorial tone. They have been making good money in the Hollywood system. Genesis tries to remain patient, but his voice rings almost too gentle now.

"I'm saying that there are certain rights of passage and initiations and explorations of one's personal thresholds, physical and spiritual, which are the province of the most holy people in most cultures; but in the Western culture these practices are actually legislated against. On the books in England, piercing is illegal. You can be arrested for it."

As our AIDS activists have argued, making something that everyone already does illegal is a way to create a society of outlaws, arrestable at the drop of a hat. But why have these particular acts been outlawed?

"The only reason those in power would bother to legislate things of this ilk is to maintain power. Therefore, these acts must empower the individual." Genesis does not mean that self-mutilation necessarily releases magical empowering energy. Breaking conventional barriers, however—merely finding gaps and exploiting them—erodes the power structure of the incumbent regime. Further, breaking the barriers between people by encouraging sex, communication, and intimate forms of magic develops an interconnected, organismic, and powerful living culture.

But how has Genesis really empowered himself? Once the leader of a popular English band, a homeowner, an archivist, a family man, university lecturer, and bank depositor, he is now a penniless exile with nothing but the clothes on his back and the thoughts in his head. Like Leary, though, whose ups and downs in public opinion and personal wealth have brought him from jail to Beverly Hills to bankruptcy and back, P-Orridge's erratic career slope has never bothered him. Staying unperturbed by what dominator society dishes out to him is precisely how he maintains his power. He simply followed Leary's advice and dropped out.

"What I think I have achieved, and what we need as a culture, is a stance which is constantly flexible," Gen says, fanning away from his face the smoke from Leary's cigarette. "It's an attitude which does not require us to believe in our own history. Our previous moves have an obsolescence on a day-to-day, moment-to-moment basis. The enemy's power of seduction is the need for a career, recognition, and reward. Because we don't have that need, we present a much larger problem for those who would control culture."

By staying out of the traditional rat race, Genesis P-Orridge and other meta-media activists feel they can break the tyrannous lineage that constructed the mediasphere in the first place. Studying, exploring, and exposing the gaps in our postmodern, highly edited media reality, virus formulators learn that the deepest, darkest power of the media is its ability to break through the perception of linear time. Just as home video feeds back to a previously top-down media, home editing—at least in theory—changes the established order of time and challenges the very nature of tradition by allowing artists and activists to reinvent reality at every edit point.

Genesis hopes to break time itself, and to thwart those who use it to maintain tyranny: "What I'm really saying is that the enemy resides in the concept of heritage and inheritance. The medium it uses to maintain its life is the culture. It's patently obvious that time is not linear. This is the imposition of an impractical and inappropriate construct. Things are really in chaos. But the policing of this inept construct damages and cripples us psychicly, emotionally, intellectually, and even physically." In order to break this illusion of linear time, media activists confront us with discontinuities ranging from UFO invasions to fractals, neurolinguistic oxymorons to quick-cut MTV videos, and computer viruses to morphed faces.

Finally, as a race, our biological link to time and inheritance resides in our own genetic code—the DNA that researchers are rapidly learning to manipulate. While the DNA is only a code—a language of codons—it directs the physical shape of the future of humanity. Likewise those who manipulate the codons of media by launching meme-rich viruses are challenging the traditional, linear process by which history is regulated. Whether there is a back room of angry and powerful elitists is irrelevant. The way in which culture moves through time has been altered.

As Gen concludes, "Everything should be vulnerable to redesigning. So a fluidity of knowledge of the language of editing, the invisible languages, and a basic understanding of the ability of each individual to investigate and interact with their own DNA or to investigate and interact with the culture through memes is essential."

For Genesis and his daring cohorts, the cultural immune response to their mimetic engineering appears to prove that they have tapped, if not yet mastered, the hidden but pervasive language of our viral media. Whether their alterations of the codons of cultural history are necessary or positive is left to be seen. But rejecting the fact that the efforts of viral activists are having a tangible effect on the architecture of our ever-increasingly mediated culture is to pretend that what goes on in your city hall is more important to your kids than what Beavis and Butt-head said to each other on MTV last night.

You can ignore media viruses if you like, but it's really too late. If you've gotten this far, you've already been infected.

NOTES

CHAPTER 1

1. Walter Lippmann, quoted in Noam Chomsky, *Media Control*, Open Pamphlet Series, Westfield, N.J., 1991.
2. Ibid.
3. Ibid.
4. Ibid.
5. William Irwin Thompson, *The American Replacement of Nature*, p. 44.
6. *Seven Days* Magazine, March 8, 1989, cited in *Whole Earth Review*, Spring 1991: "Garbage in Mind" by 'Sparrow.'

CHAPTER 2

1. James Wolcott, *The New Yorker*, February 6, 1993.
2. Ibid.
3. *Newsweek*, December 13, 1993.
4. Jonathan Alter, "The Shield of Vulnerability," *Newsweek*, September 6, 1993.

CHAPTER 3

1. Ken Auletta, "Loathing the Media," *Esquire*, November 1992.
2. Ibid.
3. *New York Times*, August 25, 1992.
4. Ibid.
5. *New York*, August 31, 1992.
6. Ibid.

7. *New York Times*, March 19, 1993.

8. *Time*, August 31, 1992.

9. Ibid.

10. *New York Times*, April 7, 1993.

11. *New York Times*, March 19, 1993.

12. *Village Voice*, September 1, 1992.

13. *New York Times*, October 8, 1992.

14. *USA Today*, September 22, 1992.

15. "Murphy Brown," airdate Monday, September 21, 1992.

16. *Time*, September 21, 1992.

17. *New York Times*, September 23, 1992.

18. *New York Times*, August 31, 1992.

19. Ibid.

20. *Village Voice*, September 1, 1992.

21. *TV Guide*, November 21–28, 1992.

22. Ibid.

23. Ibid.

24. Greil Marcus, OpEd, *New York Times*, October 27, 1992.

25. *Time*, "Election Issue," November-December 1992.

26. *Campaign* magazine, October 25, 1992.

27. *The Atlantic*, October 1992.

28. *Time*, "Election Issue," November-December 1992.

29. Ibid.

30. Ibid.

CHAPTER 4

1. *People Weekly*, August 12, 1991.

2. *The Nation*, August 26, 1991.

3. *Whole Earth Review*, Fall 1987.

4. Richard Corliss, review, *Time*, August 1, 1988.

5. *The Atlantic*, May 1987.

6. *Spin*, January 1993.

7. *Esquire*, October 1992.

8. *Reactor*, Winter 1992.

9. *Village Voice*, November 17, 1992.

10. *Esquire*, October 1992.

CHAPTER 5

1. Pat Aufderheide, "The Look of the Sound," in *Watching Television*, edited by Todd Gitlin. New York: Pantheon, 1986.

2. *Entertainment Weekly*, February 26, 1993.

3. *Newsweek*, September 6, 1993.

4. *New York Times*, January 26, 1994.

5. *Vanity Fair*, October 1992.

6. *New York Times*, October 18, 1992.

7. Ibid.

8. *Newsweek*, November 1, 1992.

9. Jean Baudrillard, *Simulation*, Semiotext(e), 1983.

10. *Rolling Stone*, "Beavis and Butt-head," August 19, 1993.

11. Frank Rich, "Public Stages: Burn, Baby, Burn!" *New York Times Magazine*, November 28, 1993.

12. *New York Times Magazine*, October 11, 1992.

13. Ibid.

14. Ice-T, interviewed in *Rolling Stone*, August 20, 1992.

15. *Spin*, October 1992.

16. Ibid.

17. Ibid.

18. Ibid.

19. *Rolling Stone*, August 20, 1992.

20. *Spin*, October 1992.

21. Ibid.

22. Five Percent Lesson, "The Five Percent Solution," *Spin*, February 1991.

23. Ibid.

24. Ibid.

25. *Rolling Stone*, August 20, 1992.

26. *Details*, November 1992.

27. *Newsweek*, November 16, 1992.

28. *Esquire*, October 1992.

29. *Village Voice*, November 10, 1992.

30. *Rolling Stone*, August 20, 1992.

31. *Mondo 2000*, Issue 8.

32. Ibid.

33. Ibid.

34. *New York Times*, November 26, 1992.

CHAPTER 6

1. In fact, the Secret Service agents eventually revealed they were concerned about Steve Jackson's company's electronic bulletin board, which they believed might have been involved in the dissemination of a telephone company document. What provoked their suspicion, among other things, was the bulletin board's conspiratorial greeting.

2. Terence McKenna, *Food of the Gods*, p. 265.

3. "Swamp Thing," no. 140, March 1994.

4. Immediast Underground: "Seize the Media."

5. "Seize the Media," a pamphlet by the Immediast Underground.

CHAPTER 7

1. David Armstrong, *A Trumpet to Arms: Alternative Media in America* (Boston: South End Press, 1981), p. 20–21.
2. Dirk Koning, *Community Television Review*, November/December 1991 (Editorial Page).
3. Janet Maslin, *New York Times*, March 1993.

CHAPTER 8

1. Bruce Sterling quoting the RAND report; in "Complete Internet History," a Literary Freeware document.
2. Brian Becker, "U.S. Military Chief Reveals Pentagon Plan for New Wars," NY Transfer News Service, January 2, 1993.
3. Harel Barzilai, posting on Activists Mailing List.
4. John DiNardo, epilogue to numerous Activist Progressive newsgroup articles, 1992–93.
5. European Counter Network on-line, November 1992 (text prepared for international info-shop meeting in Berlin).
6. Howard Rheingold, working introduction to *Virtual Communities* (Reading, Mass: Addison-Wesley, 1994).
7. Michael Synergy, in *Mondo 2000*, Issue #3.
8. Rheingold, working introduction to *Virtual Communities*.
9. Urnst Kouch, interviewed in *Gray Areas*, Issue #3, 1993.
10. Bill Me Tuesday, in *Mondo 2000: A User's Guide to the New Edge* (New York: HarperCollins, 1992).
11. Mutated from Christian Book's original text in VIRUS 23.
12. TAZ refers to a book by Hakim Bey, in which virtual communities could be considered temporary autonomous zones.
13. IRC is Internet Relay Chat, a way of having live conversations, through text, with other users on the Internet.

CHAPTER 9

1. Abbie Hoffman, Paul Krassner, and Mike Roselle quotes are from *Pranks*, a collection of interviews by Re/Search, volume #11.
2. David Foreman and Bill Haywood, *Ecodefense: A Field Guide to Monkeywrenching*, Tuscon: Ned Ludd Books, 1987, p. 284.
3. Edward Abbey, *Ecodefense*, p. 8.
4. Mike Roselle in *Pranks*, Re/Search #11.
5. Tom Brokaw, among many others, "NBC Nightly News."

CHAPTER 10

1. *New York Times*, May 16, 1993.
2. Jay Stevens, *Storming Heaven*, p. 268.
3. Genesis P-Orridge, *Genesis P-Orridge, Esoterrorist, Selected Essays, 1980–1988*, OV-Press, Denver, 1989.
4. Ibid.
5. Ibid.
6. See British newspapers for details of this bizarre case: Rosie Waterhouse, in *The Independent on Sunday*, February 23, 1992, and her series of articles over the following weeks.

BIBLIOGRAPHY

BOOKS

Abraham, Ralph, *Chaos, Gaia, and Eros*. San Francisco: Harper San Francisco, 1994.

Armstrong, David, *A Trumpet to Arms: Alternative Media in America*. Boston: South End Press, 1981.

Baudrillard, Jean, *Simulations*. New York: Semiotext(e), 1983.

Brooks, Tim and Earle Marsh, *The Complete Directory to Prime Time Network TV Shows 1946–Present*. New York: Ballantine Books, 1992.

de Bord, Guy, *The Society of the Spectacle*. New York: Zone Books, 1994.

Dean, Ward and John Morgenthaler, *Smart Drugs and Nutrients*. Santa Cruz: B & J Publications, 1991.

Foreman, David and Bill Haywood, *Ecodefense: A Field Guide to Monkeywrenching*. Tuscon: Ned Ludd Books, 1987.

Gitlin, Todd, ed. *Watching Television: A Pantheon Guide to Popular Culture*. New York: Pantheon Books, 1986.

Herman, Edward S. and Noam Chomsky, *Manufacturing Consent: The Political Economy of the Mass Media*. New York: Pantheon Books, 1988.

Juno, Andrea and V. Vale, *Re/Search #11: Pranks*. San Francisco: Re/Search, 1987.

Lovelock, J. E. Gaia, *A New Look at Life on Earth*. New York: Oxford University Press, 1979.

McKenna, Terence, *Food of the Gods*. New York: Bantam, 1992.

Morgenthaler, John and Steven Wm. Fowkes, eds. *Stop the FDA*. Menlo Park: Health Freedom Press, 1992.

P-Orridge, Genesis, *Genesis P-Orridge, Esoterrorist, Selected Essays, 1980–1988*. Denver: OV-Press, 1989.

Pratkanis, Anthony, and Elliot Aronson, *Age of Propaganda*. New York: WH Freeman, 1992.

Rheingold, Howard, *Virtual Communities*. New York: Addison Wesley, 1993.

Rucker, Rudy, R. U. Sirius, and Queen Mu, *Mondo 2000: A User's Guide to the New Edge*. New York: HarperCollins, 1992.

Sheldrake, Rupert, *The Rebirth of Nature: The Greening of Science and God*. London: Random Century, 1990.

Stevens, Jay, *Storming Heaven: LSD and the American Dream*. New York: Harper & Row, 1987.

Thompson, William Irwin, *The American Replacement of Nature*. New York: Doubleday, 1991.

USEFUL PERIODICALS

Adbusters magazine
The Atlantic
bOING bOING
Campaign magazine
Community Television Review
Details
Entertainment Weekly
Esquire
Gray Areas
Media Culture Review
Mondo 2000
Nation
New York Magazine
New York Times Magazine
The New Yorker
Open Pamphlet Series
Reactor
Rolling Stone
Seize the Media Immediast Underground Open Pamphlet Series
Spin
Swamp Thing
Village Voice
Whole Earth Review
Wired

ON-LINE SOURCES

Computer Underground Digest
European Counter Network Online
FutureCulture: ahawks@nyx.cs.du.edu

NY Transfer News Service
PHAGE magazine: TK0JUT2@NIU.BITNET)
Sterling, Bruce, *Complete Internet History*, a Literary Freeware document
Usenet Newsgroup: misc.activism.progressive
WELL (Whole Earth 'Lectronic Link) Gen X Conference, Media Conference, and Writers Conference.

INDEX

ABOUT THE AUTHOR

DOUGLAS RUSHKOFF is the first mainstream writer to cover topics like virtual reality, cyberpunks, the psychedelic revival, and rave culture. His articles have appeared in *GQ, Us, Vibe, The Miami Herald, The Wall Street Journal,* and *The Boston Globe.* He is the author of *The GenX Reader* and *Cyberia: Life in the Trenches of Hyperspace,* and was Politics Editor of *Exposure* magazine in Los Angeles. He lives in New York City.